D1881004

CHARACTERISTICS OF WOMEN

MORAL, POETICAL, AND HISTORICAL

CHARACTERISTICS
OF
WOMEN

MORAL, POETICAL, AND HISTORICAL.

by

ANNA JAMESON

THE AUTHOR'S EDITION

ILLUSTRATED BY A SERIES OF HER OWN VIGNETTE ETCHINGS, WITH A NEW PREFACE, ORIGINAL NOTES AND OTHER IMPORTANT ADDITIONS.

GYAN

Published by

GYAN

Gyan Publishing House
5, Ansari Road
Daryaganj, New Delhi-110002
Phone: 011-47034999, 9811692060
E-mail: books@gyanbooks.com

Distribution Network
gyanbooks.com
India, USA, Canada, UK, Australia, France

© Publisher

All rights reserved. No part of this work may be reproduced, stored, adapted, or transmitted in any form or by any means, electronic, mechanical, photocopying, micro-filming, recording or otherwise, or translated in any language, without the prior written permission of the copyright owner and the publisher.

ISBN : 978-81-212-2307-2 (PB)
First Published, 1837

2nd Impression 2021

Printed at: Gyan Press, Delhi.

The book is sold subject to the condition that it shall not, by way of trade or otherwise, be lent, resold, hired out, or otherwise circulated without the prior publisher's written consent.

Characteristics of Women, Moral, Poetical, and Historical.
Author: Anna Jameson

CHARACTERISTICS

OF

WOMEN,

MORAL, POETICAL, AND HISTORICAL,

BY ANNA JAMESON.

THE AUTHOR'S EDITION.

ILLUSTRATED BY A SERIES OF HER OWN VIGNETTE ETCHINGS,
WITH A NEW PREFACE, ORIGINAL NOTES AND OTHER
IMPORTANT ADDITIONS.

NEW YORK:
SAUNDERS AND OTLEY, ANN STREET.

MDCCCXXXVII.

Entered according to Act of Congress in the year 1836,
By ANNA JAMESON,
In the Clerk's Office of the Southern District of New York.

TO MRS. PIERCE BUTLER,

OF PHILADELPHIA.

I have particular pleasure, my dearest Fanny, in once more dedicating to you, by your new name, in a new land, this little book, which in its progress you cherished, and which without you would, in all probability, have never been published.

"Lieti Giorni, e felici."

Your affectionate friend,

A. J.

January 1, 1837.

CONTENTS.

HISTORICAL CHARACTERS.

PREFACE

TO THIS EDITION.

The former editions of this little book, printed in America, contained not only innumerable errors of the press, but omissions to the extent of at least ten or twelve pages. In presenting to my American friends an edition, more compact and complete, as well as more correct than any of the preceding, I seize the opportunity of adding a few words by way of preface.

Beyond a short advertisement to the second English edition, (which differed materially from the first,) I have never yet written any preface to this work, conceiving that the Introductory Dialogue sufficiently explained its intention, and its meaning. But I have reason to think, that on this point I have been mistaken; and that some misapprehension *does* exist, relative to the object I have had in view.

I am quite aware "that the work derives its chief interest from the subject; as it owes its most unhoped-for success principally to the great name of Shakspeare, that bond of sympathy among all who speak his language." But it has been justly observed, that, as an analysis of the female characters of Shakspeare's plays, the work is imperfect; for that many of them, and not the least striking, have been slightly noticed, or omitted altogether. I must therefore repeat once for all, that my object was not to present a complete commentary on Shakspeare's Women: such an undertaking would have required much more critical learning than I possess; a profounder knowledge of the spirit of past ages; and more acquaintance with the sources whence Shakspeare drew his incidents and materials. I must have dived far deeper into that vast perplexing chaos of tradition, poetry, history, romance, real life, whence he conjured up spirits of grace, intellect, grandeur, and bade them stand before us, clothed in the aspects and passions of humanity. I could not do this; but I selected a few among the creatures of his art, for particular consideration, merely to throw into a flowing and intelligible form, some observations on the natural workings of mind and feeling in my own sex, which might lead to good. More than this I never designed; more than this I never attempted; and what I *have* attempted I sincerely wish I had done better.

In general, I have only to thank my kind critics in England, America, and Germany, for the approbation with which they have honored me, and the indulgence with which they have treated my deficiencies; and I do thank them with very grateful and gratified feelings. That some among them differ from me in their view of one or two of the characters, rather pleases me than otherwise; for, as I have elsewhere remarked, it is the necessary result of the innate truth of those wondrous creations, that, like individuals in real life, they strike every observer in a different light. Forgetting the artist in his own work, we are unconsciously biased in our judgment by peculiar habits of feeling and thought, by our own opinions and prejudices. We condemn or sympathise with these beings of air, approve or disapprove their motives and actions as if they had really existed—did now exist in this veritable world. We give them, from our faith in their identity with ourselves, a sort of moral responsibility, and hence, their moral influence.

I have received some anonymous letters and confidential communications, which would induce me to believe that there exist some people who strangely misapprehend me; who imagine, that in admiring Juliet, I intended to recommed unadvised passion, disobedience, and suicide; and in pleading for Lady Macbeth, to excuse treachery and murder. I can but say, "peace to all such." On this point, and others therewith connected, I trust myself and my book to the "merciful construction of good women:" to the *good* observe! for they only can afford to be merciful.

And let me add thus much: Could we but, in real life, look into any heart as Shakspeare has permitted us to look into Juliet's and Lady Macbeth's,—could we follow the whole course of feeling in any feminine mind,—trace correctly the links that connect certain consequences with remote causes, often rendering what we most condemn, a dread necessity derived from foregone conclusions—could we, in short, see the *whole*, and clearly, what we now see only in part and darkly—all that tempted to wrong, all that blinded to right, we should not then presume, from the little known, to infer the unknown; to set ourselves up as accusers, judges, executioners, all at once: we should have more mercy on each other—as becomes "*good* women."

Men make it a general accusation against us, as a sex, that we are ill-natured, unfair, pitiless, in judging one another. They say that when women get together, "at every word a reputation dies;" they say that as a savage proves his heroism by displaying in grim array the torn scalps of his enemies, so a woman thinks she proves her virtue by exhibiting the mangled reputations of her friends; they say—but there is no end to the witty impertinences, and fag ends of rhymes from Simonides to Pope, which they fling at us on this subject. I have never heard men so eloquently satirical, as when treating with utter scorn the idea, that a woman can possibly elevate herself in the eyes of one of their sex by degrading, or suffering to be degraded, one of her own: and in their censure they are right—quite right; but wrong—quite wrong in attributing this, our worst propensity, to ill-nature and jealousy. Ignorance is the main cause; ignorance of ourselves and others: and when I have heard any female acquaintance commenting with a spiteful, or a sprightly levity on the delinquencies and mistakes of their sex, I have only said to myself, "they know not what they do." Here then, I present to woman a little elementary manual, or introduction to the knowledge of woman; in which they may learn to understand better their own nature; to judge more gently, more truly of each other.

> And in the silent hour of inward thought,
> To still *suspect*, yet still *revere* themselves
> In lowliness of heart.

A. J.

Toronto, January, 1837.

INTRODUCTORY DIALOGUE.

MEDON—ALDA.

ALDA.

You will not listen to me?

MEDON.

I do, with all the deference which befits a gentleman when a lady holds forth on the virtues of her own sex.

He is a parricide of his mother's name,
And with an impious hand murders her fame,
That wrongs the praise of woman; that dares write,
Libels on saints, or with foul ink requite
The milk they lent us.
Yours was the nobler birth,
For you from man were made—man but of earth—
The son of dust!

ALDA.

What's this?

MEDON.

"Only a rhyme I learned from one I talked withal;" 'tis a quotation from some old poet that has fixed itself in my memory—from Randolph, I think.

ALDA.

'Tis very justly thought, and very politely quoted, and my best curtsey is due to him and to you;—but now will you listen to me?

MEDON.

With most profound humility.

ALDA.

Nay then! I have done, unless you will lay aside these mock airs of gallantry, and listen to me for a moment! Is it fair to bring a second-hand accusation against me, and not attend to my defence?

MEDON.

Well, I will be serious.

ALDA.

Do so, and let us talk like reasonable beings.

MEDON.

Then tell me, (as a reasonable woman you will not be affronted with the question,) do you really expect that any one will read this little book of yours?

ALDA.

I might answer, that it has been a great source of amusement and interest to me for several months, and that so far I am content; but no one writes a book without a hope of finding readers, and I shall find a few. Accident first made me an authoress; and not now, or ever, have I written to flatter any prevailing fashion of the day for the sake of profit, though this is done, I know, by many who have less excuse for thus coining their brains. This little book was undertaken without a thought of fame or money: out of the fullness of my own heart and soul have I written it. In the pleasure it has given me, in the new and various views of human nature it has opened to me, in the beautiful and soothing images it has placed before me, in the exercise and improvement of my own faculties, I have already been repaid; if praise or profit come beside, they come as a surplus. I should be gratified and grateful, but I have not sought for them, nor worked for them. Do you believe this?

MEDON.

I do: in this I cannot suspect you of affectation, for the profession of disinterestedness is uncalled for, and the contrary would be too far countenanced by the custom of the day to be matter of reserve or reproach. But how could you, (saving the reverence due to a lady authoress, and speaking as one reasonable being to another,) choose such a threadbare subject?

ALDA.

What do you mean?

MEDON.

I presume you have written a book to maintain the superiority of your sex over ours; for so I judge by the names at the heads of some of your chapters; women, fit indeed to inlay heaven with stars, but, pardon me, very unlike those who at present walk upon this earth.

ALDA.

Very unlike the fine ladies of your acquaintance, I grant you; but as to maintaining the superiority, or speculating on the rights of women—nonsense! why should you suspect me of such folly?—it is quite out of date. Why should there be competition or comparison?

MEDON.

Both are ill judged and odious; but did you ever meet with a woman of the world, who did not abuse most heartily the whole race of men?

ALDA.

Did you ever talk with a man of the world, who did not speak with levity or contempt of the whole race of women?

MEDON.

Perhaps I might answer like Voltaire—"Hélas! ils pourraient bien avoir raison tous deux." But do you thence infer that both are good for nothing?

ALDA.

Thence I infer that the men of the world and the women of the world are neither of them—good for much.

MEDON.

And you have written a book to make them better?

ALDA.

Heaven forbid! else I were only fit for the next lunatic asylum. Vanity run mad never conceived such an impossible idea.

MEDON.

Then, in few words, what is the subject, and what the object of your book?

ALDA.

I have endeavored to illustrate the various modifications of which the female character is susceptible, with their causes and results. My life has been spent in observing and thinking; I have had, as you well know, more opportunities for the first, more leisure for the last, than have fallen to the lot of most people. What I have seen, felt, thought, suffered, has led me to form certain opinions. It appears to me that the condition of women in society, as at present constituted, is false in itself, and injurious to them,—that the education of women, as at present conducted, is founded in mistaken principles, and tends to increase fearfully the sum of misery and error in both sexes; but I do not choose presumptuously to fling these opinions in the face of the world, in the form of essays on morality, and treatises on education. I have rather chosen to illustrate certain positions by examples, and leave my readers to deduce the moral themselves, and draw their own inferences.

MEDON.

And why have you not chosen your examples from real life? you might easily have done so. You have not been a mere spectator, or a mere actor, but a lounger behind the scenes of existence—have even assisted in preparing the puppets for the stage: you might have given us an epitome of your experience, instead of dreaming over Shakspeare.

ALDA.

I might so, if I had chosen to become a female satirist, which I will never be.

MEDON.

You would at least stand a better chance of being read.

ALDA.

I am not sure of that. The vile taste for satire and personal gossip will not be eradicated, I suppose, while the elements of curiosity and malice remain in human nature; but as a fashion of literature, I think it is passing away;—at all events it is not my *forte*. Long experience of what is called "the world," of the folly, duplicity, shallowness, selfishness, which meet us at every turn, too soon unsettles our youthful creed. If it only led to the knowledge of good and evil, it were well; if it only taught us to despise the illusions and retire from the pleasures of the world, it would be better. But it destroys our belief—it dims our perception of all abstract truth, virtue, and happiness; it turns life into a jest, and a very dull one too. It makes us indifferent to beauty, and incredulous of goodness; it teaches us to consider *self* as the centre on which all actions turn, and to which all motives are to be referred.

MEDON.

But this being so, we must either revolve with these earthly natures, and round the same centre, or seek a sphere for ourselves, and dwell apart.

ALDA.

I trust it is not necessary to do either. While we are yet young, and the passions, powers, and feelings, in their full activity, create to us a world within, we cannot look fairly on the world without:—all things then are good. When first we throw ourselves forth, and meet burrs and briars on every side, which stick in our very hearts;—and fair tempting fruits which turn to bitter ashes in the taste, then we exclaim with impatience, all things are evil. But at length comes the calm hour, when they who look beyond the superficies of things begin to discern their true bearings; when the perception of evil, or sorrow, or sin, brings also the perception of some opposite good, which awakens our indulgence, or the knowledge of the cause which excites our pity. Thus it is with me. I can smile,—nay, I can laugh still, to see folly, vanity, absurdity, meanness, exposed by scornful wit, and depicted by others, in fictions light and brilliant. But these very things, when I encounter the reality, rather make me sad than merry, and take away all the inclination, if I had the power, to hold them up to derision.

MEDON.

Unless by doing so, you might correct them.

ALDA.

Correct them! Show me that one human being who

has been made essentially better by satire! Oh no, no! there is something in human nature which hardens itself against the lash—something in satire which excites only the lowest and worst of our propensities. That avowal in Pope—

> I must be proud to see
> Men not afraid of God, afraid of me!

—has ever filled me with terror and pity.

MEDON.

From its truth perhaps?

ALDA.

From its arrogance,—for the truth is that a vice never corrected a vice. Pope might be proud of the terror he inspired in those who feared no God; in whom vanity was stronger than conscience; but that terror made no individual man better; and while he indulged his own besetting sin, he administered to the malignity of others. Your professed satirists always send me to think upon the opposite sentiment in Shakspeare, on "the mischievous foul sin of chiding sin." I remember once hearing a poem of Barry Cornwall's (he read it to me,) about a strange winged creature that, having the lineaments of a man, yet preyed on a man, and afterwards coming to a stream to drink, and beholding his own face therein, and discovering that he had made his prey of a creature like himself, pined away with repentance. So should those do, who having made themselves mischievous mirth out of the sins and sorrows of others, remembering their own humanity, and seeing within themselves the same lineaments—so should *they* grieve and pine away, self-punished.

MEDON.

'Tis an old allegory, and a sad one—and but too much to the purpose.

ALDA.

I abhor the spirit of ridicule, I dread it, and I despise it. I abhor it, because it is in direct contradiction to the mild and serious spirit of Christianity; I fear it, because we find that in every state of society in which it has prevailed as a fashion, and has given the tone to the manners and literature, it has marked the moral degradation and approaching destruction of that society; and I despise it because it is the usual resource of the shallow and the base mind, and, when wielded by the strongest hand with the purest intentions, an inefficient means of good. The spirit of satire, reversing the spirit of mercy which is twice blessed, seems to me twice accursed;—evil in those who indulge it—evil to those who are the objects of it.

MEDON.

"Peut-être fallait-il que la punition des imprudens et des faibles fut confiée á la malignité, car la pure vertu n'eût jamais été assez cruelle."

ALDA.

That is a woman's sentiment.

MEDON.

True—it *was*; and I have pleasure in reminding you that a female satirist by profession is yet an anomaly in the history of our literature, as a female schismatic is yet unknown in the history of our religion. But to what do you attribute the number of satirical women we meet in society?

ALDA.

Not to our nature; but to a state of society in which the levelling spirit of *persiflage* has been long a fashion, to a perverse education which fosters it; to affections disappointed or unemployed, which embitter the temper; to faculties misdirected or wasted, which oppress and irritate the mind; to an utter ignorance of ourselves, and the common lot of humanity, combined with the quick and refined perceptions, and much superficial cultivation; to frivolous habits which make serious thought a burthen, and serious feeling a bane if suppressed,—if betrayed, a ridicule. Women, generally speaking, are by nature too much subjected to suffering in many forms—have too much of fancy and sensibility, and too much of that faculty which some philosophers call *veneration*, to be naturally satirical. I have known but one woman eminently gifted in mind and person, who is also distinguished for powers of satire as bold as merciless; and she is such a compound of all that nature can give of good, and all that society can teach of evil—

MEDON.

That she reminds us of the dragon of old, which was generated between the sunbeams from heaven and the slime of earth?

ALDA.

No such thing. Rather of the powerful and beautiful fairy Melusina, who had every talent and every charm under heaven; but once in so many hours, was fated to become a serpent. No, I return to my first position: it is not by exposing folly and scorning fools that we make other people wiser, or ourselves happier. But to soften the heart by images and examples of the kindly and generous affections,—to show how the human soul is disciplined and perfected by suffering—to prove how much of possible good may exist in things evil and perverted—how much hope there is for those who despair—how much comfort for those whom a heartless world has taught to contemn both others and themselves, and so put barriers to the hard, cold, selfish, mocking, and levelling spirit of the day——O would I could do this!

MEDON.

On the same principle, I suppose, that they have changed the treatment of lunatics; and whereas they used to condemn poor distempered wretches to straw and darkness, stripes and a strait-waistcoat, they now send them to sunshine and green fields, to wander in gardens among birds and flowers, and soothe them with soft music and kind flattering speech.

ALDA.

You laugh at me!—perhaps I deserve it.

MEDON.

No, in truth: I am a little amused, but most honestly attentive, and perhaps wish I could think more like you. But to proceed: I allow that with this view of the case, you could not well have chosen your illustrations from real life. But why not from history?

ALDA.

As far as history could guide me I have taken her with me in one or two recent publications, which all tend to the same object. Nor have I here lost sight of her; but I have entered on a land where she alone is not to be trusted, and may make a pleasant companion, but a most fallacious guide. To drop metaphor: history informs us that such things have been done or have occurred; but when we come to inquire into motives and characters, it is the most false and partial and unsatisfactory authority we can refer to. Women are illustrious in history, not from what they have been in themselves, but generally in proportion to the mischief they have done or caused. Those characters best fitted to my purpose are precisely those of which history never heard, or disdains to speak: of those which have been handed down to us by many different authorities under different aspects we cannot judge without prejudice; in others there occur certain chasms which it is difficult to supply; and hence inconsistencies we have no means of reconciling, though doubtless they *might* be reconciled if we knew the whole, instead of a part.

MEDON.

But instance—instance!

ALDA.

Examples crowd upon me: but take the first that occurs. Do you remember that Duchess de Longueville, whose beautiful picture we were looking at yesterday?—the heroine of the Fronde? Think of that woman—bold, intriguing, profligate, vain, ambitious, factious!—who made men rebels with a smile,—or if that were not enough,—the lady was not scrupulous,—apparently without principle as without shame, nothing was *too* much!—And then think of the same woman protecting the virtuous philosopher Arnauld, when he was denounced and condemned; and, from motives which her worst enemies could not malign, secreting him in her house, unknown even to her own servants—preparing his food herself, watching for his safety, and at length saving him. Her tenderness, her patience, her discretion, her disinterested benevolence, not only defied danger, (that were little to a woman of her temper,) but endured a lengthened trial, all the ennui caused by the necessity of keeping her house, continual self-control, and the thousand small daily sacrifices which, to a vain, dissipated, proud, impatient woman, must have been hard to bear. Now, if Shakspeare had drawn the character of the Duchess de Longueville, he would have shown us the same individual woman in both situations;—for the same being, with the same faculties, and passions, and powers, it surely was: whereas in history, we see in one case a fury of discord, a woman without modesty or pity; and in the other an angel of benevolence, and a worshipper of goodness; and nothing to connect the two extremes in our fancy.

MEDON.

But these are contradictions which we meet on every page of history, which make us giddy with doubt or sick with belief; and are the proper subjects of inquiry for the moralist and the philosopher.

ALDA.

I cannot say that professed moralists and philosophers did much to help *me* out of the dilemma; but the riddle which history presented I found solved in the pages of Shakspeare. There the crooked appeared straight; the inaccessible, easy; the incomprehensible, plain. All I sought, I found there; his characters combine history and real life; they are complete individuals, whose hearts and souls are laid open before us—all may behold and all judge for themselves.

MEDON.

But all will not judge alike.

ALDA.

No; and herein lies a part of their wonderful truth. We

hear Shakspeare's men and women discussed, praised and dispraised, liked, disliked, as real human beings; and in forming our opinions of them, we are influenced by our own characters, habits of thought, prejudices, feelings, impulses, just as we are influenced with regard to our acquaintances and associates.

MEDON.

But we are then as likely to misconceive and misjudge them.

ALDA.

Yes, if we had only the same imperfect means of studying them. But we can do with them what we cannot do with real people: we can unfold the whole character before us, stripped of all pretensions of self-love, all disguises of manner. We can take leisure to examine, to analyze, to correct our own impressions, to watch the rise and progress of various passions: we can hate, love, approve, condemn, without offence to others, without pain to ourselves.

MEDON.

In this respect they may be compared to those exquisite anatomical preparations of wax; which those who could not without disgust and horror dissect a real specimen, may study, and learn the mysteries of our frame, and all the internal workings of the wondrous machine of life.

ALDA.

And it is the safer and the better way—for us, at least. But look—that brilliant rain-drop trembling there in the sunshine, suggests to me another illustration. Passion, when we contemplate it through the medium of imagination, is like a ray of light transmitted through a prism; we can calmly, and with undazzled eye, study its complicate nature, and analyze its variety of tints; but passion brought home to us in its reality, through our own feelings and experience, is like the same ray transmitted through a lens—blinding, burning, consuming where it falls.

MEDON.

Your illustration is the most poetical, I allow; but not the most just. But tell me, is the ground you have taken sufficiently large?—is the foundation you have chosen strong enough to bear the moral superstructure you raise upon it? You know the prevalent idea is, that Shakspeare's women are inferior to his men. This assertion is constantly repeated, and has been but tamely refuted.

ALDA.

Professor Richardson?—

MEDON.

He is as dry as a stick, and his refutation not successful even as a piece of logic. Then it is not sufficient for critics to assert this inferiority and want of variety; they first assume the fallacy, then argue upon it. Cibber accounts for it from the circumstance that all the female parts in Shakspeare's time were acted by boys—there were no women on the stage; and Mackenzie, who ought to have known better, says that he was not so happy in his delineations of love and tenderness, as of the other passions; because, forsooth, the majesty of his genius could not stoop to the refinements of delicacy:—preposterous!

ALDA.

Stay! before we waste epithets of indignation, let us

consider. If these people mean that Shakspeare's women are inferior in power to his men, I grant it at once ; for in Shakspeare the male and female characters bear precisely the same relation to each other that they do in nature and in society—they are not equal in prominence or in power—they are subordinate throughout. Richardson remarks, that "if situation influences the mind, and if uniformity of conduct be frequently occasioned by uniformity of condition, there *must* be a greater diversity of male than of female characters," which is true ; add to this, our limited sphere of action, consequently of experience,—and the habits of self-control rendering the outward distinctions of character and passion less striking and less strong—all this we see in Shakspeare as in nature ; for instance, Juliet is the most impassioned of his female characters, but what are *her* passions compared to those which shake the soul of Othello?

> "Eevn as the dew-drop on the myrtle leaf,
> To the vexed sea."

Look at Constance, frantic for the loss of her son—then look at Lear, maddened by the ingratitude of his daughters ; why it is the west wind blowing those aspen tops that wave before our window, compared to the tropic hurricane, when forests crash and burn, and mountains tremble to their bases!

MEDON.

True ; and Lady Macbeth, with all her soaring ambition, her vigor of intellect, her subtlety, her courage, and her cruelty—what is she, compared to Richard III.?

ALDA.

I will tell you what she is—she is a woman. Place

Lady Macbeth in comparison with Richard III., and you see at once the essential distinction between masculine and feminine ambition—though both in extreme, and overleaping all restraints of conscience or mercy. Richard says of himself, that he has "neither pity, love, nor fear." Lady Macbeth is susceptible of all three. You smile! but that remains to be proved. The reason that Shakspeare's wicked women have such a singular hold upon our fancy, is from the consistent preservation of the feminine character, which renders them more terrible, because more credible and intelligible; not like those monstrous caricatures we meet with in history—

MEDON.

In history?—this is new!

ALDA.

Yes! I repeat, in history, where certain isolated facts and actions are recorded, without any relation to causes or motives, or connecting feelings; and pictures exhibited, from which the considerate mind turns in disgust, and the feeling heart has no relief but in positive, and, I may add, reasonable incredulity. I have lately seen one of Correggio's finest pictures, in which the three furies are represented, not as ghastly deformed hags, with talons, and torches, and snaky hair, but as young women, with fine luxuriant forms and regular features, and a single serpent wreathing the tresses like a bandeau—but *such* countenances!—such a hideous expression of malice, cunning and cruelty!—and the effect is beyond conception appalling. Leonardo da Vinci worked upon the same grand principle of art in his Medusa—

> Where it is less the horror than the grace
> Which turns the gazer's spirit into stone—

* * * * * *

> 'Tis the melodious tints of beauty thrown
> Athwart the hue of guilt and glare of pain,
> That humanise and harmonise the strain.

And Shakspeare, who understood all truth, worked out his conceptions on the same principle, having said himself, that " proper deformity shows not in the fiend so horrid as in woman." Hence it is that whether he portrayed the wickedness founded in perverted power, as in Lady Macbeth; or the wickedness founded in weakness, as in Gertrude, Lady Anne, or Cressida, he is the more fearfully impressive, because we cannot claim for ourselves an exemption from the same nature, before which, in its corrupted state, we tremble with horror, or shrink with disgust.

MEDON.

Do you remember that some of the commentators of Shakspeare have thought it incumbent on their gallantry to express their utter contempt for the scene between Richard and Lady Anne, as a monstrous and incredible libel on your sex?

ALDA.

They might have spared themselves the trouble. Lady Anne is just one of those women whom we see walking in crowds through the drawing-rooms of the world—the puppets of habit, the fools of fortune, without any particular inclination for vice, or any steady principle of virtue; whose actions are inspired by vanity, not affection, and regulated by opinion, not by conscience: who are good while there is no temptation to be otherwise, and ready victims of the first soliciting to evil. In the case of Lady

Anne, we are startled by the situation; not three months a widow, and following to the sepulchre the remains of a husband and a father, she is met and wooed and won by the very man who murdered them. In such a case it required perhaps either Richard or the arch-fiend himself to tempt her successfully; but in a less critical moment, a far less subtle and audacious seducer would have sufficed. Cressida is another modification of vanity, weakness, and falsehood drawn in stronger colors. The world contains many Lady Annes and Cressidas, polished and refined externally, whom chance and vanity keep right, whom chance and vanity lead wrong, just as it may happen. When we read in history of the enormities of certain women, perfect scare-crows and ogresses, we can safely, like the Pharisee in Scripture, hug ourselves in our secure virtue, and thank God that we are not as others are:—but the wicked women in Shakspeare are portrayed with such perfect consistency and truth, that they leave us no such resource—they frighten us into reflection—they make us believe and tremble. On the other hand, his amiable women are touched with such exquisite simplicity—they have so little external pretension—and are so unlike the usual heroines of tragedy and romance, that they delight us more "than all the nonsense of the beau-ideal!" We are flattered by the perception of our own nature in the midst of so many charms and virtues: not only are they what we could wish to be, or ought to be, but what we persuade ourselves we might be, or would be, under a different and a happier state of things, and perhaps, some time or other, *may* be. They are not stuck up, like the cardinal virtues, all in a row, for us to admire and wonder at: they are not mere poetical abstractions—nor (as they have been termed) mere abstractions of the affections,—

But common clay, ta'en from the common earth,
Moulded by God, and tempered by the tears
Of angels, to the perfect form of—*woman*.

MEDON.

Beautiful lines!—Where are they?

ALDA.

I quote from memory, and I am afraid inaccurately, from a poem of Alfred Tennyson's.

MEDON.

Well, between argument, and sentiment, and logic, and poetry, you are making out a very plausible case. I think with you, that in the instances you have mentioned, (as Lady Macbeth and Richard, Juliet and Othello, and others,) the want of comparative power is only an additional excellence; but to go to an opposite extreme of delineation, we must allow that there is not one of Shakspeare's women, that, as a dramatic character, can be compared to Falstaff.

ALDA.

No; because any thing like Falstaff in the form of a woman—any such compound of wit, sensuality, and selfishness, unchecked by the moral sentiments and the affections, and touched with the same vigorous painting, would be a gross and monstrous caricature. If it could exist in nature we might find it in Shakspeare; but a moment's reflection shows us that it would be essentially an impossible combination of faculties in a female.

MEDON.

It strikes me, however, that his humorous women are

feebly drawn, in comparison with some of the female wits of other writers.

ALDA.

Because his women of wit and humor are not introduced for the sole purpose of saying brilliant things, and displaying the wit of the author; they are, as I will show you, real, natural women, in whom *wit* is only a particular and occasional modification of intellect. They are all, in the first place, affectionate, thinking beings, and moral agents; and *then* witty, as if by accident, or as the Duchess de Chaulnes said of herself, "par la grace de Dieu." As to humor, it is carried as far as possible in Mrs. Quickly; in the termagant Catherine; in Maria, in "Twelfth Night;" in Juliet's nurse; in Mrs. Ford and Mrs. Page. What can exceed in humorous naivete, Mrs. Quickly's upbraiding Falstaff, and her concluding appeal—"Didst thou not kiss me, and bid me fetch thee thirty shillings?" Is it not exquisite—irresistible? Mrs. Ford and Mrs. Page are both "merry wives," but how perfectly discriminated! Mrs. Ford has the most good nature—Mrs. Page is the cleverer of the two, and has more sharpness in her tongue, more mischief in her mirth. In these instances, I allow that the humor is more or less vulgar; but a humorous woman, whether in high or low life, has always a tinge of vulgarity.

MEDON.

I should like to see that word *vulgar* properly defined, and its meaning limited—at present it is the most arbitrary word in the language.

ALDA.

Yes; like the word romantic, it is a convenient "exploding word," and in its general application signifies nothing more than "see how much finer I am than other people!"* but in literature and character, I shall adhere to the definition of Madame de Stael, who uses the word *vulgar* as the reverse of *poetical.* Vulgarity, (as I wish to apply the word) is the negative in all things. In literature it is the total absence of elevation, and depth in the ideas, and of elegance and delicacy in the expression of them. In character, it is the absence of truth, sensibility and reflection. The vulgar in manner is the result of vulgarity of character, it is grossness, hardness, or affectation—If you would see how Shakspeare has discriminated, not only different degrees, but different kinds of plebian vulgarity in women, you have only to compare the Nurse in Romeo and Juliet with Mrs. Quickly. On the whole, if there are people, who, taking the strong and essential distinction of sex into consideration, still maintain that Shakspeare's female characters are not, in truth, in variety, in power, equal to his men—I think I shall prove the contrary.

MEDON.

I observe that you have divided your illustrations into classes; but shades of character so melt into each other, and the various faculties and powers are so blended and balanced, that all classification must be arbitrary. I am at a loss to conceive where you have drawn the line; here at the head of your first chapter I find "Characters of Intellect"—do you call Portia intellectual, and Hermione and Constance not so?

ALDA.

I know that Schlegel has said that it is impossible to arrange Shakspeare's characters in classes: yet some

* See Forster's Essay on the application of the word *romantic.*—*Essays*, vol. i.

classification was necessary for my purpose. I have therefore divided them into Characters, in which intellect and wit predominate; Characters in which fancy and passion predominate; and Characters in which the moral sentiments and affections predominate. The historical characters I have considered apart, as requiring a different mode of illustration. Portia I regard as a perfect model of an intellectual woman, in whom wit is tempered by sensibility, and fancy regulated by strong reflection. It is objected to her, to Beatrice, and others of Shakspeare's women, that the display of intellect is tinged with a coarseness of manner belonging to the age in which he wrote. To remark that the conversation and letters of high-bred and virtuous women of that time, were more bold and frank in expression than any part of the dialogue appropriated to Beatrice and Rosalind, may excuse it to our judgment, but does not reconcile it to our taste. Much has been said, and more might be said, on this subject—but I would rather not discuss it. It is a mere difference of manner which is to be regretted, but has nothing to do with the essence of the character.

MEDON.

I think you have done well in avoiding the topic altogether; but between ourselves, do you really think that the refinement of mere manner, the censorious, hypocritical, verbal scrupulosity, which is carried so far in this "picked age" of ours, is a true sign of superior refinement of taste, and purity of morals? Is it not rather a whiting of the sepulchre? I will not even allude to individual instances whom we both know; but does it not remind you, on the whole, of the tone of French manners previous to the revolution? that "décence," which Horace Walpole so admired,*

* Correspondence, vol. iii.

veiling the moral degradation, the inconceivable profligacy, of the higher classes?—Stay—I have not yet done—not to you, but *for* you, I will add thus much:—our modern idea of delicacy apparently attaches more importance to words than to things—to manners than to morals. You will hear people inveigh against the improprieties of Shakspeare, with Don Juan, or one of those infernal French novels—I beg your pardon—lying on their toilet table. Lady Florence is shocked at the sallies of Beatrice, and Beatrice, would certainly stand aghast to see Lady Florence dressed for Almack's; so you see that in both cases the fashion makes the indecorum. Let her ladyship new-model her gowns!

ALDA.

Well, well, leave Lady Florence—I would rather hear you defend Shakspeare.

MEDON.

I think it is Coleridge who so finely observes, that Shakspeare ever kept the high road of human life, whereon all travel, that he did not pick out by-paths of feeling and sentiment; in him we have no moral highway-men, and sentimental thieves and rat-catchers, and interesting villains, and amiable, elegant adulteresses,—*a-la-mode Germanorum*,—no delicate entanglements of situation, in which the grossest images are presented to the mind, disguised under the superficial attraction of style and sentiment. He flattered no bad passions, disguised no vice in the garb of virtue, trifled with no just nor generous principle. He can make us laugh at folly, and shudder at crime, yet still preserve our love for our fellow beings, and our reverence for ourselves. He has a lofty and a fearless trust in his own powers, and in the beauty and excellence of virtue; and, with his eye fixed on the lode-star of truth, steers us triumphantly among shoals and quicksands, where with any other pilot we had been wrecked:—for instance, who but himself would have dared to bring into close contact two such characters as Iago and Desdemona? Had the colors in which he has arrayed Desdemona been one atom less transparently bright and pure, the charm had been lost: she could not have borne the approximation: some shadow from the overpowering blackness of *his* character must have passed over the sunbright purity of *hers*. For observe, that Iago's disbelief in the virtue of Desdemona is not pretended, it is real. It arises from his total want of faith in all virtue; he is no more capable of conceiving goodness than she is capable of conceiving evil. To the brutal coarseness and fiendish malignity of this man, her gentleness appears only a contemptible weakness; her purity of affection, which "saw Othello's visage in his mind," only a perversion of taste; her bashful modesty, only a cloak for evil propensities;—so he represents them with all the force of language and self-conviction, and we are obliged to listen to him. He rips her to pieces before us—he would have bedeviled an angel! yet such is the unrivalled, though passive delicacy of the delineation, that it can stand it unhurt, untouched. It is wonderful!—yet natural as it is wonderful! After all there are people in the world, whose opinions and feelings are tainted by an habitual acquaintance with the evil side of society, though in action and intention they remain right; and who without the real depravity of heart and malignity of intention of Iago, judge as he does of the characters and productions of others.

ALDA.

Heavens bless me from such critics!—yet if genius,

youth, and innocence could not escape unslurred, can I hope to do so? I pity from my soul the persons you allude to—for to such minds there can exist few uncontaminated sources of pleasure, either in nature or in art.

MEDON.

Aye! "The perfumes of Paradise were poison to the Dives and made them melancholy." You pity them, and they will sneer at you. But what have we here?—"Characters of imagination—Juliet—Viola;"—are these romantic young ladies the pillars which are to sustain your moral edifice? Are they to serve as examples or as warnings for the youth of this enlightened age?

ALDA.

As warnings of course—what else?

MEDON.

Against the dangers of romance? but where are they? "Vraiment," as B. Constant says, ', je ne vois pas qu'en fait d'enthousiasme, le feu soit a là maison." Where are they—these disciples of poetry and romance, these victims of disinterested devotion and believing truth, these unblown roses—all conscience and tenderness—whom it is so necessary to guard against too much confidence in others, and to little in themselves—where are they?

ALDA.

Wandering in the Elysian fields, I presume, with the romantic young gentlemen who are too generous, too zealous in defence of innocence, too enthusiastic in their admiration of virtue, too violent in their hatred of vice, too sincere in friendship, too faithful in love, too active and disinterested in the cause of truth—

MEDON.

Very fair! But seriously, do you think it necessary to guard young people in this selfish and calculating age, against an excess of sentiment and imagination? Do you allow no distinction between the romance of exaggerated sentiment, and the romance of elevated thought? Do *you* bring cold water to quench the smouldering ashes of enthusiasm? Methinks it is rather superfluous; and that another doctrine is needed to withstand the heartless system of expediency which is the favorite philosophy of the day. The warning you speak of may be gently hinted to the few who are in danger of being misled by an excess of the generous impulses of fancy and feeling; but need hardly, I think, be proclaimed by sound of trumpet amid the mocks of the world. No, no; there are young women in these days, but there is no such thing as youth—the bloom of existence is sacrificed to a fashionable education, and where we should find the rose-buds of the spring, we see only the full-blown, flaunting, precocious roses of the hot-bed.

ALDA.

Blame then that *forcing* system of education, the most pernicious, the most mistaken, the most far-reaching in its miserable and mischievous effects, that ever prevailed in this world. The custom which shut up women in convents till they were married, and then launched them innocent and ignorant on society, was bad enough; but not worse than a system of education which inundates us with hard, clever, sophisticated girls, trained by knowing mothers and all-accomplished governesses, with whom vanity and expediency take place of conscience and affection—(in other words, of romance)—"frutto senile in sul giovenil fiore;" with feelings and passions suppressed or contracted not governed by higher faculties and purer pinciples; with whom opinion—the same false honor which sends men out to fight duels—stands instead of the strength and the light of virtue within their own souls. Hence the strange anomalies of artificial society—girls of sixteen who are models of manner, miracles of prudence, marvels of learning, who sneer at sentiment, and laugh at the Juliets and the Imogens; and matrons of forty, who, when the passions should be tame and wait upon the judgment, amaze the world and put us to confusion with their doings.

MEDON.

Or turn politicians to vary the excitement.—How I hate political women!

ALDA.

Why do you hate them?

MEDON.

Because they are mischievous.

ALDA.

But why are they mischievous?

MEDON.

Why!—why are they mischievous? Nay, ask them, or ask the father of all mischief, who has not a more efficient instrument to further his designs in this world, than a woman run mad with politics. The number of political intriguing women of this time, whose boudoirs and drawing-rooms are the *foyers* of party-spirit, is another trait of resemblance between the state of society now, and that which existed at Paris before the revolution.

ALDA.

And do you think, like some interesting young lady in

Miss Edgeworth's tales, that "women have nothing to do with politics?"* Do you mean to say that women are not capable of comprehending the principles of legislation, or of feeling an interest in the government and welfare of their country? that they are incapable of perceiving and sympathizing in the progress of great events?—That they

* The real sentiments of Maria Edgeworth on this oft contested subject, (or at least what I presume and hope to be her own sentiments,) may be found in the tale of "Helen," published since the first edition of this little work: they are spoken of by Lady Davenant, the most splendid and vigorous of all her female portraits, and have a characteristic beauty and propriety as well as general truth and sound practical sense. "Let me observe to you," says Lady Davenant, "that the position of women in society is somewhat different from what it was a hundred years ago, or as it was sixty, or I will say thirty years since. Women are now so highly cultivated, and political subjects are at present of so much importance, of such high interest to all human creatures who live together in society, you can hardly expect, Helen, that you as a rational being, can go through the world as it now is, without forming any opinion on points of public importance. You cannot, I conceive, satisfy yourself with the common namby-pamby, little missy phrase, 'Ladies have nothing to do with politics.'—but a little farther on she adds with equal truth, "Of the public dangers and private inconveniences, that result from Women becoming politicians, or as you better express our meaning, interfering with public affairs, no one can be more aware than I am. *Interfering*, observe I say, for I would mark and keep the line between influence and interference. Female influence must, will, and ought to exist on all political subjects as on all others; but this influence should be domestic, not public; the customs of society have to mould it."

"The customs of society" vary from age to age and cannot make wrong right,—but in this case *nature* as it seems to me "has so ruled it." This indirect but powerful female influence in politics and government, allowed in its fullest extent even by those who most bitterly denounce it, ought surely to awaken some considerations on the possibility of converting what has hitherto been a fertile cause of misery and mischief, into a source of ennobling interest for ourselves, and of pure motive and high action in the other sex.

cannot feel patriotism? Believe me, when we do feel it, our patriotism, like our courage and our love, has a purer source than with you; for a man's patriotism has always some tinge of egotism, while a woman's patriotism is generally a sentiment of the noblest kind.

MEDON.

I agree in all this: and all this does not mitigate my horror of political women in general, who are I repeat it, both mischievous and absurd. If you could but hear the reasoning in these feminine coteries!——but you never talk politics.

ALDA.

Indeed I do, when I can get any one to listen to me; but I prefer listening to others. As for the evil you complain of, impute it to that imperfect education which at once cultivates and enslaves the intellect, and loads the memory, while it fetters the judgment. Women, however well read in history, never generalize in politics; never argue an any broad or general principle; never reason from a consideration of past events, their causes and consequences. But they are always political, through their affections, their prejudices, their personal *liaisons*, their hopes, their fears.

MEDON.

If it were no worse, I could stand it; for *that* is at least feminine.

ALDA.

But most mischievous. For hence it is, that we make such blind partizans, such violent party women, and such wretched politicians. I never heard a woman *talk* politics, as it is termed, that I could not discern at once the motive, the affection, the secret bias, which swayed her opinions and inspired her arguments. If it appeared to the Grecian sage so "difficult for a man not to love himself, nor the things that belong to him, but justice only?" —how much more for woman!

MEDON.

Then you think that a better education, based on truer moral principles, would render women more reasonable politicians, or at least give them some right to meddle with politics?

ALDA.

It would cease in that case to be *meddling*, as you term it, for it would be legitimatized. It is easy to sneer at political and mathematical ladies, and quote Lord Byron—but O leave those angry common-places to others—they do not come well from you. Do not force me to remind you, that women have achieved enough to silence them for ever;* and how often must that truism be repeated, that it is not a woman's attainments which make her amiable or unamiable, estimable or the contrary, but her qualities? A time is coming perhaps when the education of women will be considered with a view to their future destination as the mothers and nurses of legislators and statesmen; and the cultivation of their power of reflection and moral feelings supersede the exciting drudgery by which they are now crammed with knowledge and accomplishments.

MEDON.

Well—till that blessed period arrives, I wish you would leave us the province of politics to ourselves. I see here

* In our own time Madame de Stael, Mrs. Somerville, Harriet Martineau, Mrs. Marcet; we need not go back to the Rolands and Agnesi, nor even to our own Lucy Hutchinson.

you have treated of a very different class of beings, "*women in whom the affections and the moral sentiments predominate.*" Are there many such, think you, in the world?

ALDA.

Yes, many such. The development of affection and sentiment is more quiet and unobtrusive than that of passion and intellect, and less observed; it is more common, too, therefore less remarked; but in women it generally gives the prevailing tone to the character, except where vanity has been made the ruling motive.

MEDON.

Except! I admire your exception! You make in this case the rule the exception. Look round the world.

ALDA.

You are not one of those with whom that common phrase "the world" signifies the circle, whatever and wherever that may be, which limits our individual experience—as a child considers the visible horizon as the bounds which shut in the mighty universe? Believe me, it is a sorry, vulgar kind of wisdom, if it be wisdom—a shallow and confined philosophy, if it be philosophy—which resolves all human motives and impulses into egotism in one sex, and vanity in the other. Such may be in the way of *the world*, as it is called, the result of a very artificial and corrupt state of society, but such is not general nature, nor female nature. Would you see the kindly self-sacrificing affections developed under their most honest but least poetical guise—displayed without any mixture of vanity, and unchecked in the display by any fear of being thought vain?—you will see it, not among the prosperous, the high-born, the educated, "far, far removed from want, and grief, and fear," but among the poor, the miserable, the perverted—among those habitually exposed to all influences that harden and deprave.

MEDON.

I believe it—nay, I know it; but how should *you* know it?—or know any thing of the strange places of refuge which truth and nature have found in the two extremes of society?

ALDA.

It is no matter what I have seen or known; and for the two extremes of society, I leave them to the author of Paul Clifford, and that most exquisite painter of living manners, Mrs. Gore. St. Giles's is no more *nature* than St. James's. I wanted character in its essential truth, not modified by particular customs, by fashion, by situation. I wished to illustrate the manner in which the affections would naturally display themselves in women—whether combined with high intellect, regulated by reflection, elevated by imagination, or purified by the moral sentiments; or existing with perverted dispositions or contending with untoward fate. I found all these in Shakspeare; and his delineations of women, in whom the virtuous and calm affections predominate, and triumph over shame, fear, pride, resentment, vanity, jealousy, are particularly worthy of consideration—and perfect in their kind, because so quiet in their effect.

MEDON.

Most true; and I believe some of his commentators have remarked in general terms on those beautiful pictures of female friendship, and of the generous affection of women for each other, which we find in Shakspeare. Other writers, especially dramatic writers, have found ample food for wit and satiric delineation in the littleness of feminine spite and rivalry, in the mean spirit of competition, the petty jealousy of superior charms, the mutual slander and mistrust, the transient leagues of folly or selfishness miscalled friendship; all the result of an education which makes vanity the ruling principle, and of a false position in society. Shakspeare, who looked upon women with the spirit of humanity, wisdom and deep love, has done justice to their natural good tendency and kindly sympathies. In the friendship of Beatrice and Hero, of Rosalind and Celia; in the description of the girlish attachment of Helena and Hermia, he has represented truth and generous affection rising superior to all the usual sources of female rivalry and jealousy; and with such force, and simplicity, and obvious self-conviction, that he absolutely forces the same conviction on us.

ALDA.

Add to these the generous feeling of Viola for her rival Olivia; of Julia for her rival Sylvia; of Helena for Diana; of the Old Countess for Helena, in the same play; and even the affection of the wicked queen in Hamlet for the gentle Ophelia, which prove that Shakspeare thought—(and when did he ever think other than the truth?)—that women have by nature "virtues that are merciful," and can be just, tender, and true to their sister women, whatever wits and wordlings, and satirists and fashionable poets, may say or sing of us to the contrary. There is another thing which he has most deeply felt and beautifully represented,—the distinction between masculine and feminine *courage*. A man's courage is often a mere animal quality, and in its most elevated form a point of honor. But a woman's courage is always a virtue, because it is not required of us; it is not one of the means through which we seek admiration and applause; on the contrary, we are courageous through our affections and mental energies, not through our vanity or our strength. A woman's heroism is always the excess of sensibility. Do you remember Lady Fanshawe putting on a sailor's jacket, and his "blue thrum cap," and standing at her husband's side, unknown to him during a sea fight? there she stood, all bathed in tears, but fixed to that spot. Her husband's exclamation when he turned and discovered her—"Good God! that love should make such a change as this!" is applicable to all the acts of courage which we read or hear of in women. This is the courage of Juliet when, after summing up all the possible consequences of her own act, till she almost maddens herself with terror, she drinks the sleeping potion; and for that passive fortitude which is founded in piety and pure strength of affection, such as the heroism of Lady Russel and Gertrude de Wart, he has given us some of the noblest modifications of it in Hermione, in Cordelia, in Imogen, in Katharine of Arragon.

MEDON.

And what then do you call the courage of Lady Macbeth?—

> My hands are of your color, but I shame
> To wear a heart so white.

And again,

> A little water clears us of this deed.
> How easy is it then!

If this is not mere masculine indifference to blood and death, mere firmness of nerve, what is it?

ALDA.

Not *that*, at least which apparently you deem it; you will find, if you have patience to read me to the end, that I have judged Lady Macbeth very differently. Take these frightful passages with the context—take the whole situation, and you will see that it is no such thing. A friend of mine truly observed, that if Macbeth had been a ruffian without any qualms of conscience, Lady Macbeth would have been the one to shrink and tremble: but that which quenched *him* lent her fire. The absolute necessity for self-command, the strength of her reason, and her love for her husband, combine at this critical moment to conquer all fear but the fear of detection, leaving her the full possession of her faculties. Recollect that the same woman who speaks with such horrible indifference of a little water clearing the blood-stain from her hand, sees in imagination that hand for ever reeking, for ever polluted; and when reason is no longer awake and paramount over the violated feelings of nature and womanhood, we behold her making unconscious efforts to wash out that "damned spot," and sighing, heart-broken, over that "little hand" which all the perfumes of Arabia will never sweeten more.

MEDON.

I hope you have given her a place among the women in whom the tender affections and moral sentiments predominate.

ALDA.

You laugh; but, jesting apart, perhaps it would have been a more accurate classification than placing her among the historical characters.

MEDON.

Apropos to the historical characters, I hope you have refused that *insolent* assumption, (shall I call it so?) that Shakspeare tampered inexcusably with the truth of history. He is the truest of all historians. His anachronisms always remind me of those in the fine old Italian pictures; either they are insignificant, or, if properly considered, are really beauties: for instance, every one knows that Correggio's St. Jerome presenting his books to the Virgin involves half a dozen anachronisms, to say nothing of that heavenly figure of the Magdalen, in the same picture, kissing the feet of the infant Saviour. Some have ridiculed, some have excused this strange combination of inaccuracies; but is it less one of the divinest pieces of sentiment and poetry that ever breathed and glowed from the canvas? You remember too the famous Nativity, by some Neapolitan painter, who had placed Mount Vesuvius and the Bay of Naples in the back ground?—In these and a hundred other instances, no one seems to feel that the apparent absurdity involves the highest truth, and that the sacred beings thus represented, if once allowed as objects of faith and worship, are eternal under every aspect, and independent of all time and all locality. So it is with Shakspeare and his anachronisms; the learned scorn of Johnson and some of his brotherhood of commentators, and the eloquent defence of Schlegel, seem in this case both superfluous. If he chose to make the Delphic oracle, and Giulio Romano cotemporary—what does it signify? he committed no anachronisms of character. He has not metamorphosed Cleopatra into a turtle-dove, nor Katharine of Arragon into a sentimental heroine. He is true to the spirit and generally even to the *letter* of history: where he deviates from the latter, the reason always may be found in some higher beauty and more universal truth.

ALDA.

I have proved this, I think, by placing parallel with the dramatic character all the historic testimony I could collect relative to Constance, Cleopatra, Katharine of Arragon, &c.

MEDON.

Analyzing the character of Cleopatra must have been something like catching a meteor by the tail, and making it sit for its picture.

ALDA.

Something like it, in truth; but those of Miranda and Ophelia were more embarrassing, because they seemed to defy all analysis. It was like intercepting the dew-drop or the snow-flake ere it fell to earth, and subjecting it to a chemical process.

MEDON.

Some one said the other day that Shakspeare had never drawn a coquette. What is Cleopatra but the empress and type of all the coquettes that ever were—or are? But now for the moral.

ALDA.

The moral!—of what.

MEDON.

Of your book. It *has* a moral, I suppose.

ALDA.

It has indeed a very deep one, which those who seek will find. If now I have answered all your considerations and objections, and sufficiently explained my own views, may I proceed?

MEDON.

If you please—I am now prepared to listen in earnest.

CHARACTERS OF INTELLECT.

PORTIA.

We hear it asserted, not seldom by way of compliment to us women, that intellect is of no sex. If this mean that the same faculties of mind are common to men and women, it is true; in any other signification it appears to me false, and the reverse of a compliment. The intellect of woman bears the same relation to that of man as her physical organization;—it is inferior in power, and different in kind. That certain women have surpassed certain men in bodily strength or intellectual energy, does not contradict the general principle founded in nature. The essential and invariable distinction appears to me this : in men the intellectual faculties exist more self-poised and self-directed—more independent of the rest of the character, than we ever find them in women, with whom talent, however predominant, is in a much greater degree modified by the sympathies and moral qualities.

In thinking over all the distinguished women I can at this moment call to mind, I recollect but one, who, in the exercise of all rare talent, belied her sex, but the moral qualities had been first perverted.* It is from not knowing, or not allowing, this general principle, that men of genius have committed some signal mistakes ; they have given us exquisite and just delineations of the more peculiar characteristics of women, as modesty, grace, tenderness ; and when they have attempted to portray them with the powers common to both sexes, as wit, energy, intellect, they have plundered in some respect ; they could form no conception of intellect which was not masculine, and therefore have either suppressed the feminine attributes altogether and drawn coarse caricatures, or they have made them completely artificial.† Women distinguished for wit may sometimes appear masculine and flippant, but the cause must be sought elsewhere than in nature, who disclaims all such. Hence the witty and intellectual ladies of our comedies and novels are all in the fashion of some particular time ;

* Artemisia Gentileschi, an Italian artist of the seventeenth century, painted one or two pictures, considered admirable as works of art, of which the subjects are the most vicious and barbarous conceivable. I remember one of these in the gallery of Florence, which I looked at once, but once, and wished then as I do now, the privilege of burning it to ashes.

† Lucy Ashton, in the Bride of Lammermoor, may be placed next to Desdemona ; Diana Vernon is (comparatively) a failure, as every woman will allow ; while the masculine lady Geraldine, in Miss Edgeworth's tale of Ennui, and the intellectual Corinne, are consistent, essential women : the distinction is more easily felt than analyzed

they are like some old portraits which can still amuse and please by the beauty of the workmanship, in spite of the graceless costume or grotesque accompaniments, but from which we turn to worship with ever new delight the Floras and goddesses of Titian—the saints and virgins of Raffaelle and Domenichino. So the Millamants and Belindas, the Lady Townleys, the Lady Teazles are out of date, while Portia and Rosalind, in whom nature and the feminine character are paramount, remain bright and fresh to the fancy as when first created.

Portia, Isabella, Beatrice, and Rosalind, may be classed together, as characters of intellect, because, when compared with others, they are at once distinguished by their mental superiority. In Portia it is intellect, kindled into romance by a poetical imagination; in Isabel, it is intellect elevated by religious principle; in Beatrice, intellect animated by spirit; in Rosalind, intellect softened by sensibility. The wit which is lavished on each is profound, or pointed, or sparkling, or playful—but always feminine, like spirits distilled from flowers, it always remind us of its origin;— it is a volatile essence, sweet as powerful; and to pursue the comparison a step further the wit of Portia is like attar of roses, rich and concentrated; that of Rosalind, like cotton dipped in aromatic vinegar; the wit of Beatrice is like sal volatile; and that of Isabel, like the incense wafted to heaven. Of these four exquisite characters, considered as dramatic and poetical conceptions, it is difficult to pronounce which is most perfect in its way, most admirably drawn, most highly finished. But if considered in another point of view, as women and individuals, as breathing realities, clothed in flesh and blood, I believe we must assign the first rank to Portia, as uniting in herself in a more eminent degree than the others, all the noblest and most loveable qualities that ever met together in woman;

and presenting a complete personification of Petrarch's exquisite epitome of female perfection :

> Il vago spirito ardento,
> E'n alto intelletto, un puro core.

It is singular, that hitherto no critical justice has been done to the character of Portia : it is yet more wonderful, that one of the finest writers on the eternal subject of Shakspeare and his perfections, should accuse Portia of pedantry and affectation, and confess she is not a great favorite of his,—a confession quite worthy of him, who avers his predilection for servant maids, and a preference of the Fannys and the Pamelas over the Clementinas and Clarissas.* Schlegel, who has given several pages to a rapturous eulogy on the Merchant of Venice, simply designates Portia, as a "rich, beautiful, clever heiress." If Portia had been created as a mere instrument to bring about a dramatic catastrophe—if she had merely detected the flaw in Antonio's bond, and used it as a means to baffle the Jew, she might have been pronounced a clever woman. But what Portia does, is forgotten in what she *is*. The rare and harmonious blending of energy, gentleness, wisdom, and feeling, in her fine character, make the epithet *clever* sound like a discord as applied to *her*, and places her infinitely beyond the slight praise of Richardson and Schlegel, neither of whom appear to have fully comprehended her.†

* Hazlitt's Essays, vol. ii. p. 167.

† In the first edition I protested against the word *clever* as quite inapplicable to Portia. I find that Schlegel's word is *geistreich*, literally *rich in soul or spirit*, a strong and beautiful expression, and just as it is beautiful. Would it not be well, if this common and comprehensive word clever were more accurately defined, or at least, more accurately used? It signifies properly, not so much the possession of high powers, as dexterity in the adaptation of certain faculties (not necessarily of a high order) to a certain end or aim—not always the worthiest. It implies something common-place, inasmuch as it speaks the presence of the *active* and *perceptive*, with a deficiency of the *feeling* and *reflective* powers : and, applied to a woman, does it not almost invariably suggest the idea of something we should

These and other critics have been aparently so dazzled and engrossed by the amazing character of Shylock that Portia has received less than justice at their hands: while the fact is, that Shylock is not a finer or more finished character in his way, than Portia in her's. These two splendid figures are worthy of each other; worthy of being placed together within the same rich frame-work of enchanting poetry, and glorious and graceful forms. She hangs beside the terrible, the inexorable Jew, the brilliant lights of her character set off by the shadowy power of his, like a magnificent beauty-breathing Titian by the side of a gorgeous Rembrandt.

Portia is endued with her own share of those delightful qualities, which Shakspeare has lavished on many of his female characters; but, besides the dignity, the sweetness, and tenderness which should distinguish her sex generally, she is individualized by qualities peculiar to herself: by her high mental powers, her enthusiasm of temperament, her decision of purpose, and her buoyancy of spirit. These are innate: she has other distinguishing qualities more external, and which are the result of the circumstances in which she is placed. Thus she is the heiress of a princely name and countless wealth: a train of obedient pleasures have ever waited round her; and from infancy she has breathed an atmosphere redolent of perfume and blandishment. Accordingly there is a commanding grace, a high-bred, airy elegance, a spirit of magnificence, in all that she does and says, as one to whom splendor had been familiar from her very birth. She treads as though her foot-

distrust or shrink from, if not allied to a higher nature? The profligate French women, who ruled the councils of Europe in the middle of the last century, were clever women; and that *philosopheress* Madame Du Chatelet, who managed at one and the same moment, the thread of an intrigue, her cards at piquet, and a calculation in algebra, was a very clever woman.

steps had been among marble palaces, beneath roofs of fretted gold, o'er cedar floors and pavements of jasper and porphyry—amid gardens full of statues, and flowers, and fountains and haunting music. She is full of penetrative wisdom, and genuine tenderness, and lively wit; but as she has never known want, or grief, or fear, or disappointment, her wisdom is without a touch of the sombre or the sad; her affections are all mixed up with faith, hope, and joy; and her wit has not a particle of malevolence or causticity.

It is well known that the Merchant of Venice is founded on two different tales; and in weaving together his double plot in so masterly a manner, Shakspeare has rejected altogether the character of the astutious lady of Belmont with her magic potions, who figures in the Italian novel. With yet more refinement, he has thrown out all the licentious part of the story, which some of his cotemporary dramatists would have seized on with avidity, and made the best or the worst of it possible; and he has substituted the trial of the caskets from another source.* We are not told expressly where Belmont is situated; but as Bassanio takes ship to go thither from Venice, and as we find them afterwards ordering horses from Belmont to Padua, we will imagine Portia's hereditary palace as standing on some lovely promontory between Venice and Trieste, overlooking the blue Adriatic, with the Friuli mountains or the Euganean hills for its back ground, such as we often see in one of Claude's or Poussin's elysian landscapes. In a scene, in a home like this, Shakspeare having first ex-

* In the "Mercatante di Venezia" of Ser. Giovanni, we have the whole story of Antonio and Bassanio, and part of the story, but not the character of Portia. The incident of the caskets is from the Gesta Romanorum.

orcised the original possessor has placed his Portia; and so endowed her, that all the wild, strange, and moving circumstances of the story become natural, probable, and necessary in connexion with her. That such a woman should be chosen by the solving of an enigma, is not surprising: herself and all around her, the scene, the country, the age in which she is placed, breathe of poetry, romance and enchantment.

From the four quarters of the earth they come
To kiss this shrine, this mortal breathing saint.
The Hyrcanian deserts, and the vasty wilds
Of wide Arabia, are as thoroughfares now,
For princes to come view fair Portia;
The watery kingdom, whose ambitious head
Spits in the face of heaven, is no bar
To stop the foreign spirits; but they come
As o'er a brook to see fair Portia.

The sudden plan which she forms for the release of her husband's friend, her disguise, and her deportment as the young and learned doctor, would appear forced and improbable in any other woman; but in Portia are the simple and natural result of her character.* The quickness with which she perceives the legal advantage which may be taken of the circumstances; the journey to consult her learned cousin the Doctor Bellario, the spirit of adventure with which she engages in the masquerading, and the decision, firmness, and intelligence with which she executes her generous purpose, are all in perfect keeping, and nothing appears forced—nothing as introduced merely for theatrical effect.

* In that age, delicate points of law were not determined by the ordinary judges of the provinces, but by doctors of law, who were called from Bologna, Padua, and other places celebrated for their legal colleges.

But all the finest parts of Portia's character are brought to bear in the trial scene. There she shines forth all her divine self. Her intellectual powers, her elevated sense of religion, her high honorable principles, her best feelings as a woman, are all displayed. She maintains at first a calm self-command, as one sure of carrying her point in the end; yet the painful heart-thrilling uncertainty in which she keeps the whole court until suspense verges upon agony, is not contrived for effect merely; it is necessary and inevitable. She has two objects in view; to deliver her husband's friend, and to maintain her husband's honor by the discharge of his just debt, though paid out of her own wealth ten times over. It is evident that she would rather owe the safety of Antonio to any thing, rather than the legal quibble with which her cousin Bellario had armed her, and which she reserves as a last resource. Thus all the speeches addressed to Shylock in the first instance, are either direct or indirect experiments on his temper and feelings. She must be understood from the beginning to the end, as examining with intense anxiety the effect of her own words on his mind and countenance; as watching for that relenting spirit, which she hopes to awaken either by reason or persuasion. She begins by an appeal to his mercy, in that matchless piece of eloquence which, with an irresistible and solemn pathos, falls upon the heart like "gentle dew from heaven:"—but in vain; for that blessed dew, drops not more fruitless and unfelt on the parched sand of the desert, than do those heavenly words upon the ear of Shylock. She next attacks his avarice;

> Shylock, there's *thrice* thy money offered thee!

Then she appeals, in the same breath, both to his avarice and his pity:

Be merciful!
Take thrice thy money. Bid me tear the bond.

All that she says afterwards—her strong expressions, which are calculated to strike a shuddering horror through the nerves—the reflections she interposes—her delays and circumlocution, to give time for any latent feeling of commiseration to display itself—all, all are premeditated, and tend in the same manner to the object she has in view. Thus—

You must prepare your bosom for his knife.
Therefore lay bare your bosom!

These two speeches, though addressed apparently to Antonio, are spoken *at* Shylock, and are evidently intended to penetrate *his* bosom. In the same spirit, she asks for the balance to weigh the pound of flesh; and entreats of Shylock to have a surgeon ready—

Have by some surgeon, Shylock, on your charge,
To stop his wounds, lest he do bleed to death!

SHYLOCK.
Is it so nominated in the bond?

PORTIA.
It is not so expressed—but what of that?
'Twere good you do so much, for *charity!*

So unwilling is her sanguine and generous spirit to resign all hope, or to believe that humanity is absolutely extinct in the bosom of the Jew, that she calls on Antonio, as a last resource to speak for himself. His gentle yet manly resignation—the deep pathos of his farewell, and the affectionate allusion to herself in his last address to Bassanio—

Commend me to your honorable wife;
Say how I lov'd you, speak me fair in death, &c.

are well calculated to swell that emotion, which through the whole scene must have been laboring suppressed within her heart.

At length the crisis arrives, for patience and womanhood can endure no longer; and when Shylock, carrying his savage bent "to the last hour of act," springs on his victim—"A sentence! come, prepare!" then the smothered scorn, indignation, and disgust, burst forth with an impetuosity which interferes with the judicial solemnity she had at first affected;—particularly in the speech—

> Therefore, prepare thee to cut off the flesh.
> Shed thou no blood; nor cut thou less nor more
> But just the pound of flesh: if thou tak'st more,
> Or less than, a just pound,—be it but so much
> As makes it light, or heavy, in the substance,
> Or the division of the twentieth part
> Of one poor scruple; nay, if the scale do turn
> But in the estimation of a hair,—
> Thou diest, and all thy goods are confiscate.

But she afterwards recovers her propriety, and triumphs with a cooler scorn and a more self-possessed exultation.

It is clear that, to feel the full force and dramatic beauty of this marvellous scene, we must go along with Portia as well as with Shylock; we must understand her concealed purpose, keep in mind her noble motives, and pursue in our fancy the under current of feeling, working in her mind throughout. The terror and the power of Shylock's character,—his deadly and inexorable malice,—would be too oppressive; the pain and pity too intolerable, and the horror of the possible issue too overwhelming, for the intellectual relief afforded by this double source of interest and contemplation.

I come now to that capacity for warm and generous affection, that tenderness of heart which render Portia no less loveable as a woman than admirable for her mental endowments. The affections are to the intellect, what the forge is to the metal; it is they which temper and shape it to all good purposes, and soften, strengthen, and purify it. What an exquisite stroke of judgment in the poet, to make the mutual passion of Portia and Bassanio, though unacknowledged to each other. anterior to the play! Bassanio's confession very properly comes first;—

BASSANIO.

In Belmont is a lady richly left,
And she is fair, and fairer than that word,
Of wond'rous virtues; sometimes from her eyes
I did receive fair speechless messages;
* * * * *

and prepares us for Portia's half betrayed, unconscious election of this most graceful and chivalrous admirer—

NERISSA.

Do you not remember, lady, in your father's time, a Venetian, a scholar and a soldier, that came hither in company of the Marquis of Montferrat?

PORTIA.

Yes, yes, it was Bassanio; as I think, so he was called.

NERISSA.

True, madam; he, of all the men that ever my foolish eyes looked upon, was the best deserving a fair lady.

PORTIA.

I remember him well; and I remember him worthy of thy praise.

Our interest is thus awakened for the lovers from the very first; and what shall be said of the casket scene with Bassanio, where every line which Portia speaks is so worthy of herself, so full of sentiment and beauty, and poetry and passion? Too naturally frank for disguiso, too modest to confess her depth of love while the issue of the trial remains in suspense,—the conflict between love and fear, and maidenly dignity, cause the most delicious confusion that ever tinged a woman's cheek, or dropped in broken utterance from her lips.

I pray you, tarry; pause a day or two,
Before you hazard: for, in choosing wrong,
I lose your company; therefore, forbear a while:
There's something tells me, (but it is not love,)
I would not lose you; and you know yourself,
Hate counsels not in such a quality:
But lest you should not understand me well,
(And yet a maiden hath no tongue but thought,)
I would detain you here some month or two,
Before you venture for me. I could teach you
How to choose right,—but then I am forsworn;—
So will I never be; so you may miss me;
But if you do, you'll make me wish a sin,
That I had been forsworn. Beshrew your eyes,
They have overlooked me, and divided me;
One half of me is yours, the other half yours,—
My own, I would say; but if mine, then yours,
And so all yours!

The short dialogue between the lovers is exquisite.

BASSANIO.

Let me choose:
For, as I am, I live upon the rack.

PORTIA.

Upon the rack, Bassanio? Then confess
What treason there is mingled with your love.

BASSANIO.

None, but that ugly treason of mistrust,
Which makes me fear the enjoying of my love;
There may as well be amity and life
'Tween snow and fire, as treason and my love.

PORTIA.
Ay, but I fear you speak upon the rack,
Where men enforced do speak any thing.

BASSANIO.
Promise me life, and I'll confess the truth.

PORTIA.
Well, then, confess, and live.

BASSANIO.
Confess and love
Had been the very sum of my confession!
O happy torment, when my torturer
Doth teach me answers for deliverance!

A prominent feature in Portia's character, is that confiding, buoyant spirit, which mingles with all her thoughts and affections. And here let me observe, that I never yet met in real life, nor ever read in tale or history, of any woman, distinguished for intellect of the highest order, who was not also remarkable for this trusting spirit, this hopefulness and cheerfulness of temper, which is compatible with the most serious habits of thought, and the most profound sensibility. Lady Wortley Montagu was one instance; and Madame de Staël furnishes another much more memorable. In her Corinne, whom she drew from herself, this natural brightness of temper is a prominent part of the character. A disposition to doubt, to suspect, and to despond, in the young, argues, in general, some inherent weakness, moral or physical, or some miserable and radical error of education: in the old, it is one of the first symptoms of age; it speaks of the influence of sorrow and experience, and foreshows the decay of the stronger and more generous powers of the soul. Portia's strength of intellect takes a natural tinge from the flush and bloom of her young and prosperous existence, and from her fervid imagination. In the casket scene, she fears indeed the issue of the trial, on which more than her life is hazarded; but while she trembles, her hope is stronger than her fear. While Bassanio is contemplating the caskets, she suffers herself to dwell for one moment on the possibility of disappointment and misery.

> Let music sound, while he doth make his choice;
> Then if he lose, he makes a swan-like end,
> Fading in music: that the comparison
> May stand more proper, my eye shall be the stream
> And wat'ry death-bed for him.

Then immediately follows that revulsion of feeling, so beautifully characteristic of the hopeful, trusting, mounting spirit of this noble creature:

> But he may win!
> And what is music then! then music is
> Even as the flourish, when true subjects bow
> To a new-crown'd monarch: such it is
> As are those dulcet sounds in break of day,
> That creep into the dreaming bridegroom's ear,
> And summon him to marriage. Now he goes
> With no less presence, but with much more love
> Than young Alcides, when he did redeem
> The virgin tribute paid by howling Troy
> To the sea-monster. I stand here for sacrifice.

Here, not only the feeling itself, born of the elastic and sanguine spirit which had never been touched by grief; but the images in which it comes arrayed to her fancy,—the bridegroom waked by music on his wedding morn,—the new-crowned monarch,—the comparison of Bassanio to the young Alcides, and of herself to the daughter of Laomedon,—are all precisely what would have suggested themselves to the fine poetical imagination of Portia, in such a moment.

Her passionate exclamations of delight, when Bassanio has fixed on the right casket, are as strong as though she had despaired before. Fear and doubt she could repel; the native elasticity of her mind bore up against them; yet she makes us feel, that as the sudden joy overpowers her almost to fainting, the disappointment would as certainly have killed her.

> How all the other passions fleet to air,
> As doubtful thoughts, and rash-embraced despair,
> And shudd'ring fear, and green-eyed jealousy!
> O love! be moderate, allay thy ecstacy;
> In measure rein thy joy, scant this excess:
> I feel too much thy blessing; make it less,
> For fear I surfeit!

Her subsequent surrender of herself in heart and soul, of her maiden freedom and her vast possessions, can never be read without deep emotion; for not only all the tenderness and delicacy of a devoted woman, are here blended with all the dignity which becomes the princely heiress of Belmont, but the serious, measured self-possession of her address to her lover when all suspense is over, and all concealment superfluous, is most beautifully consistent with the character. It is, in truth, an awful moment, that in which a gifted woman first discovers, that besides talents and powers, she has also passions and affections; when she first begins to suspect their vast importance in the sum of her existence; when she first confesses that her happiness is no longer in her own keeping, but is surrendered for ever and for ever into the dominion of another. The possession of uncommon powers of mind are so far from affording relief or resource in the first intoxicating surprise—I had almost said terror—of such a revolution, that they render it more intense. The sources of thought multiply beyond calculation, the sources of feeling, and mingled, they rush together, a torrent deep as strong. Because Portia is endued with that enlarged comprehension, which looks before and after, she does not feel the less, but the more: because from the height of her commanding intellect she can contemplate the force, the tendency, the consequences of her own sentiments—because she is fully sensible of her own situation, and the value of all she concedes—the concession is not made with less entireness and devotion of heart, less confidence in the truth and worth of her lover, than when Juliet, in a similar moment, but without any such intrusive reflections—any check but the instinctive delicacy of her sex, flings herself and her fortunes at the feet of her lover:

> And all my fortunes at thy foot I'll lay,
> And follow thee, my lord, through all the world.*

In Portia's confession, which is not breathed from a moonlit balcony, but spoken openly in the presence of her attendants and vassals, there is nothing of the passionate self-abandonment of Juliet, nor of the artless simplicity of Miranda, but a consciousness and a tender seriousness, approaching to solemnity, which are not less touching.

> You see me, Lord Bassanio, where I stand,
> Such as I am: though for myself alone,
> I would not be ambitious in my wish,
> To wish myself much better; yet, for you,
> I would be trebled twenty times myself;
> A thousand times more fair, ten thousand times
> More rich; that only to stand high in your account,
> I might in virtues, beauties, livings, friends,
> Exceed account: but the full sum of me
> Is sum of something; which to term in gross,
> Is an unlesson'd girl, unschool'd, unpractis'd,
> Happy in this, she is not yet so old
> But she may learn: and happier than this,
> She is not bred so dull but she can learn;

* Romeo and Juliet, Act ii. Scene 2.

Happiest of all is, that her gentle spirit
Commits itself for yours, to be directed,
As from her lord, her governor, her king.
Myself, and what is mine to you and yours
Is now converted. But now I was the lord
Of this fair mansion, master of my servants,
Queen o'er myself; and even now, but now,
This house, these servants, and this same myself
Are yours, my lord.

We must also remark that the sweetness, the solicitude, the subdued fondness which she afterwards displays, relative to the letter, are as true to the softness of her sex, as the generous self-denial with which she urges the departure of Bassanio, (having first given him a husband's right over herself and all her countless wealth,) is consistent with a reflecting mind, and a spirit at once tender, reasonable, and magnanimous.

It is not only in the trial scene, that Portia's acuteness, eloquence, and lively intelligence, are revealed to us; they are displayed in the first instance, and kept up consistently to the end. Her reflections, arising from the most usual aspects of nature, and from the commonest incidents of life, are in such a poetical spirit and are at the same time so pointed, so profound, that they have passed into familiar and daily application, with all the force of proverbs.

If to do were as easy as to know what were good to do, chapels had been churches, and poor men's cottages princes' palaces.

I can easier teach twenty what were good to be done, than be one of the twenty to follow mine own teaching.

The crow doth sing as sweetly as the lark,
When neither is attended; and I think
The nightingale, if she should sing by day,
When every goose is cackling, would be thought
No better a musician than the wren.
How many things by season, season'd are
To their right praise and true perfection!

How far that little candle throws its beams!
So shines a good deed in a naughty world.

A substitute shines as brightly as a king,
Until a king be by; and then his state
Empties itself, as doth an inland brook,
Into the main of waters.

Her reflections on the friendship between her husband and Antonio, are as full of deep meaning as of tenderness; and her portrait of a young coxcomb, in the same scene, is touched with a truth and spirit which show with what a keen observing eye she has looked upon men and things.

I'll hold thee any wager,
When we are both accouter'd like young men,
I'll prove the prettier fellow of the two,
And wear my dagger with the braver grace:
And speak between the change of man and boy,
With a reed voice; and turn two mincing steps
Into a manly stride; and speak of frays
Like a fine bragging youth: and tell quaint lies,
How honorable ladies sought my love,
Which I denying, they fell sick and died;
I could not do with all:—then i'll repent,
And wish, for all that, that I had not killed them:
And twenty of these puny lies I'll tell,
That men shall swear I have discontinued school
Above a twelvemonth.

And in the description of her various suitors, in the first scene with Nerissa, what infinite power, wit, and vivacity! She half checks herself as she is about to give the reins to her sportive humor: "In truth I know it is a sin to be a mocker." But if it carries her away, it is so perfectly good-natured, so temperately bright, so lady-like, it is ever without offence; and so far, most unlike the satirical, poignant, unsparing wit of Beatrice, "Misprising what she looks on." In fact, I can scarce conceive a greater contrast than between the vivacity of Portia and the vivacity of Beatrice. Portia, with all her airy brilliance, is supremely soft and dignified; every thing she says or does displays her capability for profound thought and feeling, as well as her lively and romantic disposition; and as I have seen in an Italian garden a fountain flinging round its wreaths of showery light, while the many-colored Iris hung brooding above it, in its calm and soul-felt glory, so in Portia the wit is ever kept subordinate to the poetry, and we still feel the tender, the intellectual, and the imaginative part of the character, as superior to, and presiding over, its spirit and vivacity.

In the last act, Shylock and his machinations being dismissed from our thoughts, and the rest of the *dramatis personæ* assembled together at Belmont, all our interest and all our attention are riveted on Portia, and the conclusion leaves the most delightful impression on the fancy. The playful equivoque of the rings, the sportive trick she puts on her husband, and her thorough enjoyment of the jest, which she checks just as it is proceeding beyond the bounds of propriety, show how little she was displeased by the sacrifice of her gift, and are all consistent with her bright and buoyant spirit. In conclusion, when Portia invites her company to enter her palace to refresh themselves after their travels, and talk over "these events at full," the imagination, unwilling to lose sight of the brilliant group, follows them in gay procession from the lovely moonlight garden to marble halls and princely revels, to splendor and festive mirth, to love and happiness!

Many women have possessed many of those qualities which render Portia so delightful. She is in herself a piece of reality, in whose possible existence we have no doubt: and yet a human being, in whom the moral, intellectual, and sentient faculties, should be so exquisitely blended and proportioned to each other, and these again in harmony with all outward aspects and influences, probably never existed—certainly could not now exist. A woman constituted like Portia, and placed in this age, and in the actual state of society, would find society armed against her; and instead of being like Portia a gracious, happy, beloved, and loving creature, would be a victim immolated in fire to that multitudinous Moloch termed Opinion. With her, the world without would be at war with the world within: in the perpetual strife, either her nature would "be subdued to the element it worked in," and bending to a necessity it could neither escape nor approve, lose at last something of its original brightness; or otherwise—a perpetual spirit of resistance, cherished as a safeguard, might perhaps in the end destroy the equipoise; firmness would become pride and self-assurance; and the soft, sweet, feminine texture of the mind, settle into rigidity. Is there then no sanctuary for such a mind? Where shall it find a refuge from the World?—Where seek for strength against itself? Where but in heaven?

Camiola in Massinger's Maid of Honor, is said to emulate Portia; and the real story of Camiola (for she is an historical personage) is very beautiful. She was a lady of Messina, who lived in the beginning of the fourteenth century; and was the cotemporary of Queen Joanna, of Petrarch and Boccacio. It fell out in those days, that Prince Orlando of Arragon, the younger brother of the King of Sicily, having taken the command of a naval armament against the Neapolitans, was defeated, wounded, taken prisoner and confined by Robert of Naples, (the father of Queen Joanna,) in one of his strongest castles. As the prince had distinguished himself by his enmity to the Neapolitans, and by many exploits against them, his ransom was fixed at an exorbitant sum, and his captivity was unusually severe; while the King of Sicily, who had some cause of displeasure against his brother, and imputed to him the defeat of his armament, refused either to negotiate for his release, or to pay the ransom demanded.

Orlando, who was celebrated for his fine person and reckless valor, was apparently doomed to languish away the rest of his life in a dungeon, when Camiola Turinga, a rich Sicilian heiress, devoted the half of her fortune to release him. But as such an action might expose her to evil comments, she made it a condition, that Orlando should marry her. The prince gladly accepted the terms, and sent her the contract of marriage, signed by his hand; but no sooner was he at liberty, than he refused to fulfil it, and even denied all knowledge of his benefactress.

Camiola appealed to the tribunal of state, produced the written contract, and described the obligations she had heaped on this ungrateful and ungenerous man; sentence was given against him, and he was adjudged to Camiola, not only as her rightful husband, but as a property which, according to the laws of war in that age, she had purchased with her gold. The day of marriage was fixed; Orlando presented himself with a splendid retinue; Camiola also appeared, decorated as for her bridal; but instead of giving her hand to the recreant, she reproached him in the presence of all with his breach of faith, declared her utter contempt for his baseness; and then freely bestowing on him the sum paid for his ransom, as a gift worthy of his mean soul, she turned away, and dedicated herself and her heart to heaven. In this resolution she remained inflexible, though the king and all the court united in entreaties to soften her. She took the veil; and Orlando, henceforth regarded as one who had stained his knighthood, and violated his faith, passed the rest of his life as a dishonored man, and died in obscurity.

Camiola, in "The Maid of Honor," is like Portia, a

wealthy heiress, surrounded by suitors, and "queen o'er herself:" the character is constructed upon the same principles,—as great intellectual power, magnanimity of temper, and feminine tenderness; but not only do pain and disquiet, and the change induced by unkind and inauspicious influences, enter into this sweet picture to mar and cloud its happy beauty,—but the portrait itself may be pronounced out of drawing;—for Massinger apparently had not sufficient delicacy of sentiment to work out his own conception of the character with perfect consistency. In his adaptation of the story, he represents the mutual love of Orlando and Camiola as existing previous to the captivity of the former, and on his part declared with many vows of eternal faith, yet she requires a written contract of marriage before she liberates him. It will perhaps be said that she has penetrated his weakness, and anticipates his falsehood: miserable excuse!—how could a magnanimous woman love a man, whose falsehood she believes but *possible?*—or loving him, how could she deign to secure herself by such means against the consequences? Shakspeare and Nature never committed such a solecism. Camiola doubts before she has been wronged; the firmness and assurance in herself border on harshness. What in Portia is the gentle wisdom of a noble nature, appears in Camiola too much a spirit of calculation: it savors a little of the counting-house. As Portia is the heiress of Belmont, and Camiola a merchant's daughter, the distinction may be proper and characteristic, but it is not in favor of Camiola. The contrast may be thus illustrated:

CAMIOLA.

You have heard of Bertoldo's captivity, and the king's neglect; the greatness of his ransom; fifty thousand crowns, Adorni! Two parts of my estate! Yet I so love the gentleman, for to you I will confess my weakness, that I purpose now, when he is forsaken by the king, and his own hopes, to ransom him.

Maid of Honor, Act 3.

PORTIA.
What sum owes he the Jew?

BASSANIO.
For me three thousand ducats,

PORTIA.
What! *no more!*
Pay him six thousand and deface the bond,
Double six thousand and then treble that,
Before a friend of this description
Shall lose a hair thro' my Bassanio's fault.
——You shall have gold
To pay the *petty debt* twenty times o'er.

Merchant of Venice.

Camiola, who is a Sicilian, might as well have been born at Amsterdam: Portia could only have existed in Italy. Portia is profound as she is brilliant; Camiola is sensible and sententious: she asserts her dignity very successfully; but we cannot for a moment imagine Portia as reduced to the necessity of *asserting* her's. The Idiot Sylli, in "The Maid of Honor," who follows Camiola like one of the deformed dwarfs of old time, is an intolerable violation of taste and propriety, and it sensibly lowers our impression of the principal character. Shakspeare would never have placed Sir Andrew Aguecheek in constant and immediate approximation with such a woman as Portia.

Lastly, the charm of the poetical coloring is wholly wanting in Camiola, so that when she is placed in contrast with the glowing eloquence, the luxuriant grace, the buoyant spirit of Portia, the effect is somewhat that of coldness and formality. Notwithstanding the dignity and the beauty of Massinger's delineation, and the noble self-devotion of Camiola, which I acknowledge and admire, the two characters will admit of no comparison as sources of contemplation and pleasure.

It is observable that something of the intellectual brilliance of Portia is reflected on the other female characters of the "Merchant of Venice," so as to preserve in the midst of contrast a certain harmony and keeping. Thus Jessica, though properly kept subordinate, is certainly

> A most beautiful Pagan—a most sweet Jew.

She cannot be called a sketch—or if a sketch, she is like one of those dashed off in such glowing colors from the rainbow pallette of a Rubens; she has a rich tinge of orientalism shed over her, worthy of her eastern origin. In any other play, and in any other companionship than that of the matchless Portia, Jessica would make a very beautiful heroine of herself. Nothing can be more poetically, more classically fanciful and elegant, than the scenes between her and Lorenzo;—the celebrated moonlight dialogue, for instance, which we all have by heart. Every sentiment she utters interests us for her:—more particularly her bashful self-reproach, when flying in the disguise of a page:

> I am glad 'tis night, you do not look upon me,
> For I am much ashamed of my exchange;
> But love is blind, and lovers cannot see
> The pretty follies that themselves commit;
> For if they could, Cupid himself would blush
> To see me thus transformed to a boy.

And the enthusiastic and generous testimony to the superior graces and accomplishments of Portia comes with a peculiar grace from her lips.

> Why if two gods should play some heavenly match,
> And on the wager lay two earthly women,
> And Portia one, there must be something else
> Pawned with the other; for the poor rude world
> Hath not her fellow.

We should not, however, easily pardon her for cheating her father with so much indifference, but for the perception that Shylock values his daughter far beneath his wealth.

I would my daughter were dead at my foot, and the jewels in her ear!—would she were hearsed at my foot, and the ducats in her coffin!

Nerissa is a good specimen of a common genus of characters; she is a clever confidential waiting-woman, who has caught a little of her lady's elegance and romance; she affects to be lively and sententious, falls in love, and makes her favor conditional on the fortune of the caskets, and, in short, mimics her mistress with good emphasis and discretion. Nerissa and the gay talkative Gratiano are as well matched as the incomparable Portia and her magnificent and captivating lover.

ISABELLA.

(MEASURE FOR MEASURE.)

The character of Isabella, considered as a poetical delineation, is less mixed than that of Portia; and the dissimilarity between the two appears, at first view, so complete, that we can scarce believe, that the same elements enter into the composition of each. Yet so it is: they are portrayed as equally wise, gracious, virtuous, fair, and young; we perceive in both the same exalted principle and firmness of character; the same depth of reflection and persuasive eloquence; the same self-denying generosity and capability of strong affections; and we must wonder at that marvellous power, by which qualities and endowments, essentially and closely allied, are so combined and modified as to produce a result altogether different. "O nature! O Shakspeare! which of ye drew from the other?"

Isabella is distinguished from Portia, and strongly individualized by a certain moral grandeur, a saintly grace, something of vestal dignity and purity, which render her less attractive and more imposing; she is "severe in youthful beauty," and inspires a reverence which would have placed her beyond the daring of one unholy wish or thought, except in such a man as Angelo—

> O cunning enemy! that to catch a saint,
> With saints dost bait thy hook.

This impression of her character is conveyed from the very first, when Lucio, the libertine jester, whose coarse audacious wit checks at every feather, thus expresses his respect for her—

> I would not, though 'tis my familiar sin
> With maids to seem the lapwing, and to jest,
> Tongue far from heart—play with all virgins so.
> I hold you as a thing enskyed and sainted;
> By your renouncement, an immortal spirit,
> And to be talked with in sincerity,
> As with a saint.

A strong distinction between Isabella and Portia is produced by the circumstances in which they are respectively placed. Portia is a high-born heiress, "Lord of a fair mansion, master of her servants, queen o'er herself;" easy and decided, as one born to command, and used to it. Isabella has also the innate dignity which renders her "queen o'er herself," but she has lived far from the world and its pomps and pleasures; she is one of a consecrated sisterhood—a novice of St. Clare; the power to command obedience, and to confer happiness, are to her unknown. Portia is a splendid creature, radiant with confidence, hope, and joy; she is like the orange-tree, hung at once with golden fruit and luxuriant flowers, which has expanded into bloom and fragance beneath favoring skies, and has been nursed into beauty by the sunshine and the dews of heaven. Isabella is like a stately and graceful cedar towering on some Alpine cliff, unbowed and unscathed amid the storm. She gives us the impression of one who had passed under the ennobling discipline of suffering and self-denial: a melancholy charm tempers the natural vigor of her mind: her spirit seems to stand upon an eminence and look down upon the world as if already "enskyed and sainted;" and yet when brought in contact with that world which she inwardly despises, she shrinks back with all the timidity natural to her cloistral education.

This union of natural grace and grandeur with the habits and sentiments of a recluse,—of austerity of life with gentleness of manner,— of inflexible moral principle with humility and even bashfulness of deportment, is delineated with the most beautiful and wonderful consistency. Thus when her brother sends to her, to entreat her mediation, her first feeling is fear, and a distrust in her own powers:

> . . . Alas! what poor ability's in me
> To do him good?
>
> LUCIO.
>
> Essay the power you have.
>
> ISABELLA.
>
> My power, alas! I doubt.

In the first scene with Angelo she seems divided between her love for her brother and her sense of his fault; between her self-respect and her maidenly bashfulness. She begins with a kind of hesitation, "at war 'twixt will and will not:" and when Angelo quotes the law, and insists on the justice of his sentence, and the responsibility of his station, her native sense of moral rectitude and severe principles takes the lead, and she shrinks back.

> O just, but severe law!
> I *had* a brother then—Heaven keep your honor!
>
> (*Retiring.*)

Excited and encouraged by Lucio, and supported by her own natural spirit, she returns to the charge—she gains energy and self-possession as she proceeds—grows more earnest and passionate from the difficulty she encounters, and displays that eloquence and power of reasoning for which we had been already prepared by Claudio's first allusion to her:

> In her youth
> There is a prone and speechless dialect,
> Such as moves men; beside, she hath prosperous art,
> When she will play with reason and discourse,
> And well she can persuade.

It is a curious coincidence, that Isabella, exhorting Angelo to mercy, avails herself of precisely the same arguments, and insists on the self-same topics which Portia addresses to Shylock in her celebrated speech; but how beautifully and how truly is the distinction marked! how like, and yet how unlike! Portia's eulogy on mercy is a piece of heavenly rhetoric; it falls on the ear with a solemn measured harmony; it is the voice of a descended angel addressing an inferior nature: if not premeditated, it is at least part of a preconcerted scheme: while Isabella's pleadings are poured from the abundance of her heart in broken sentences, and with the artless vehemence of one who feels that life and death hang upon her appeal. This will be best understood by placing the corresponding passages in immediate comparison with each other.

PORTIA.

The quality of mercy is not strained;
It droppeth as the gentle dew from heaven
Upon the place beneath; it is twice bless'd:
It blesseth him that gives and him that takes.
'Tis mightiest in the mightiest; it becomes
The throned monarch better than his crown;
His sceptre shows the force of temporal power,
The attribute to awe and majesty,
Wherein doth sit the dread and fear of kings;
But mercy is above this sceptre'd sway—
It is enthroned in the hearts of kings.

ISABELLA.

Well, believe this,
No ceremony that to great ones 'longs,
Not the king's crown, nor the deputed sword,
The marshal's truncheon, nor the judge's robe,
Become them with one half so good a grace
As mercy does.

PORTIA.

Consider this—
That in the course of justice, none of us
Should see salvation. We do pray for mercy;
And that same prayer doth teach us all to render
The deeds of mercy.

ISABELLA.

Alas! alas!
Why all the souls that are, were forfeit once;
And He, that might the 'vantage best have took,
Found out the remedy. How would you be,
If He, which is the top of judgment, should
But judge you as you are? O think on that,
And mercy then will breathe within your lips
Like man new made!

The beautiful things which Isabella is made to utter, have, like the sayings of Portia, become proverbial; but in spirit and character, they are as distinct as are the two women. In all that Portia says, we confess the power of a rich poetical imagination, blended with a quick practical spirit of observations familiar with the surfaces of things; while there is a profound yet simple morality, a depth of religious feeling, a touch of melancholy, in Isabella's sentiments, and something earnest and authoritative in the manner and expression, as though they had grown up in her mind from long and deep meditation in the silence and solitude of her convent cell.

O it is excellent
To have a giant's strength: but it is tyrannous
To use it like a giant.

Could great men thunder
As Jove himself does, Jove would ne'er be quiet:
For every pelting, petty officer
Would use his heaven for thunder; nothing but thunder.
Merciful heaven!
Thou rather, with thy sharp and sulphurous bolt
Split'st the unwedgable and gnarled oak
Than the soft myrtle. O but man, proud man!
Drest in a little brief authority,
Most ignorant of what he's most assur'd,
His glassy essence, like an angry ape,
Plays such fantastic tricks before high Heaven
As make the angels weep.

Great men may jest with saints, 'tis wit in them;
But, in the less, foul profanation.
That is the captain's but a choleric word,
Which in the soldier is flat blasphemy.

Authority, although it err like others,
Hath yet a kind of medicine in itself
That skins the vice o' the top. Go to your bosom;
Knock there, and ask your heart what it doth know
That's like my brother's fault: if it confess
A natural guiltiness such as his is,
Let it not sound a thought upon your tongue
Against my brother's life.

Let me be ignorant, and in nothing good,
But graciously to know I am no better.

The sense of death is most in apprehension;

And the poor beetle that we tread upon,
In corporal sufferance finds a pang as great,
As when a giant dies!

'Tis not impossible
But one, the wicked'st caitiff on the ground
May seem as shy, as grave, as just, as absolute
As Angelo; even so may Angelo,
In all his dressings, charaets, titles, forms,
Be an arch-villain.

Her fine powers of reasoning, and that natural uprightness and purity which no sophistry can warp, and no allurement betray, are further displayed in the second scene with Angelo.

ANGELO.
What would you do?

ISABELLA.
As much for my poor brother as myself;
That is, were I under the terms of death,
The impression of keen whips I'd wear as rubies,
And strip myself to death, as to a bed
That, longing, I have been sick for, ere I'd yield
My body up to shame.

ANGELO.
Then must your brother die.

ISABELLA.
And 'twere the cheaper way:
Better it were a brother died at once,
Than that a sister, by redeeming him,
Should die for ever.

ANGELO.
Were not you then as cruel as the sentence,
That you have slandered so?

ISABELLA.
Ignominy in ransom, and free pardon,
Are of two houses: lawful mercy is
Nothing akin to foul redemption.

ANGELO.

You seem'd of late to make the law a tyrant;
And rather proved the sliding of your brother
A merriment than a vice.

ISABELLA.

O pardon me, my lord; it oft falls out,
To have what we'd have, we speak not what we mean;
I something do excuse the thing I hate,
For his advantage that I dearly love.

Isabella's confession of the general frailty of her sex, has a peculiar softness, beauty, and propriety. She admits the imputation with all the sympathy of woman for woman; yet with all the dignity of one who felt her own superiority to the weakness she acknowledges.

ANGELO.

Nay, women are frail too.

ISABELLA.

Ay, as the glasses where they view themselves:
Which are as easy broke as they make forms.
Women! help, heaven! men their creation mar
In profiting by them. Nay, call us ten times frail;
For we are soft as our complexions are,
And credulous to false prints.

Nor should we fail to remark the deeper interest which is thrown round Isabella, by one part of her character, which is betrayed rather then exhibited in the progress of the action; and for which we are not at first prepared, though it is so perfectly natural. It is the strong undercurrent of passion and enthusiasm flowing beneath this calm and saintly self-possession;—it is the capacity for high feeling and generous and strong indignation, veiled beneath the sweet austere composure of the religious recluse which, by the very force of contrast, powerfully impresses the imagination. As we see in real life that where, from some external or habitual cause, a strong control is exercised over naturally quick feelings and an impetuous temper, they display themselves with a proportionate vehemence when that restraint is removed; so the very violence with which her passions burst forth, when opposed or under the influence of strong excitement, is admirably characteristic.

Thus in her exclamation, when she first allows herself to perceive Angelo's vile design—

> Ha! little honor to be much believed
> And most pernicious purpose!—seeming! seeming!
> I will proclaim thee, Angelo: look for it!
> Sign me a present pardon for my brother,
> Or with an outstretched throat I'll tell the world
> Aloud, what man thou art!

And again, where she finds that the "outward sainted deputy" has deceived her—

> O! I will to him, and pluck out his eyes!

> Unhappy Claudio! wretched Isabel!
> Injurious world! most damned Angelo!

She places at first a strong and high-souled confidence in her brother's fortitude and magnanimity, judging him by her own lofty spirit:

> I'll to my brother,
> Though he hath fallen by prompture of the blood,
> Yet hath he in him such a mind of honor,
> That had he twenty heads to tender down,
> On twenty bloody blocks, he'd yield them up
> Before his sister should her body stoop
> To such abhor'd pollution.

But when her trust in his honor is deceived by his momentary weakness, her scorn has a bitterness, and her indignation a force of expression almost fearful; and both are carried to an extreme which is perfectly in character:

> O faithless coward! O dishonest wretch!
> Wilt thou be made a man out of my vice?
> Is 't not a kind of incest to take life
> From thine own sister's shame? What should I think?
> Heaven shield, my mother play'd my father fair!
> For such a warped slip of wilderness
> Ne'er issued from his blood. Take my defiance:
> Die! perish! might but my bending down
> Reprieve thee from thy fate, it should proceed.
> I'll pray a thousand prayers for thy death,
> No word to save thee.

The whole of this scene with Claudio is inexpressibly grand in the poetry and the sentiment: and the entire play abounds in those passages and phrases which must have become trite from familiar and constant use and abuse, if their wisdom and unequalled beauty did not invest them with an immortal freshness and vigor, and a perpetual charm.

The story of Measure for Measure is a tradition of great antiquity, of which there are several versions, narrative and dramatic. A contemptible tragedy, the *Promos and Cassandra* of George Whetstone, is supposed, from various coincidences, to have furnished Shakspeare with the groundwork of the play; but the character of Isabella is, in conception and execution, all his own. The commentators have collected with infinite industry all the sources of the plot; but to the grand creation of Isabella, they award either silence, or worse than silence. Johnson, and the rest of the black letter crew, pass her over without a word.

One critic, a lady-critic too, whose name I will be so merciful as to suppress, treats Isabella as a coarse vixen. Hazlitt, with that strange perversion of sentiment and want of taste, which sometimes mingle with his piercing and powerful intellect, dismisses Isabella with a slight remark, that "we are not greatly enamored of her rigid chastity, nor can feel much confidence in the virtue that is sublimely good at another's expense." What shall we answer to such criticism? Upon what ground can we read the play from beginning to end, and doubt the angel-purity of Isabella, or contemplate her possible lapse from virtue? Such gratuitous mistrust is here a sin against the light of heaven.

> Having waste ground enough,
> Shall we desire to raise the sanctuary,
> And pitch our evils there?

Professor Richardson is more just, and truly sums up her character as "amiable, pious, sensible, resolute, determined, and eloquent;" but his remarks are rather superficial.

Schlegel's observations are also brief and general, and in no way distinguish Isabella from many other characters; neither did his plan allow him to be more minute.

Of the play altogether, he observes very beautifully, "that the title Measure for Measure is in reality a misnomer, the sense of the whole being properly the triumphof mercy over strict justice;" but it is also true that there is "an original sin in the nature of the subject, which prevents us from taking a cordial interest in it."* Of all the characters, Isabella alone has our sympathy. But though she triumphs in the conclusion, her triumph is not produced in a pleasing manner. There are too many disguises and tricks, too many "by-paths and indirect crooked ways," to conduct us to the natural and foreseen catastrophe, which the duke's presence throughout renders inevitable.

* Characters of Shakspeare's Plays.

This duke seems to have a predilection for bringing about justice by a most unjustifiable succession of falsehoods and counter-plots. He really deserves Lucio's satirical designation, who somewhere styles him, "The Fantastical Duke of Dark Corners." But Isabella is ever consistent in her pure and upright simplicity, and, in the midst of this simulation, expresses a characteristic disapprobation of the part she is made to play,

> To speak so indirectly I am loth:
> I would say the truth.*

She yields to the supposed Friar with a kind of forced docility, because her situation as a religious novice, and his station, habit, and authority, as her spiritual director, demand this sacrifice. In the end we are made to feel, that her transition from the convent to the throne has but placed this noble creature in her natural sphere: for though Isabella as Duchess of Vienna would not more command our highest reverence than Isabel the novice of Saint Clare, yet a wider range of usefulness and benevolence, of trial and action was better suited to the large capacity, the ardent affections, the energetic intellect and firm principle of such a woman as Isabella than the walls of a cloister. The philosophical duke observes in the very first scene—

> Spirits are not finely touch'd,
> But to fine issues: nor nature never lends
> The smallest scruple of her excellence,
> But like a thrifty goddess she determines,
> Herself the glory of a creditor,
> Both thanks and use.†

This profound and beautiful sentiment is illustrated in

* Act iv. scene 5. † *Use*, i. e. usury interest.

the character and destiny of Isabella. She says, of herself, that "she has spirit to act whatever her heart approves;" and what her heart approves we know.

In the convent, (which may stand here poetically for any narrow and obscure situation in which such a woman might be placed,) Isabella would not have been unhappy, but happiness would have been the result of an effort, or of the concentration of her great mental powers to some particular purpose; as St. Theresa's intellect, enthusiasm, tenderness, restless activity, and burning eloquence, governed by one overpowering sentiment of devotion, rendered her the most extraordinary of saints. Isabella, like St. Theresa, complains that the rules of her order are not sufficiently severe, and from the same cause,—that either from the consciousness of strong intellectual and imaginable power, and of overflowing sensibility, she desires a "more strict restraint;" or from the continual involuntary struggle against the trammels imposed, feels its necessity.

ISABELLA.
And have you nuns no further privileges?

FRANCISCA.
Are not these large enough?

ISABELLA.
Yes truly; I speak, not as desiring more,
But rather wishing a more strict restraint
Upon the sisterhood.

Such women as Desdemona and Ophelia would have passed their lives in the seclusion of a nunnery, without wishing like Isabella for stricter bonds, or planning, like St. Theresa the reformation of their order, simply because any restraint would have been efficient, as far as they were concerned.

Isabella "dedicate to nothing temporal," might have found resignation through self-government, or have become a religious enthusiast: while "place and greatness" would have appeared to her strong and upright mind only a more extended field of action, a trust and a trial. The mere trappings of power and state, the gemmed coronal, the ermined robe, she would have regarded as the outward emblems of her earthly profession; and would have worn them with as much simplicity as her novice's hood and scapular; still, under whatever guise she might tread this thorny world—the same "angel of light."

BEATRICE.

SHAKSPEARE has exhibited in Beatrice a spirited and faithful portrait of the fine lady of his own time. The deportment, language, manners, and allusions, are those of a particular class in a particular age; but the individual and dramatic character which forms the ground work is strongly discriminated; and being taken from general nature, belongs to every age. In Beatrice, high intellect and high animal spirits meet, and excite each other like fire and air. In her wit, (which is brilliant without being imaginative,) there is a touch of insolence not unfrequent in women, when the wit predominates over reflection and imagination. In her temper, too, there is a slight infusion of the termagant, and her satirical humor plays with such an unrespective levity over all subjects alike, that it required a profound knowledge of women to bring such a character within the pale of our sympathy. But Beatrice, though wilful, is not wayward,—she is volatile, not unfeeling. She has not only an exuberance of wit and gayety, but of heart, and soul, and energy of spirit; and is no more like the fine ladies of modern comedy,—whose wit consists in a temporary allusion or a play upon words, and whose petulance is displayed in a toss of the head, a flirt of the fan, or a flourish of the pocket handkerchief,—than one of our modern dandies is like Sir Philip Sydney.

In Beatrice, Shakspeare has contrived that the poetry of the character shall not only soften, but heighten its comic effect. We are not only inclined to forgive Beatrice all her scornful airs, all her biting jests, all her assumption of superiority; but they amuse and delight us the more, when we find her, with all the head-long simplicity of a child falling at once into the snare laid for her affections. When we see *her*,—who thought a man of God's making not good enough for her,—who disdained to be o'er-mastered by "a piece of valiant dust," stooping like the rest of her sex, vailing her proud spirit, and taming her wild heart to the loving hand of him whom she had scorned, flouted, and misused, "past the endurance of a block." And we are yet more completely won by her generous enthusiastic attachment to her cousin. When the father of Hero believes the tale of her guilt; when Claudio, her lover, without remorse or a lingering doubt, consigns her to shame; when the Friar remains silent, and the generous Benedick himself knows not what to say,—Beatrice, confident in her affections, and guided only by the impulses of her own feminine heart, sees through the inconsistency, the impossibility of the charge, and exclaims, without a moment's hesitation—

O, on my soul! my cousin is belied!

Schlegel, in his remarks on the play of "Much Ado about Nothing," has given us an amusing instance of that sense of reality with which we are impressed by Shakspeare's characters. He says of Benedick and Beatrice, as if he had known them personally, that the exclusive direction of their pointed raillery against each other "is a proof of a growing inclination:" this is not unlikely; and the same inference would lead us to suppose that this mutual inclination had commenced before the opening of the play. The very first words uttered by Beatrice, are an inquiry after Benedick, though expressed with her usual arch impertinence:—

I pray you, is Signior Montanto returned from the wars, or no?

I pray you, how many hath he killed and eaten in these wars? But how many hath he killed? for indeed I promised to eat all of his killing.

And in the unprovoked hostility with which she falls upon him in his absence, in the pertinacity and bitterness of her satire, there is certainly great argument that he occupies much more of her thoughts than she would have been willing to confess even to herself. In the same manner Benedick betrays a lurking partiality for his fascinating enemy; he shows that he has looked upon her with no careless eye, when he says,

There's her cousin, (meaning Beatrice,) an' she were not possessed with a fury, excels her as much in beauty as the first of May does the last of December.

Infinite skill, as well as humor, is shown in making this pair of airy beings the exact counterpart of each other; but of the two portraits, that of Benedick is by far the most pleasing, because the independence and gay indifference of temper, the laughing defiance of love and marriage, the satirical freedom of expression common to both, are more becoming to the masculine than to the feminine character. Any woman might love such a cavalier as Benedick, and be proud of his affection; his valor, his wit, and his gayety, sit so gracefully upon him! and his light scoffs against the power of love are but just sufficient to render more piquant the conquest of this "heretic in despite of beauty." But a man might well be pardoned who should shrink from encountering such a spirit as that of Beatrice, unless, indeed, he had "served an apprenticeship to the taming school." The wit of Beatrice, is less good-humored than that of Benedick, or, from the difference of sex, appears so. It is observable, that the power is throughout on her side, and the sympathy and interest on his, which, by reversing the usual order of things, seems to excite us *against the grain*, if I may use such an expression. In all their encounters she constantly gets the better of him, and the gentleman's wits go off halting, if he is not himself fairly *hors de combat*. Beatrice, woman-like, generally has the first word, and will have the last. Thus, when they first meet, she begins by provoking the merry warfare:—

I wonder that you will still be talking, Signior Benedick, nobody marks you.

BENEDICK.

What, my dear Lady Disdain! are you yet living?

BEATRICE.

Is it possible Disdain should die, while she hath such meet food to feed it as Signior Benedick? Courtesy itself must convert to disdain, if you come in her presence.

It is clear that she cannot for a moment endure his neglect, and he can as little tolerate her scorn. Nothing that Benedick addresses to Beatrice personally can equal the malicious force of some of her attacks upon him; he is either restrained by a feeling of natural gallantry, little as she deserves the consideration due to her sex,—(for a female satirist ever places herself beyond the pale of such forbearance,) or he is subdued by her superior volubility. He revenges himself, however, in her absence; he abuses her with such a variety of comic invective, and pours forth his pent-up wrath with such a ludicrous extravagance and exaggeration, that he betrays at once how deep is his mortification, and how unreal his enmity.

In the midst of all this tilting and sparring of their nimble and fiery wits, we find them infinitely anxious for the good opinion of each other, and secretly impatient of each other's scorn, but Beatrice is the most truly indifferent of the two, the most assured of herself. The comic effect produced by their mutual attachment, which, however natural and expected, comes upon us with all the force of a surprise, cannot be surpassed; and how exquisitely characteristic the mutual avowal!

BENEDICK.

By my sword, Beatrice, thou lovest me.

BEATRICE.

Do not swear by it, and eat it.

BENEDICK.

I will swear by it, that you love me; and I will make him eat it that says I love not you.

BEATRICE.

Will you not eat your word?

BENEDICK.

With no sauce that can be devised to it: I protest, I love thee.

BEATRICE.

Why, then, God forgive me!

BENEDICK.

What offence, sweet Beatrice?

BEATRICE.

You stayed me in a happy hour. I was about to protest I loved you.

BENEDICK.

And do it with all thy heart.

BEATRICE.

I love you with so much of my heart, that there is none left to protest.

But here again the dominion rests with Beatrice, and she appears in a less amiable light than her lover. Benedick surrenders his whole heart to her and to his new passion. The revulsion of feeling even causes it to overflow in an excess of fondness; but with Beatrice temper has still the mastery. The affection of Benedick induces him to challenge his intimate friend for her sake, but the affection of Beatrice does not prevent her from risking the life of her lover.

The character of Hero is well contrasted with that of Beatrice, and their mutual attachment is very beautiful and natural. When they are both on the scene together, Hero has but little to say for herself: Beatrice asserts the rule of a master spirit, eclipses her by her mental superiority, abashes her by her raillery, dictates to her, answers for her, and would fain inspire her gentle-hearted cousin with some of her own assurance.

Yes, faith; it is my cousin's duty to make a curtsey, and say,

"Father, as it please you;" but yet, for all that, cousin, let him be a handsome fellow, or else make another curtsey, and "Father, as it please me."

But Shakspeare knew well how to make one character subordinate to another, without sacrificing the slightest portion of its effect; and Hero, added to her grace and softness, and all the interest which attaches to her as the sentimental heroine of the play, possesses an intellectual beauty of her own. When she has Beatrice at an advantage, she repays her with interest, in the severe, but most animated and elegant picture she draws of her cousin's imperious character and unbridled levity of tongue: the portrait is a little overcharged, because administered as a corrective, and intended to be overheard.

But nature never fram'd a woman's heart
Of prouder stuff than that of Beatrice:
Disdain and scorn ride sparkling in her eyes,
Misprising what they look on; and her wit
Values itself so highly, that to her
All matter else seems weak; she cannot love,
Nor take no shape nor project of affection,
She is so self-endeared.

URSULA.

Sure, sure, such carping is not commendable.

HERO.

No: not to be so odd, and from all fashions,
As Beatrice is, cannot be commendable:
But who dare tell her so? If I should speak,
She'd mock me into air; O she would laugh me
Out of myself, press me to death with wit.
Therefore let Benedick, like cover'd fire,
Consume away in sighs, waste inwardly:
It were a better death than die with mocks,
Which is as bad as die with tickling.

Beatrice never appears to greater advantage than in

her soliloquy after leaving her concealment "in the pleached bower where honey-suckles, ripened by the sun, forbid the sun to enter;" she exclaims, after listening to this tirade against herself,

> What fire is in mine ears? Can this be true?
> Stand I condemned for pride and scorn so much?

The sense of wounded vanity is lost in bitter feelings, and she is infinitely more struck by what is said in praise of Benedick, and the history of his supposed love for her, than by the dispraise of herself. The immediate success of the trick is a most natural consequence of the self-assurance and magnanimity of her character; she is so accustomed to assert dominion over the spirits of others, that she cannot suspect the possibility of a plot laid against herself.

A haughty, excitable, and violent temper is another of the characteristics of Beatrice, but there is more of impulse than of passion in her vehemence. In the marriage scene, where she has beheld her gentle spirited cousin,—whom she loves the more for those very qualities which are most unlike her own,—slandered, deserted, and devoted to public shame, her indignation, and the eagerness with which she hungers and thirsts after revenge, are, like the rest of her character, open, ardent, impetuous, but not deep or implicable. When she bursts into that outrageous speech—

> Is he not approved in the height a villain that hath slandered, scorned, dishonored my kinswoman? O that I were a man! What! bear her in hand until they come to take hands; and then, with public accusation, uncovered slander, unmitigated rancor—O God, that I were a man! I would eat his heart in the market-place!

And when she commends her lover, as the first proof of his affection, "to kill Claudio," the very consciousness of the exaggeration,—of the contrast between the real good-nature of Beatrice and the fierce tenor of her language, keeps alive the comic effect, mingling the ludicrous with the serious. It is remarkable that, notwistanding the point and vivacity of the dialogue, few of the speeches of Beatrice are capable of a general application, or engrave themselves distinctly on the memory: they contain more mirth than matter; and though wit be the predominant feature in the dramatic portrait, Beatrice more charms and dazzles us by what she is, than by what she *says*. It is not merely her sparkling repartees and saucy jests, it is the soul of wit, and the spirit of gayety in forming the whole character,—looking out from her brilliant eyes, and laughing on her full lips that pout with scorn,—which we have before us, moving and full of life. On the whole, we dismiss Benedick and Beatrice to their matrimonial bonds, rather with a sense of amusement, than a feeling of congratulation or sympathy; rather with an acknowledgment that they are well-matched, and worthy of each other, than with any well-founded expectation of their domestic tranquility. If, as Benedick asserts, they are both "too wise, to woo peaceably," it may be added, that both are too wise, too witty, and too wilful, to live peaceably together. We have some misgivings about Beatrice—some apprehensions, that poor Benedick will not escape the "predestinated scratched face," which had been foretold to him who should win and wear this quick-witted and pleasant-spirited lady; yet when we recollect that to the wit and imperious temper of Beatrice is united a magnanimity of spirit which would naturally place her far above all selfishness, and all paltry struggles of power—when we perceive in the midst of her sarcastic levity and volubility of tongue, so much of generous affection, and such a high sense of female virtue and honor, we are inclined to hope the best. We think it possible that though the gentleman may now and then swear, and the lady scold, the native good humor of the one, the really fine understanding of the other, and the value they so evidently attach to each other's esteem, will insure them a tolerable portion of domestic felicity,—and in this hope we leave them.

ROSALIND.

I COME now to Rosalind whom I should have ranked before Beatrice, inasmuch as a greater degree of her sex's softness and sensibility, united with equal wit and intellect, give her the superiority as a woman ; but that as a dramatic character, she is inferior in force. The portrait is one of infinitely more delicacy and variety, but of less strength and depth. It is easy to seize on the prominent features in the mind of Beatrice, but extremely difficult to catch and fix the more fanciful graces of Rosalind. She is like a compound of essences, so volatile in their nature, and so exquisitely blended, that on any attempt to analyze them, they seem to escape us. To what else shall we compare her, all enchanting as she is?—to the silvery summer clouds, which even while we gaze on them, shift their hues and forms, dissolving into air and light, and rainbow showers?—to the May-morning, flush with opening flowers and roseate dews, and "charm of earliest birds?—to some wild and beautiful melody, such as some shepherd boy might pipe to Amarillis in the shade?–to a mountain streaming now smooth as a mirror in which the skies may glass themselves and anon leaping and sparkling in the sunshine—or rather to the very sunshine itself? for so her genial spirit touches into life and beauty whatever it shines on!

But this impression, though produced by the complete development of the character, and in the end possessing the whole fancy, is not immediate. The first introduction of Rosalind is less striking than interesting; we see her a dependant, almost a captive, in the house of her usurping uncle; her genial spirits are subdued by her situation, and the remembrance of her banished father: her playfulness is under a temporary eclipse.

> I pray thee, Rosalind, sweet my coz, be merry!

is an adjuration which Rosalind needed not, when once at liberty, and sporting "under the greenwood tree." The sensibility and even pensiveness of her demeanor in the first instance, render her archness and gayety afterwards, more graceful, and more fascinating.

Though Rosalind is a princess, she is a princess of Arcady; and notwithstanding the charming effect produced by her first scenes, we scarcely ever think of her with a reference to them, or associate her with a court, and the artificial appendages of her rank. She was not made to "lord it o'er a fair mansion," and take state upon her like the all-accomplished Portia; but to breathe the free air of heaven, and frolic among green leaves. She was not made to stand the siege of daring profligacy, and oppose high action and high passion to the assaults of adverse fortune, like Isabel; but to "fleet the time carelessly, as they did i' the golden age." She was not made to bandy wit with lords, and tread courtly measures with plumed and warlike cavaliers, like Beatrice; but to dance on the green sward, and "murmur among living brooks a music sweeter than their own."

Though sprightliness is the distinguishing characteristic of Rosalind, as of Beatrice, yet we find her much more nearly allied to Portia in temper and intellect. The tone of her mind is, like Portia's, genial and buoyant: she has something too of her softness and sentiment: there is the same confiding abandonment of self in her affections; but the characters are otherwise as distinct as the situations are dissimilar. The age, the manners, the circumstance in which Shakspeare has placed his Portia, are not beyond the bounds of probability; nay, have a certain reality and locality. We fancy her a cotemporary of Titian and Ariosto; the sea-wedded Venice, its merchants, and Magnificos,—the Rialto, and the long canals,—rise before us when we think of her. But Rosalind is surrounded with the purely ideal and imaginative; the reality is in the characters and in the sentiments, not in the circumstances or situation. Portia is dignified, splendid and romantic, Rosalind is playful, pastoral and picturesque: both are in the highest degree poetical, but the one is epic and the other lyric.

Every thing about Rosalind breathes of "youth and youth's sweet prime." She is fresh as the morning, sweet as the dew-awakened blossoms, and light as the breeze that plays among them. She is as witty as voluble, as sprightly as Beatrice; but in style altogether distinct. In both, the wit is equally unconscious; but in Beatrice it plays about us like the lightning, dazzling but also alarming; while the wit of Rosalind bubbles up and sparkles like the living fountain, refreshing all around. Her volubility is like the bird's song; it is the outpouring of a heart filled to overflowing with life, love, and joy, and all sweet and affectionate impulses. She has as much tenderness as mirth, and in her most petulant raillery there is a touch of softness—"By this hand it will not hurt a fly!" As her vivacity never lessens our impression of her sensibility, so she wears her masculine attire without the slightest impugnment of her delicacy. Shakspeare did not make the modesty of his women depend on their dress, as we shall see further when we come to Viola and Imogen, Rosalind has in truth "no doublet and hose in her disposition." How her heart seems to throb and flutter under her page's vest! What depth of love in her passion for Orlando! whether disguised beneath a saucy playfulness, or breaking forth with a fond impatience, or half betrayed in that beautiful scene where she faints at the sight of the 'kerchief stained with his blood! Here her recovery of her self-possession—her fears lest she should have revealed her sex—her presence of mind, and quick-witted excuse—

> I pray you, tell your brother how well I counterfeited—

and the characteristic playfulness which seems to return so naturally with her recovered senses,—are all as amusing as consistent. Then how beautifully is the dialogue managed between herself and Orlando! how well she assumes the airs of a saucy page, without throwing off her feminine sweetness! How her wit flutters free as air over every subject! With what a careless grace, yet with what exquisite propriety!

> For innocence hath a privilege in her
> To dignify arch jests and laughing eyes.

And if the freedom of some of the expressions used by Rosalind or Beatrice be objected to, let it be remembered that this was not the fault of Shakspeare or the women, but generally of the age. Portia, Beatrice, Rosalind, and the rest, lived in times when more importance was attached to things than to words; now we think more of words than of things; and happy are we in these latter days of super-refinement, if we are to be saved by our verbal morality. But this is meddling with the province of the melancholy Jaques, and our argument is Rosalind.

The impression left upon our hearts and minds by the character of Rosalind—by the mixture of playfulness, sensibility, and what the French, (and we for lack of a better expression) call *naivete*—is like a delicious strain of music. There is a depth of delight, and a subtlety of words to express that delight, which is enchanting. Yet when we call to mind particular speeches and passages, we find that they have a relative beauty and propriety, which renders it difficult to separate them from the context without injuring their effect. She says some of the most charming things in the world, and some of the most humorous; but we apply them as phrases rather than as maxims, and remember them rather for their pointed felicity of expression and fanciful application, than for their general truth and depth of meaning. I will give a few instances:—

I was never so berhymed since Pythagoras' time—that I was an Irish rat—which I can hardly remember.*

Good, my complexion! Dost thou think, though I am caparisoned like a man, that I have a doublet and hose in my disposition?

We dwell here on the skirts of a forest, like fringe upon a petticoat.

Love is merely a madness; and I tell you, deserves as well a dark house and a whip as madmen do; and the reason why they are not so punished and cured is, that the lunacy is so ordinary, that the whippers are in love too.

A traveller! by my faith, you have great reason to be sad. I fear you have sold your own lands to see other men's; then to have seen much, and to have nothing, is to have rich eyes and poor hands.

Farewell, Monsieur Traveller. Look you lisp, and wear strange suits; disable all the benefits of your own country; be out of love with your nativity, and almost chide God for making you that countenance you are; or I will scarce think you have swam in a gondola.

Break an hour's promise in love! He that will divide a minute into a thousand parts, and break but a part of the thousandth part of a minute in the affairs of love, it may be said of him that Cupid hath clapp'd him on the shoulder, but I warrant him heart-whole.

* In Shakspeare's time there were people in Ireland, (there may be such still, for aught I know,) who undertook to charm rats to death, by chanting certain verses which acted as a spell. "Rhyme them to death, as they do rats in Ireland," is a line in one of Ben Jonson's comedies: this will explain Rosalind's humorous allusion.

Men have died from time to time, and worms have eaten them—but not for love.

I could find in my heart to disgrace my man's apparel, and to cry like a woman; but I must comfort the weaker vessel, as doublet and hose ought to show itself courageous to petticoat.

Rosalind has not the impressive eloquence of Portia, nor the sweet wisdom of Isabella. Her longest speeches are not her best: nor is her taunting address to Phebe, beautiful and celebrated as it is, equal to Phebe's own description of her. The latter, indeed, is more in earnest.*

Celia is more quiet and retired; but she rather yields to Rosalind, than is eclipsed by her. She is as full of sweetness, kindness, and intelligence, quite as susceptible, and almost as witty, though she makes less display of wit. She is described as less fair and less gifted; yet the attempt to excite in her mind a jealousy of her lovelier friend, by placing them in comparison—

Thou art a fool; she robs thee of thy name;
And thou wilt show more bright, and seem more virtuous,
When she is gone—

fails to awaken in the generous heart of Celia any other feeling than an increased tenderness and sympathy for her cousin. To Celia, Shakspeare has given some of the most striking and animated parts of the dialogue; for instance when Rosalind playfully talks of "*falling in love in sport*," Celia replies with that excellent piece of advice,

* Rousseau could describe such a character as Rosalind, but failed to represent it consistently. "Nest-ce pas de ton cœur que viennent les graces de ton enjouement? Tes railleries sont des signes d'interet plus touchants que les compliments d'un autre. Tu caresses quand tu folatres. Tu ris, mais ton rire penetre l'ame; tu ris, mais tu fais pleurer de tendresse, et je te vois presque toujours serieuse avec les indifférentes."—*Heloise.*

"Love no man farther in sport than with safety of a pure blush thou may'st in honor come off again." When Rosalind exclaims—"O how full of briars is this working-day world!" Celia replies as truly as beautifully "they are but burrs, if we walk not in the trodden path our very petticoats will catch them." And further on is that exquisite description of the friendship between her and Rosalind:

> If she be a traitor,
> Why so am I; we have still slept together,
> Rose at an instant, learned, played, eat together,
> And wheresoe'er we went, like Juno's swans,
> Still we were coupled and inseparable.

The feeling of interest and admiration thus excited for Celia at the first, follows her through the whole play. We listen to her as to one who has made herself worthy of our love; and her silence expresses more than eloquence.

Phebe is quite an Arcadian coquette; she is a piece of pastoral poetry; while Audrey is only rustic. A very amusing effect is produced by the contrast between the frank and free bearing of the two princesses in disguise, and the scornful airs of the real shepherdess. In the speeches of Phebe, and in the dialouge between her and Sylvius, Shakspeare has anticipated all the beauties of the Italian pastoral, and surpassed Tasso and Guarini. We find two among the most poetical passages of the play, appropriated to Phebe; the taunting speech to Sylvius, and the description of Rosalind in her page's costume;—which last is finer than the portrait of Bathyllus in Anacreon.

CHARACTERS OF PASSION AND IMAGINATION.

JULIET.

O Love! thou teacher—O Grief! thou tamer—and Time, thou healer of human hearts!—bring hither all your deep and serious revelations!—And ye too, rich fancies of unbruised, unbowed youth—ye visions of long perished hopes—shadows of unborn joys—gay colorings of the dawn of existence! whatever memory hath treasured up of bright and beautiful in nature and in art; all soft and delicate images—all lovely forms—divinest voices and entrancing melodies—gleams of sunnier skies and fairer climes—Italian moon-lights, and airs that "breathe of the sweet South"—now, if it be possible, revive to my imagination—live once more to my heart! Come, thronging around me, all inspirations that wait on passion, on power, on beauty;—give me to tread, not bold, and yet unblamed, within the inmost sanctuary of Shakspeare's genius, in Juliet's moon-light bower, and Miranda's enchanted isle!

* * * * *

It is not without emotion, that I attempt to touch upon the character of Juliet. Such beautiful things have been said of her—only to be exceeded in beauty by the subject that inspired them!—it is impossible to say any thing better; but it is possible to say something more. Such in fact is the simplicity, the truth, and the loveliness of Juliet's character, that we are not at first aware of its complexity, its depth, and its variety. There is in it an intensity of passion, a singleness of purpose, an entireness, a completeness of effect, which we feel as a whole; and to attempt to analyze the impression thus conveyed at once to the soul and sense, is as if while hanging over a half blown rose, and revelling in its intoxicating perfume, we should pull it asunder, leaflet by leaflet, the better to display its bloom and fragrance. Yet how otherwise should we disclose the wonders of its formation, or do justice to the skill of the divine hand that has thus fashioned it in its beauty?

Love, as a passion, forms the groundwork of the drama. Now, admitting the axiom of Rochefoucauld, that there is but one love, though a thousand different copies, yet the true sentiment itself has as many different aspects as the human soul of which it forms a part. It is not only modified by the individual character and temperament; but it is under the influence of climate and circumstance. The love that is calm in one moment, shall show itself vehement and tumultuous in another. The love that is wild and passionate in the south, is deep and contemplative in the north: as the Spanish or Roman girl perhaps poisons a rival, or stabs herself for the sake of a living lover, and the German or Russian girl pines into the grave for love of the false, the absent, or the dead. Love is ardent or deep, bold or timid, jealous or confiding, impatient or humble, hopeful or desponding—and yet there are not many loves, but one love.

All Shakspeare's women, being essentially women, either love, or have loved, or are capable of loving; but Juliet is love itself. The passion is her state of being, and out of it she has no existence. It is the soul within her soul; the pulse within her heart; the life blood along her veins, blending with every atom of her frame. The love that is so chaste and dignified in Portia—so airy-delicate and fearless in Miranda—so sweetly confiding in Perdita—so playfully fond in Rosalind—so constant in Imogen—so devoted in Desdemona—so fervent in Helen—so tender in Viola,—is each and all of these in Juliet. All these remind us of her; but she reminds us of nothing but her own sweet self: or if she does, it is of the Gismunda, or the Lisetta, or the Fiammetta of Boccaccio, to whom she is allied, not in the character or circumstances, but in the truly Italian spirit, the glowing national complexion of the portrait.*

* Lord Byron remarked of the Italian women, (and he could speak *avec connaisance de fait*,) that they are the only women in the world capable of impressions, at once very sudden and very durable; which he adds, is to be found in no other nation. Mr. Moore observes afterwards, how completely an Italian woman, either from nature or her social position, is led to invert the usual course of frailty among ourselves, and, weak in resisting the first impulses of passion, to reserve the whole strength of her character for a display of constancy and devotedness afterwards.—Both these traits of national character are exemplified in Juliet.—*Moore's Life of Byron*, vol. ii. p. 303. 338. 4to edit.

There was an Italian painter who said that the secret of all effect in color consisted in white upon black, and black upon white. How perfectly did Shakspeare understand this secret of effect! and how beautifully he has exemplified it in Juliet!

> So shows a snowy dove trooping with crows,
> As yonder lady o'er her fellows shows.

Thus she and her lover are in contrast with all around them. They are all love surrounded with all hate; all harmony, surrounded with all discord; all pure nature, in the midst of polished and artificial life. Juliet, like Portia, is the foster-child of opulence and splendor: she dwells in a fair city—she has been nurtured in a palace—she clasps her robe with jewels—she braids her hair with rainbow-tinted pearls; but in herself she has no more connection with the trappings around her, than the lovely exotic transplanted from some Eden-like climate, has with the carved and gilded conservatory which has reared and sheltered its luxuriant beauty.

But in this vivid impression of contrast, there is nothing abrupt or harsh. A tissue of beautiful poetry weaves together the principal figures and the subordinate personages. The consistent truth of the costume, and the exquisite gradations of relief with which the most opposite hues are approximated, blend all into harmony. Romeo and Juliet are not poetical beings placed on a prosaic back ground: nor are they, like Thekla and Max in the Wallenstein, two angels of light amid the darkest and harshest, the most debased and revolting aspects of humanity; but every circumstance, and every personage, and every shade of character in each, tends to the development of the sentiment which is the subject of the drama. The poetry, too, the richest that can possibly be conceived, is interfused through all the characters; the splendid imagery lavished upon all with the careless prodigality of genius, and the whole is lighted up into such a sunny brilliance of effect, as though Shakspeare had really transported himself into Italy, and had drunk to intoxication of her genial atmosphere. How truly it has been said, that "although Romeo and Juliet are in love, they are not love-sick!" What a false idea would any thing of the mere whining amoroso, give us of Romeo, such as he is really in Shakspeare—the noble, gallant, ardent, brave, and witty! And Juliet—with even less truth could the phrase or idea apply to her! The picture in "Twelfth Night" of the wan girl dying of love, "who pined in thought, and with a green and yellow melancholy," would never surely occur to us, when thinking on the enamored and impassioned Juliet, in whose bosom love keeps a fiery vigil, kindling tenderness into enthusiasm, enthusiasm into passion, passion into heroism! No, the whole sentiment of the play is of a far different cast. It is flushed with the genial spirit of the south; it tastes of youth, and of the essence of youth; of life, and of the very sap of life.* We have indeed the struggle of love against evil destinies and a thorny world; the pain, the grief, the anguish, the terror, the despair:—the aching adieu; the pang unutterable of parted affection; and rapture, truth, and tenderness trampled into an early grave: but still an Elysian grace lingers round the whole, and the blue sky of Italy bends over all!

In the delineation of that sentiment which forms the groundwork of the drama, nothing in fact can equal the power of the picture, but its inexpressible sweetness and its perfect grace: the passion which has taken possession of Juliet's whole soul, has the force, the rapidity, the re-

* *La seve de la vie*, is an expression used somewhere by Madame de Stael.

sistless violence of the torrent; but she is herself as "moving delicate," as fair, as soft, as flexible, as the willow that bends over it, whose light leaves tremble even with the motion of the current which hurries beneath them. But at the same time that the pervading sentiment is never lost sight of, and is one and the same throughout, the individual part of the character in all its variety is developed, and marked with the nicest discrimination. For instance, the simplicity of Juliet is very different from the simplicity of Miranda: her innocence is not the innocence of a desert island. The energy she displays does not once remind us of the moral grandeur of Isabel, or the intellectual power of Portia;—it is founded in the strength of passion, not in the strength of character:—it is accidental rather than inherent, rising with the tide of feeling or temper, and with it subsiding. Her romance is not the pastoral romance of Perdita, nor the fanciful romance of Viola; it is the romance of a tender heart and a poetical imagination. Her inexperience is not ignorance; she has heard that there is such a thing as falsehood, though she can scarcely conceive it. Her mother and her nurse have perhaps warned her against flattering vows and man's inconstancy: or she has even

> —— Turned the tale by Ariosto told,
> Of fair Olimpia, loved and left of old!

Hence that bashful doubt, dispelled almost as soon as felt—

> Ah, gentle Romeo!
> If thou dost love pronounce it faithfully.

That conscious shrinking from her own confession—

> Fain would I dwell on form; fain, fain deny
> What I have spoke!

The ingenious simplicity of her avowal—

> Or if thou think'st I am too quickly won,
> I'll frown and be perverse, and say thee nay,
> So thou wilt woo—but else, not for the world!
> In truth fair Montague I am too fond
> And therefore thou may'st think my 'haviour light,
> But trust me gentleman I'll prove more true
> Than those who have more cunning to be strange.

And the proud yet timid delicacy, with which she throws herself for forbearance and pardon, upon the tenderness of him she loves even for the love she bears him—

> Therefore pardon me,
> And not impute this yielding to light love,
> Which the dark night hath so discovered.

In the alternative which she afterwards places before her lover with such a charming mixture of conscious delicacy and girlish simplicity, there is that jealousy of female honor which precept and education have infused into her mind, without one real doubt of his truth, or the slightest hesitation in her self-abandonment; for she does not even wait to hear his asservations:

> But if thou means't not well, I do beseech thee
> To cease thy suit and leave me to my grief.
>
> ROMEO.
>
> So thrive my soul ——
>
> JULIET.
>
> A thousand times, good night!

But all these flutterings between native impulses and maiden fears become gradually absorbed, swept away, lost and swallowed up, in the depth and enthusiasm of confiding love.

> My bounty is as boundless as the sea,
> My love as deep; the more I give to you
> The more I have—for both are *infinite!*

What a picture of the young heart, that sees no bound to its hopes, no end to its affections! For "what was to hinder the thrilling tide of pleasure which had just gushed from her heart, from flowing on without stint or measure, but experience, which she was yet without? What was to abate the transport of the first sweet sense of pleasure which her heart had just tasted, but indifference, to which she was yet a stranger? What was there to check the ardour of hope, of faith, of constancy, just rising in her breast, but disappointment, which she never yet felt?"*

Lord Byron's Haidée is a copy of Juliet in the Oriental costume, but the development is epic, not dramatic. †

* Characters of Shakspeare's Plays.

† I must allude, but with reluctance to another character, which I have heard likened to Juliet, and often quoted as the heroine *par excellence* of amatory fiction—I mean the Julie of Rousseau's Nouvelle Heloise; I protest against her altogether. As a creation of fancy the portrait is a compound of the most gross and glaring inconsistencies; as false and impossible to the reflecting and philosophical mind, as the fabled Syrens, Hamadriads and Centaurs to the eye of the anatomist. As a woman, Julie belongs neither to nature, nor to artificial society; and if the pages of melting and dazzling eloquence in which Rousseau has garnished out his idol did not blind and intoxicate us, as the incense and the garlands did the votaries of Isis we should be disgusted. Rousseau having composed his Julie of the commonest clay of the earth, does not animate her with fire from heaven, but breathes his own spirit into her, and then calls the "impetticoated" paradox a *woman*. He makes her a peg on which to hang his own visions and sentiments—and what sentiments! but that I fear to soil my pages, I would pick out a few of them, and show the difference between this strange combination of youth and innocence, philosopy and pedantry, sophistical prudery, and detestable grossierete, and our own Juliet. No! if we seek a French Juliet, we must go far—far back to the real Heloise, to her eloquence, her sensibility, her fervor of passion, her devotedness of truth. She at least, married the man she loved, and loved the man she married, and more than died for him; but enough of both.

I remember no dramatic character conveying the same impression of singleness of purpose, and devotion of heart and soul, except the Thekla of Schiller's Wallenstein : she is the German Juliet; far unequal, indeed, but conceived, nevertheless, in a kindred spirit. I know not if critics have ever compared them, or whether Schiller is supposed to have had the English, or rather the Italian, Juliet in his fancy when he portrayed Thekla ; but there are some striking points of coincidence, while the national distinction in the character of the passion leaves to Thekla a strong cast of originality.* The *Princess* Thekla is, like Juliet, the heiress of rank and opulence ; her first introduction to us, in her full dress and diamonds, does not impair the impression of her softness and simplicity. We do not think of them, nor do we sympathize with the complaint of her lover,

> The dazzle of the jewels which played round you
> Hid the beloved from me.

We almost feel the reply of Thekla before she utters it.

> Then you saw me
> Not with your heart, but with your eyes !

The timidity of Thekla in her first scene, her trembling silence in the commencement, and the few words she addresses to her mother, remind us of the unobtrusive simplicity of Juliet's first appearance ; but the impression is

* B. Constant describes her beautifully—"Sa voix si douce au travers le bruit des armes, sa forme delicate au milieu de ces hommes tout converts de fer, la purete de son ame opposee a leurs calculs avides, son calme celeste qui contraste avec leur agitations, remplisent le spectateur d'une emotion constant et melancholique, telle que ne la fait ressentir nulle tragedie ordinaire."

different;—the one is the shrinking violet, the other the unexpanded rose-bud. Thekla and Max Piccolomini are, like Romeo and Juliet, divided by the hatred of their fathers. The death of Max, and the resolute despair of Thekla, are also points of resemblance; and Thekla's complete devotion, her frank yet dignified abandonment of all disguise, and her apology for her own unreserve, are quite in Juliet's style,—

> I ought to be less open, ought to hide
> My heart more from thee—so decorum dictates:
> But where in this place wouldst thou seek for truth,
> If in my mouth thou didst not find it?

The same confidence, innocence, and fervor of affection, distinguish both heroines; but the love of Juliet is more vehement, the love of Thekla is more calm, and reposes more on itself; the love of Juliet gives us the idea of infinitude, and that of Thekla of eternity: the love of Juliet flows on with an increasing tide, like the river pouring to the ocean; and the love of Thekla stands unalterable, and enduring as the rock. In the heart of Thekla love shelters as in a home; but in the heart of Juliet he reigns a crowned king,—"he rides on its pants triumphant!" As women they would divide the loves and suffrages of mankind, but not as dramatic characters; the moment we come to look nearer, we acknowledge that it is indeed "rashness and ignorance to compare Schiller with Shakspeare."* Thekla is a fine conception in the German spirit, but Juliet is a lovely and palpable creation. The coloring in which Schiller has arrayed his Thekla is pale, sombre, vague, compared with the strong individual marking, the rich glow of life and reality, which distinguish

* Coleridge—Preface to Wallenstein.

Juliet. One contrast in particular has always struck me; the two beautiful speeches in the first interview between Max and Thekla—that in which she describes her father's astrological chamber, and that in which he replies with reflections on the influence of the stars, are said to "form in themselves a fine poem." They do so; but never would Shakspeare have placed such extraneous description and reflection in the mouth of *his* lovers. Romeo and Juliet speak of themselves only; they see only themselves in the universe, all things else are as an idle matter. Not a word they utter, though every word is poetry—not a sentiment or description, though dressed in the most luxuriant imagery, but has a direct relation to themselves, or to the situation in which they are placed, and the feelings that engross them: and besides, it may be remarked of Thekla, and generally of all tragedy heroines in love, that however beautifully and distinctly characterized, we see the passion only under one or two aspects at most, or in conflict with some one circumstance or contending duty or feeling. In Juliet alone we find it exhibited under every variety of aspect, and every gradation of feeling it could possibly assume in a delicate female heart; as we see the rose, when passed through the colors of the prism, catch and reflect every tint of the divided ray, and still it is the same sweet rose.

I have already remarked the quiet manner in which Juliet steals upon us in her first scene, as the serene, graceful girl, her feelings as yet unawakened, and her energies all unknown to herself, and unsuspected by others. Her silence and her filial deference are charming:

> I'll look to like, if looking, liking move;
> But no more deep will I endart mine eye
> Than your consent shall give it strength to fly.

Much in the same unconscious way we are impressed with an idea of her excelling loveliness:

> Beauty too rich for use, for earth too dear!

and which could make the dark vault of death "a feasting presence full of light." Without any elaborate description, we behold Juliet, as she is reflected in the heart of her lover, like a single bright star mirrored in the bosom of a deep transparent well. The rapture with which he dwells on the "white wonder of her hand;" on her lips,

> That even in pure and vestal modesty
> Still blush, as thinking their own kisses sin.

And on her eyes, "two of the fairest stars in all the heavens!" his exclamation in the sepulchre,

> Ah, dear Juliet, why art thou yet so fair!

where life and death, beauty and horror, rapture and anguish are combined; the Friars' description of her approach,

> O, so light a step
> Will ne'er wear out the everlasting flint!

and her father's similitude,

> Death lies upon her like an untimely frost
> Upon the sweetest flower of all the field;—

all these mingle into a beautiful picture of youthful, airy delicate grace,—feminine sweetness, and patrician elegance.

And our impression of Juliet's loveliness and sensibility is enhanced, when we find it overcoming in the bosom of Romeo a previous love for another. His visionary passion for the cold, inaccessible Rosaline, forms but the prologue, the threshold, to the true—the real sentiment which succeeds to it. The incident which is found in the original story has been retained by Shakspeare with equal feeling and judgment;—and far from being a fault in taste and sentiment, far from prejudicing us against Romeo, by casting on him, at the outset of the piece, the stigma of inconstancy, it becomes, if properly considered, a beauty in the drama, and adds a fresh stroke of truth to the portrait of the lover. Why, after all, should we be offended at what does not offend Juliet herself? for in the original story we find that her attention is first attracted towards Romeo, by seeing him "fancy sick, and pale of cheer," for love of a cold beauty. We must remember, that in those times every young cavalier of any distinction devoted himself, at his first entrance into the world, to the service of some fair lady, who was selected to be his fancy's queen: and the more rigorous the beauty, and the more hopeless the love, the more honorable the slavery. To go about "metamorphosed by a mistress," as Speed humorously expresses it,*—to maintain her supremacy in charms at the sword's point; to sigh; to walk with folded arms; to be negligent and melancholy, and to show "a careless desolation," was the fashion of the day. The Surreys, the Sydneys, the Bayards, the Herberts of the time—all those who were the mirrors "in which the noble youth did dress themselves," were of this fantastic school of gallantry—the last remains of the age of chivalry; and it was especially prevalent in Italy. Shakspeare has ridiculed it in many places with exquisite humor; but he wished to show us that it has its serious as well as its comic aspect. Romeo, then, is introduced to us with per-

* In the Two Gentlemen of Verona.

fect truth of costume, as the thrall of a dreaming, fanciful passion for the scornful Rosaline, who had forsworn to love; and on her charms and coldness, and on the power of love generally, he descants to his companions in pretty phrases, quite in the style and taste of the day.*

> Why then, O brawling love, O loving hate,
> O any thing, of nothing first create!
> O heavy lightness, serious vanity,
> Misshapen chaos of well-seeming forms!
>
> Love is a smoke, raised with the fume of sighs,
> Being purg'd, a fire sparkling in lover's eyes;
> Being vex'd, a sea, nourished with lover's tears.

But when once he has beheld Juliet, and quaffed intoxicating draughts of hope and love from her soft glance, how all these airy fancies fade before the soul-absorbing reality! The lambent fire that played round his heart, burns to that heart's very core. We no longer find him adorning his lamentations in picked phrases, or making a confidant of his gay companions; he is no longer "for the numbers that Petrarch flowed in;" but all is concentrated,

* There is an allusion to this court language of love in "All's Well that Ends Well," where Helena says,

> There shall your master have a thousand loves—
> A guide, a goddess, and a sovereign;
> A counsellor, a traitress, and a dear,
> His humble ambition, proud humility,
> His jarring concord, and his discord dulcet,
> His faith, his sweet disaster, with a world
> Of pretty fond adoptious Christendoms
> That blinking Cupid gossips.—*Act* 1. *Scene* 1.

The courtly poets of Elizabeth's time, who copied the Italian sonnetteers of the sixteenth century, are full of these quaint conceits.

earnest, rapturous, in the feeling and the expression. Compare, for instance, the sparkling antithetical passages just quoted with one or two of his passionate speeches to or of Juliet:

> Heaven is here,
> Where Juliet lives! &c.
>
> Ah, Juliet! if the measure of thy joy
> Be heaped like mine, and that thy skill be more
> To blazon it, then sweeten with thy breath
> This neighbor air, and let rich music's tongue
> Unfold the imagin'd happiness, that both
> Receive in either by this dear encounter!
>
> Come what sorrow may,
> It cannot countervail the exchange of joy
> That one short minute gives me in her sight.

How different! and how finely the distinction is drawn! His first passion is indulged as a waking dream, a reverie of the fancy: it is depressing, indolent, fantastic; his second elevates him to the third heaven, or hurries him to despair. It rushes to its object through all impediments, defies all dangers, and seeks at last a triumphant grave, in the arms of her he so loved. Thus Romeo's previous attachment to Rosaline, is so contrived as to exhibit to us another variety in that passion, which is the subject of the poem, by showing us the distinction between the fancied and the real sentiment. It adds a deeper effect to the beauty of Juliet; it interests us in the commencement for the tender and romantic Romeo; and gives an individual reality to his character, by stamping him like an historical, as well as a dramatic portrait, with the very spirit of the age in which he lived.*

* Since this was written I have met with some remarks of a similar tendency in that most interesting book, "The Life of Lord E. Fitzgerald."

It may be remarked of Juliet as of Portia, that we not only trace the component qualities in each as they expand before us in the course of the action, but we seem to have known them previously, and mingle a consciousness of their past, with the interest of their present and their future. Thus in the dialogue between Juliet and her parents, and in the scenes with the Nurse, we seem to have before us the whole of her previous education and habits: we see her, on the one hand, kept in severe subjection by her austere parents; and on the other fondled and spoiled by a foolish old nurse—a situation perfectly accordant with the manners of the time. Then Lady Capulet comes sweeping by with her train of velvet, her black hood, her fan and rosary—the very *beau-ideal* of a proud Italian matron of the fifteenth century, whose offer to poison Romeo in revenge for the death of Tybalt, stamps her with one very characteristic trait of the age and country. Yet she loves her daughter; and there is a touch of remorseful tenderness in her lamentation over her, which adds to our impression of the timid softness of Juliet, and the harsh subjection in which she has been kept:

> But one, poor one!—one poor and loving child,
> But one thing to rejoice and solace in,
> And cruel death hath catched it from my sight!

Capulet, as the jovial, testy old man, the self-willed, violent, tyrannical father,—to whom his daughter is but a property, the appanage of his house, and the object of his pride, is equal as a portrait: but both must yield to the Nurse, who is drawn with the most wonderful power and discrimination. In the prosaic homeliness of the conception, and the magical allusion of the coloring, she reminds us of some of the marvellous Dutch paintings, from which, with all their coarseness, we start back as from a reality.

Her low humor, her shallow garrulity, mixed with the dotage and petulance of age—her subserviency, her secrecy, and her total want of elevated principle, or even of common honesty—are brought before us like a living and palpable truth.

Among these harsh and inferior spirits is Juliet placed; her haughty parents, and her plebeian nurse, not only throw into beautiful relief her own native softness and elegance, but are at once the cause and the excuse of her subsequent conduct. She trembles before her stern mother and her violent father; but like a petted child, alternately cajoles and commands her nurse. It is her old foster-mother who is the confidant of her love. It is the woman who cherished her infancy, who aids and abets her in her clandestine marriage. Do we not perceive how immediately our impression of Juliet's character would have been lowered, if Shakspeare had placed her in connexion with any common-place dramatic waiting-woman?—even with Portia's adroit Nerissa, or Desdemona's Emilia? By giving her the Nurse for her confidant, the sweetness and dignity of Juliet's character are preserved inviolate to the fancy, even in the midst of all the romance and wilfulness of passion.

The natural result of these extremes of subjection and independence, is exhibited in the character of Juliet, as it gradually opens upon us. We behold it in the mixture of self-will and timidity, of strength and weakness, of confidence and reserve, which are developed as the action of the play proceeds. We see it in the fond eagerness of the indulged girl, for whose impatience the nimblest of the "lightning winged loves" had been too slow a messenger; in her petulance with her nurse; in those bursts of vehement feeling, which prepare us for the climax of passion and the catastrophe; in her invectives against Romeo, when she hears of the death of Tybalt; in her indignation when the Nurse echoes those reproaches, and the rising of her temper against unwonted contradiction:

NURSE.
Shame come to Romeo!
JULIET
Blistered be thy tongue
For such a wish—he was not born to shame!

Then comes that revulsion of strong feeling, that burst of magnificent exultation in the virtue and honor of her lover:

Upon *his* brow Shame is asham'd to sit,
For 'tis a throne where Honor may be crown'd
Sole monarch of the universal earth!

And this, by one of those quick transitions of feeling which belong to the character, is immediately succeeded by a gush of tenderness and self-reproach—

Ah, poor my lord, what tongue shall smooth thy name,
When I, thy three hours wife, have mangled it?

With the same admirable truth of nature, Juliet is represented as at first bewildered by the fearful destiny that closes round her; reverse is new and terrible to one nursed in the lap of luxury, and whose energies are yet untried.

Alack, alack, that heaven should practice stratagems
Upon so soft a subject as myself!

While a stay remains to her amid the evils that encompass her, she clings to it. She appeals to her father—to her mother—

Good father, I beseech you on my knees,
Hear me with patience but to speak one word!
* * * * *
Ah, sweet my mother, cast me not away!
Delay this marriage for a month,—a week!

And rejected by both, she throws herself upon her nurse in all the helplessness of anguish, of confiding affection, of habitual dependence—

> O God! O nurse! how shall this be prevented?
> Some comfort, nurse!

The old woman, true to her vocation, and fearful lest her share in these events should be discovered, counsels her to forget Romeo and marry Paris; and the moment which unveils to Juliet the weakness and the baseness of her confidant, is the moment which reveals her to herself. She does not break into upbraidings; it is no moment for anger; it is incredulous amazement succeeded by the extremity of scorn and abhorrence which takes possesion of her mind. She assumes at once and asserts all her own superiority, and rises to majesty in the strength of her despair.

> JULIET.
> Speakest thou from thy heart?
> NURSE.
> Aye, and from my soul too;—or else
> Behrew them both!
> JULIET.
> AMEN!

This final severing of all the old familiar ties of her childhood—

> Go, counsellor!
> Thou and my bosom henceforth shall be twain!

and the calm, concentrated force of her resolve,

> If all else fail,—myself have power to die!

have a sublime pathos. It appears to me also an admirable touch of nature, considering the master passion which, at this moment, rules in Juliet's soul, that she is as much shocked by the Nurse's dispraise of her lover, as by her wicked, time-serving advice.

This scene is the crisis in the character; and henceforth we see Juliet assume a new aspect. The fond, impatient, timid girl, puts on the wife and the woman: she has learned heroism from suffering, and subtlety from oppression. It is idle to criticise her dissembling submission to her father and mother; a higher duty has taken place of that which she owed to them; a more sacred tie has severed all others. Her parents are pictured as they are, that no feeling for them may interfere in the slightest degree with our sympathy for the lovers. In the mind of Juliet there is no struggle between her filial and her conjugal duties, and there ought to be none. The Friar, her spiritual director, dismisses her with these instructions:

> Go home,—be merry,—give consent
> To marry Paris;

and she obeys him. Death and suffering in every horrid form she is ready to brave, without fear or doubt, "to live an unstained wife;" and the artifice to which she has recourse, which she is even instructed to use, in no respect impairs the beauty of the character: we regard it with pain and pity, but excuse it, as the natural and inevitable consequence of the situation in which she is placed. Nor should we forget, that the dissimulation, as well as the courage of Juliet, though they spring from passion, are justified by principle:—

> My husband is on earth, my faith in heaven:
> How shall my faith return again to earth,
> Unless that husband send it me from heaven!

In her successive appeals to her father, her mother, her

nurse, and the Friar, she seeks those remedies which would first suggest themselves to a gentle and virtuous nature, and grasps her dagger only as the last resource against dishonor and violated faith :

> God joined my heart with Romeo's—thou our hands,
> And ere this hand by thee to Romeo seal'd,
> Shall be the label to another deed,
> Or my true heart, with treacherous revolt
> Turn to another,—*this* shall slay them both !

Thus, in the very tempest and whirlwind of passion and terror, preserving, to a certain degree, that moral and feminine dignity which harmonizes with our best feelings, and commands our unreproved sympathy.

In the extreme vivacity of her imagination, and its influence upon the action, the language, the sentiments of the drama, Juliet resembles Portia : but with this striking difference. In Portia, the imaginative power, though developed in a high degree, is so equally blended with the other intellectual and moral faculties, that it does not give us the idea of access. It is subject to her nobler reason ; it adorns and heightens all her feelings ; it does not overwhelm or mislead them. In Juliet, it is rather a part of her southern temperament, controlling and modifying the rest of her character ; springing from her sensibility, hurried along by her passions, animating her joys, darkening her sorrows, exaggerating her terrors, and, in the end, overpowering her reason. With Juliet, imagination is, in the first instance, if not the source, the medium of passion ; and passion again kindles her imagination. It is through the power of imagination that the eloquence of Juliet is so vividly poetical ; that every feeling, every sentiment comes to her, clothed in the richest imagery, and is thus reflected, from her mind to ours. The poetry is not here the mere adornment, the outward garnishing of the character; but its result, or rather blended with its essence. It is indivisible from it, and interfused through it like moonlight through the summer air. To particularize is almost impossible, since the whole of the dialogue appropriated to Juliet, is one rich stream of imagery: she speaks in pictures; and sometimes they are crowded one upon another; thus in the balcony scene—

> I have no joy of this contract to night:
> It is too rash, too unadvised, too sudden,
> Too like the lightning which doth cease to be
> Ere one can say it lightens.
>
> This bud of love, by summer's ripening breath,
> May prove a beauteous flower when next we meet.

Again,

> O for a falconer's voice
> To lure this tassel—gentle back again!
> Bondage is hoarse, and may not speak aloud,
> Else would I tear the cave where echo lies,
> And make her airy tongue more harsh than mine,
> With repetition of my Romeo's name.

Here then are three images in the course of six lines. In the same scene, the speech of twenty-two lines, beginning,

> Thou knowest the mask of night is on my face,

contains but one figurative expression, the *mask of night;* and every one reading this speech with the context must have felt the peculiar propriety of its simplicity, though perhaps without examining the cause of an omission which certainly is not fortuitous.

The reason lies in the situation and in the feeling of the moment; where confusion, and anxiety, and earnest self-defence predominate, the excitability and play of the imagination would be checked and subdued for the time.

In the soliloquy of the second act, where she is chiding at the Nurse's delay:—

> O she is lame! love's heralds should be thoughts
> That ten times faster glide than the sun's beams,
> Driving back shadows over lowering hills;
> Therefore do nimble-pinion'd doves draw love,
> And therefore hath the wind-swift Cupid wings!

How beautiful! how the lines mount and float responsive to the sense! She goes on—

> Had she affections, and warm youthful blood,
> She'd be as swift in motion as a ball;
> My words should bandy her to my sweet love,
> And his to me!

The famous soliloquy, "Gallop apace, ye fiery-footed steeds," teems with luxuriant imagery. The fond adjuration, "Come night! Come Romeo! *come thou day in night!*" expresses that fulness of enthusiastic admiration for her lover, which possesses her whole soul; but expresses it as only Juliet could or would have expressed it,—in a bold and beautiful metaphor. Let it be remembered, that in this speech, Juliet is not supposed to be addressing an audience, nor even a confidant. And I confess I have been shocked at the utter want of taste and refinement in those who, with coarse derision, or in a spirit of prudery, yet more gross and perverse, have dared to comment on this beautiful "Hymn to the Night," breathed out by Juliet, in the silence and solitude of her chamber. She is thinking aloud; it is the young heart "triumphing to itself in words." In the midst of all the vehemence with which she calls upon the night to bring Romeo to her arms, there is something so almost infantine in her perfect simplicity, so playful and fantastic in the imagery and language, that the charm of sentiment and innocence is thrown over the whole; and her impatience, to use her own expression, is truly that of "a child before a festival, that hath new robes and may not wear them." It is at the very moment too that her whole heart and fancy are abandoned to blissful anticipation, that the nurse enters with the news of Romeo's banishment; and the immediate transition from rapture to despair has a most powerful effect.

It is the same shaping spirit of imagination which, in the scene with the Friar, heaps together all images of horror that ever hung upon a troubled dream.

> O bid me leap, rather than marry Paris,
> From off the battlements of yonder tower,
> Or walk in thievish ways; or bid me lurk
> Where serpents are—chain me with roaring bears,
> Or shut me nightly in a charnel-house,
> O'ercovered quite with dead men's rattling bones:
> Or bid me go into a new-made grave;
> Or hide me with a dead man in his shroud;—
> Things that to hear them told, have made me tremble!

But she immediately adds,

> And I will do it without fear or doubt,
> To live an unstained wife to my sweet love!

In the scene where she drinks the sleeping potion, although her spirit does not quail, nor her determination falter for an instant, her vivid fancy conjures up one terrible apprehension after another, till gradually, and most naturally, in such a mind once thrown off its poise, the horror rises to frenzy—her imagination realizes its own hideous creations, and she *sees* her cousin Tybalt's ghost.*

* Juliet, courageously drinking off the potion, after she has placed before herself in the most fearful colors all its possible consequences, is compared by Schlegel to the famous story of Alexander and his physician.

In particular passages this luxuriance of fancy may seem to wander into excess. For instance,

> O serpent heart, hid with a flowery face!
> Did ever dragon keep so fair a cave?
> Beautiful tyrant! fiend angelical!
> Dove feather'd raven! wolfish ravening lamb, &c.

Yet this highly figurative and antithetical exuberance of language is defended by Schlegel on strong and just grounds; and to me also it appears natural, however critics may argue against its taste or propriety.* The warmth and vivacity of Juliet's fancy, which plays like a light over every part of her character—which animates every line she utters—which kindles every thought into a picture, and clothes her emotions in visible images, would naturally, under strong and unusual excitement, and in the conflict of opposing sentiments, run into some extravagance of diction.†

> *Perhaps 'tis pretty to force together
> Thoughts so all unlike each other;
> To mutter and mock a broken charm,
> To dally with wrong that does no harm!
> Perhaps 'tis tender, too, and pretty,
> At each wild word to feel within
> A sweet recoil of love and pity.
> And what if in a world of sin
> (O sorrow and shame should this be true!)
> Such giddiness of heart and brain
> Comes seldom save from rage and pain,
> So talks as it's most used to do?
>
> COLERIDGE.

These lines seem to me to form the truest comment on Juliet's wild exclamations against Romeo.

† "The censure," observes Schlegel, "originates in a fanciless way of thinking, to which every thing appears unnatural that does not suit its tame insipidity. Hence an idea has been formed of sim-

With regard to the termination of the play, which has been a subject of much critical argument, it is well known that Shakspeare, following the old English versions, has departed from the original story of Da Porta ; * and I am inclined to believe that Da Porta in making Juliet waken from her trance while Romeo yet lives, and in his terrible final scene between the lovers, has himself departed from the old tradition, and as a romance, has certainly improved it : but that which is effective in a narrative, is not always

ple and natural pathos, which consists of exclamations destitute of imagery, and nowise elevated above every-day life ; but energetic passions electrify the whole mental powers, and will, consequently, in highly-favored natures, express themselves in an ingenious and figurative manner."

* The "Giulietta" of Luigi da Porta was written about 1520. In a popular little book published in 1565, thirty years before Shakspeare wrote his tragedy, the name of Juliet occurs as an example of faithful love, and is thus explained by a note in the margin. "Juliet, a noble maiden of the citie of Verona, which loved Romeo, eldest son of the Lord Monteschi ; and being privily married together, he at last poisoned himself for love of her ; she, for sorrow of his death, slew herself with his dagger." This note, which furnishes in brief, the whole argument of Shakspeare's play, might possibly have made the first impression on his fancy.

In the novel of Da Porta the catastrophe is altogether different. After the death of Romeo, the friar Lorenzo endeavors to persuade Juliet to leave the fatal monument. She refuses : and throwing herself back on the dead body of her husband, she resolutely holds her breath and dies.—"E volta ta si al giacente corpo di Romeo, il cui capo sopra un origliere, che con lei nell' arca era stato lasciato, posto aveva ; gli occhi meglio rinchiusi avendogli, e di lagrime il freddo volto bagnandogli disse ;" Che debbo senza di te in vita piu fare, signor mio ? e che altro mi resta verso te se non colla mia morte seguirti ?" E detto questo, la sua gran sciagura nell' animo recatasi, e la perdita del caro amante ricordandosi, deliberando di piu non vivere, raccolto a se il fiato, e per buono spazio tenutolo, e poscia con un gran grido fuori mandandolo, sopra il morto corpo, morta ricadde."

calculated for the drama; and I cannot but agree with Schlegel, that Shakspeare has done well and wisely in adhering to the old story.* Can we doubt, for a moment, that he, who has given us the catastrophe of Othello, and the tempest scene in Lear, might also have adopted these additional circumstances of horror in the fate of the lovers, and have so treated them as to harrow up our very soul—had it been his object to do so? But apparently it was *not*. The tale is one,

> Such, as once heard, in gentle heart destroys
> All pain but pity.

It is in a truth a tale of love and sorrow, not of anguish and terror. We behold the catastrophe afar off with scarcely a wish to avert it. Romeo and Juliet *must* die: their destiny is fulfilled: they have quaffed off the cup of life, with all its infinite of joys and agonies, in one intoxicating draught. What have they to do more upon this earth? Young, innocent, loving, and beloved, they descend together into the tomb; but Shakspeare has made that tomb a shrine of martyred and sainted affection, consecrated for

* There is nothing so improbable in the story of Romeo and Juliet as to make us doubt the tradition that it is a real fact. "The Veronese," says Lord Byron, in one of his letters from Verona, "are tenaceous to a degree of the truth of Juliet's story, insisting on the fact, giving the date 1303, and showing a tomb. It is a plain, open, and partly decayed sarcophagus, with withered leaves in it, in a wild and desolate conventual garden—once a cemetery, now ruined to the very graves! The situation struck me as very appropriate to the legend, being blighted as their love." He might have added, that when Verona itself, with its amphitheatre and its Palladian structures, lies level with the earth, the very spot on which it stood will still be consecrated by the memory of Juliet.

When in Italy, I met a gentleman, who being then "*dans le genre romantique*," wore a fragment of Juliet's tomb set in a ring.

the worship of all hearts,—not a dark charnel vault, haunted by spectres of pain, rage, and desperation. Romeo and Juliet are pictured lovely in death as in life: the sympathy they inspire does not oppress us with that suffocating sense of horror which in the altered tragedy makes the fall of the curtain a relief: but all pain is lost in the tenderness and poetic beauty of the picture. Romeo's last speech over his bride is not like the raving of a disappointed boy: in its deep pathos, its rapturous despair, its glowing imagery, there is the very luxury of life and love. Juliet, who had drunk off the sleeping potion in a fit of frenzy, wakes calm and collected—

> I do remember well where I should be,
> And there I am,—where is my Romeo?

The profound slumber in which her senses have been steeped for so many hours has tranquillized her nerves, and stilled the fever in her blood; she wakes "like a sweet child who has been dreaming of something promised to it by its mother," and opens her eyes to ask for it—

> . . . . Where is my Romeo?

she is answered at once,

> Thy husband in thy bosom here lies dead.

This is enough: she sees at once the whole horror of her situation—she sees it with a quiet and resolved despair—she utters no reproach against the Friar—makes no inquiries, no complaints, except that affecting remonstrance—

> O churl—drink all, and leave no friendly drop,
> To help me after!

All that is left to her is to die, and she dies. The poem, which opened with the enmity of the two families, closes with their reconciliation over the breathless remains of their children; and no violent, frightful, or discordant feeling, is suffered to mingle with that soft impression of melancholy left within the heart, and which Schlegel compares to one long, endless sigh.

"A youthful passion," says Goëthe, (alluding to one of his own early attachments,) "which is conceived and cherished without any certain object, may be compared to a shell thrown from a mortar by night: it rises calmly in a brilliant track, and seems to mix, and even to dwell, for a moment, with the stars of heaven; but at length it falls—it bursts—consuming and destroying all around even as it itself expires."

* * * * *

To conclude: love, considered under its poetical aspect, is the union of passion and imagination; and accordingly to one of these, or to both, all the qualities of Juliet's mind and heart, (unfolding and varying as the action of the drama proceeds,) may be finally traced; the former concentrating all those natural impulses, fervent affections, and high energies, which lend the character its internal charm, its moral power, and individual interest; the latter diverging into all those splendid and luxuriant accompaniments which invest it with its external glow, its beauty, its vigor, its freshness and its truth.

With all this immense capacity of affection and imagination, there is a deficiency of reflection and of moral energy arising from previous habit and education; and the action of the drama, while it serves to develope the character, appears but its natural and necessary result. "Le mystère de l'existence," said Madame de Staël to her daughter, "c'est le rapport de nos erreurs avec nos peines."

HELENA.

In the character of Juliet we have seen the passionate and the imaginative blended in an equal degree, and in the highest conceivable degree as combined with delicate female nature. In Helena we have a modification of character altogether distinct; allied, indeed, to Juliet as a picture of fervent, enthusiastic, self-forgetting love, but differing wholly from her in other respects; for Helena is the union of strength of passion with strength of character.

"To be tremblingly alive to the gentle impressions, and yet be able to preserve, when the prosecution of a design requires it, an immoveable heart amidst even the most imperious causes of subduing emotion, is perhaps not an impossible constitution of mind; but it is the utmost and rarest endowment of humanity."* Such a character, almost as difficult to delineate in fiction as to find in real life, has Shakspeare given us in Helena, touched with the most soul-subduing pathos, and developed with the most consummate skill.

Helena, as a woman, is more passionate than imaginative; and as a character, she bears the same relation to Juliet that Isabel bears to Portia. There is equal unity of purpose and effect, with much less of the glow of imagery and the external coloring of poetry in the sentiments, language, and details. It is passion developed under its most profound and serious aspect; as in Isabella, we have the serious and the thoughtful, not the brilliant side of intellect. Both Helena and Isabel are distinguished by high mental powers, tinged with a melancholy sweetness; but in Isabel, the serious and energetic part of the character is founded in religious principle; in Helena it is founded in deep passion.

* Foster's Essays.

There never was, perhaps, a more beautiful picture of a woman's love, cherished in secret, not self-consuming in silent languishment—not pining in thought—not passive and "desponding over its idol"—but patient and hopeful, strong in its own intensity, and sustained by its own fond faith. The passion here reposes upon itself for all its interest; it derives nothing from art or ornament or circumstance; it has nothing of the picturesque charm, or glowing romance of Juliet; nothing of the poetical splendor of Portia, or the vestal grandeur of Isabel. The situation of Helena is the most painful and degrading in which a woman can be placed. She is poor and lowly; she loves a man who is far her superior in rank, who repays her love with indifference, and rejects her hand with scorn. She marries him against his will; he leaves her with contumely on the day of their marriage, and makes his return to her arms depend on conditions apparently impossible.* All the circumstances and details with which Helena is surrounded, are shocking to our feelings and wounding to our delicacy: and yet the beauty of the character is made to triumph over all: and Shakspeare, resting for all his effect on its internal resources and its genuine truth and sweetness, has not even availed himself of some extraneous advantages with which Helena is represented in the original story. She is the Giletta di Narbonna of Boccaccio. In the Italian tale, Giletta is the daughter of a celebrated physician attached to the court of Roussillon; she is represented as a rich heiress, who rejects many suitors of worth and rank, in consequence of her secret attachment to the young Bertram de Roussillon.

* I have read somewhere, that the play of which Helena is the heroine, (All's Well that Ends Well,) was at first entitled by Shakspeare "Love's Labor won." Why the title was altered, or by whom, I cannot discover.

She cures the King of France of a grievous distemper by one of her father's prescriptions; and she asks and receives as her reward the young Count of Roussillon as her wedded husband. He forsakes her on their wedding day, and she retires by his order, to his territory of Roussillon. There she is received with honor, takes state upon her in her husband's absence "as the lady of the land," administers justice, and rules her lord's dominions so wisely and so well, that she is universally loved and reverenced by his subjects. In the mean time, the count, instead of rejoining her, flies to Tuscany, and the rest of the story is closely followed in the drama. The beauty, wisdom, and royal demeanor of Giletta, are charmingly described, as well as her fervent love for Bertram. But Helena, in the play, derives no dignity or interest from place or circumstance, and rests for all our sympathy and respect solely upon the truth and intensity of her affections.

She is indeed represented to us as one

> Whose beauty did astonish the survey
> Of richest eyes; whose words all ears took captive;
> Whose dear perfection, hearts that scorn'd to serve,
> Humbly call'd mistress.

As her dignity is derived from mental power, without any alloy of pride, so her humility has a peculiar grace. If she feels and repines over her lowly birth, it is merely as an obstacle which separates her from the man she loves. She is more sensible to his greatness than her own littleness: she is continually looking from herself up to him, not from him down to herself. She has been bred up under the same roof with him; she has adored him from infancy. Her love is not "th' infection taken in at the eyes," nor kindled by youthful romance: it appears to have taken root in her being; to have grown with her years;

and to have gradually absorbed all her thoughts and faculties, until her fancy "carries no favor in it but Bertram's," and "there is no living, none, if Bertram be away."

It may be said that Bertram, arrogant, wayward, and heartless, does not justify this ardent and deep devotion. But Helena does not behold him with our eyes; but as he is "sanctified in her idolatrous fancy." Dr. Johnson says he cannot reconcile himself to a man who marries Helena like a coward, and leaves her like a profligate. This is much too severe; in the first place, there is no necessity that we *should* reconcile ourselves to him. In this consists a part of the wonderful beauty of the character of Helena—a part of its womanly truth, which Johnson, who accuses Bertram, and those who so plausibly defend him, did not understand. If it never happened in real life, that a woman, richly endued with heaven's best gifts loved with all her heart, and soul, and strength, a man unequal to, or unworthy of her, and to whose faults herself alone was blind—I would give up the point; but if it be in nature, why should it not be in Shakspeare? We are not to look into Bertram's character for the spring and source of Helena's love for him, but into her own. She loves Bertram, —because she loves him!—a woman's reason,—but here, and sometimes elsewhere, all sufficient.*

And although Helena tells herself that she loves in vain, a conviction stronger than reason tells her that she does not; her love is like a religion, pure, holy and deep; the blessedness to which she has lifted her thoughts is for ever before her, to despair would be a crime—it would be to cast herself away and die. The faith of her affection, combining with the natural energy of her character,

* *Lucellia*—I have no other but a woman's reason,
I think him so, because I think him so!
Two Gentlemen of Verona.

believing all things possible makes them so. It could say to the mountain of pride which stands between her and her hopes, "Be thou removed!" and it is removed. This is the solution of her behavior in the marriage scene, where Bertram, with obvious reluctance and disdain, accepts her hand, which the king, his feudal lord and guardian, forces on him. Her maidenly feeling is at first shocked and she shrinks back—

> That you are well restor'd, my lord, I am glad:
> Let the rest go.

But shall she weakly relinquish the golden opportunity, and dash the cup from her lips at the moment it is presented? Shall she cast away the treasure for which she has ventured both life and honor,—when it is just within her grasp? Shall she, after compromising her feminine delicacy by the public disclosure of her preference, be thrust back into shame, "to blush out the remainder of her life," and die a poor, lost, scorned thing! This would be very pretty, and interesting, and characteristic in Viola or Ophelia, but not at all consistent with that high determined spirit, that moral energy, with which Helena is portrayed. Pride is the only obstacle opposed to her. She is not despised and rejected as a woman, but as a poor physician's daughter; and this, to an understanding so clear, so strong, so just as Helena's, is not felt as an unpardonable insult. The mere pride of rank and birth is a prejudice of which she cannot comprehend the force, because her mind towers so immeasurably above it; and, compared to the infinite love which swells within her own bosom, it sinks into nothing. She cannot conceive that he to whom she has devoted her heart and truth, her soul, her life, her service, must not one day love her in return; and once her own beyond the reach of fate, that her cares, her caresses, her unwearied, patient tenderness, will not at last " win her lord to look upon her"—

> * * * For time will bring on summer,
> When briars shall have leaves as well as thorns,
> And be as sweet as sharp!

It is this fond faith which, hoping all things, enables her to endure all things;—which hallows and dignifies the surrender of her woman's pride, making it a sacrifice on which virtue and love throw a mingled incense.

The scene in which the Countess extorts from Helen the confession of her love, must, as an illustration, be given here. It is, perhaps, the finest in the whole play, and brings out all the striking points of Helen's character, to which I have already alluded. We must not fail to remark, that though the acknowledgment is wrung from her with an agony which seems to convulse her whole being, yet when once she has given it solemn utterance, she recovers her presence of mind, and asserts her native dignity. In her justification of her feelings and her conduct, there is neither sophistry, nor self-deception, nor presumption, but a noble simplicity, combined with the most impassioned earnestness; while the language naturally rises in its eloquent beauty, as the tide of feeling, now first let loose from the bursting heart, comes pouring forth in words. The whole scene is most exquisite.

HELENA.

What is your pleasure, madam?

COUNTESS.

You know, Helen, I am a mother to you.

HELENA.

Mine honorable mistress.

COUNTESS.

Nay, a mother;
Why not a mother? When I said a mother,

Methought you saw a serpent: what's in mother,
That you start at it? I say, I am your mother;
And put you in the catalogue of those
That were enwombed mine; 'tis often seen,
Adoption strives with nature; and choice breeds
A native slip to us from foreign seeds.
You ne'er oppressed me with a mother's groan,
Yet I express to you a mother's care.
God's mercy, maiden! does it curd thy blood
To say I am thy mother? What's the matter,
That this distempered messenger of wet,
The many-color'd Iris, rounds thine eye?
Why?—that you are my daughter?

HELENA.

That I am not.

COUNTESS.

I say, I am your mother.

HELENA.

Pardon, madam:
The Count Roussillon cannot be my brother,
I am from humble, he from honor'd name;
No note upon my parents, his all noble:
My master, my dear lord he is; and I
His servant live, and will his vassal die:
He must not be my brother.

COUNTESS.

Nor I your mother?

HELENA.

You are my mother, madam; would you were
(So that my lord, your son, were not my brother,)
Indeed my mother! or, were you both our mothers,
I care no more for, than I do for heaven,*
So I were not his sister; can't no other,
But I, your daughter, he must be my brother?

COUNTESS.

Yes Helen, you might be my daughter-in-law;
God shield, you mean it not! daughter and mother
So strive upon your pulse: what, pale again?
My fear hath catch'd your fondness; now I see
The mystery of your loneliness, and find

* i. e. I care as much for as I do for heaven.

Your salt tears, head. Now to all sense 'tis gross
You love my son; invention is asham'd,
Against the proclamation of thy passion,
To say, thou doest not: therefore tell me true;
But tell me then 'tis so;—for look, thy cheeks
Confess it, one to the other.
Speak is't so?
If it be so, you have wound a goodly clue!
If it be not, forswear't; howe'er I charge thee,
As heaven shall work in me for thy avail,
To tell me truly.

HELENA.

Good madam, pardon me!

COUNTESS.

Do you love my son?

HELENA,

Your pardon noble mistress?

COUNTESS.

Love you my son?

HELENA.

Do not you love him, madam?

COUNTESS.

Go not about; my love hath in't a bond,
Whereof the world takes note; come, come, disclose
The state of your affection; for your passions
Have to the full appeach'd.

HELENA.

Then I confess
Here on my knee, before high heaven and you,
That before you, and next unto high heaven,
I love your son;—
My friends were poor, but honest; so's my love.
Be not offended; for it hurts not him,
That he is lov'd of me; I follow him not
By any token of presumptuous suit;
Nor would I have him, till I do deserve him:
Yet never know how that desert should be.
I know I love in vain; strive against hope;
Yet in this captious and intenible sieve,
I still pour in the waters of my love,

And lack not to love still: thus, Indian-like,
Religious in mine error, I adore
The sun that looks upon his worshipper,
But knows of him no more. My dearest madam,
Let not your hate encounter with my love,
For loving where you do: but, if yourself,
Whose aged honor cites a virtuous youth,
Did ever, in so true a flame of liking,
Wish chastely, and love dearly! that your Dian
Was both herself and love; O then, give pity
To her, whose state is such, that cannot choose
But lend and give, where she is sure to loose;
That seeks not to find that her search implies,
But riddle-like, lives sweetly where she dies.

This old Countess of Roussillon is a charming sketch. She is like one of Titian's old women, who still, amid their wrinkles, remind us of that soul of beauty and sensibility which must have animated them when young. She is a fine contrast to Lady Capulet—benign, cheerful, and affectionate; she has a benevolent enthusiasm, which neither age, nor sorrow, nor pride, can wear away. Thus, when she is brought to believe that Helen nourishes a secret attachment for her son, she observes—

Even so it was with me when I was young!
This thorn
Doth to our rose of youth rightly belong,
It is the show and seal of nature's truth,
When love's strong passion is impress'd in youth.

Her fond maternal love for Helena, whom she has brought up; her pride in her good qualities overpowering all her own prejudices of rank and birth, are most natural in such a mind; and her indignation against her son, however strongly expressed, never forgets the mother.

What angel shall
Bless this unworthy husband? he cannot thrive
Unless *her* prayers, whom heaven delights to hear
And loves to grant, reprieve him from the wrath
Of greatest justice.

> Which of them both
> Is dearest to me—I have no skill in sense
> To make distinction.

This is very skilfully, as well as delicately conceived. In rejecting those poetical and accidental advantages which Giletta possesses in the original story, Shakspeare has substituted the beautiful character of the Countess; and he has contrived, that as the character of Helena should rest for its *internal* charm on the depth of her own affections, so it should depend for its *external* interest on the affection she inspires. The enthusiastic tenderness of the old Countess, the admiration and respect of the King of Lafeu, and all who are brought in connexion with her, make amends for the humiliating neglect of Bertram; and cast round Helen that collateral light, which Gilletta in the story owes to other circumstances, striking indeed, and well imagined, but not (I think) so finely harmonizing with the character.

It is also very natural that Helen, with the intuitive discernment of a pure and upright mind, and the penetration of a quick-witted woman, should be the first to detect the falsehood and cowardice of the boaster Parolles, who imposes on every one else.

It has been remarked that there is less of poetical imagery in this play than in many of the others. A certain solidity in Helen's character takes place of the ideal power, and with consistent truth of keeping, the same predominance of feeling over fancy, of the reflective over the imaginative faculty, is maintained through the whole dialogue, Yet the finest passages in the serious scenes are those appropriated to her; they are familiar and celebrated as quotations, but fully to understand their beauty and truth, they should be considered relatively to her character and situation; thus, when in speaking of Bertram, she says, "that he is one to whom she wishes well," the consciousness of the disproportion between her words and her feelings, draws from her this beautiful and affecting observation, so just in itself, and so true in her situation, and to the sentiment which fills her whole heart;

'Tis pity
That wishing well had not a body in't
Which might be felt: that we, the poorer born
Whose baser stars do shut us up in wishes,
Might with effects of them follow our friends,
And act what we must only think, which never
Returns us thanks.

Some of her general reflections have a sententious depth and a contemplative melancholy, which remind us of Isabella:

Our remedies oft in ourselves do lie
Which we ascribe to heaven; the fated sky
Gives us free scope; only doth backward pull
Our slow designs when we ourselves are dull.

Impossible be strange events to those
That weigh their pains in sense; and do suppose
What hath been, cannot be.

He that of greater works is finisher
Oft does them by the weakest minister;
So holy writ in babes hath judgment shown,
When judges have been babes.

Oft expectation fails, and most oft there
Where most it promises; and oft it hits,
Where hope is coldest, and despair most sits.

Her sentiments in the same manner are remarkable for the union of profound sense with the most passionate feeling; and when her language is figurative, which is seldom, the picture presented to us is invariably touched either with a serious, a lofty, or a melancholy beauty. For instance—

It were all one
That I should love a bright particular star,
And think to wed it—he's so far above me.

And when she is brought to choose a husband from among the young lords of the court, her heart having already made its election, the strangeness of that very privilege for which she had ventured all, nearly overpowers her, and she says beautifully—

The blushes on my cheeks thus whisper me,
"We blush that thou shouldst choose:—but be refused,
Let the white death sit on that cheek for ever,
We'll ne'er come there again!"

In her soliloquy after she has been forsaken by Bertram, the beauty lies in the intense feeling, the force and simplicity of the expressions. There is little imagery, and wherever it occurs, it is as bold as it is beautiful, and springs out of the energy of the sentiment, and the pathos of the situation. She has been reading his cruel letter.

Till I have no wife I have nothing in Framce,
Tis bitter!
Nothing in France, until he has no wife!
Thou shalt have none, Roussillon, none in France,
Then hast thou all again. Poor lord! is't I
That chase the from thy country, and expose
Those tender limbs of thine to the event
Of the none-sparing war? And is it I
That drive thee from thee sportive court, where thou
Wast shot at with fair eyes, to be the mark
Of smoky muskets? O you leaden messengers,
That ride upon the violent speed of fire,
Fly with false aim! move the still-piercing air,

That sings with piercing, do not touch my lord!
Whoever shoots at him, I set him there;
Whoever charges on his forward breast,
I am the caitiff that do hold him to it;
And, though I kill him not, I am the cause
His death was so effected: better 'twere
I met the ravin lion when he roar'd
With sharp constraint of hunger; better 'twere
That all the miseries which nature owes
Were mine at once.

No, no, although
The air of paradise did fan the house,
And angels officed all; I will be gone.

Though I cannot go the length of those who have defended Bertram on almost every point, still I think the censure which Johnson has passed on the character is much too severe. Bertram is certainly not a pattern hero of romance, but full of faults such as we meet with every day in men of his age and class. He is a bold, ardent, self-willed youth, just dismissed into the world from domestic indulgence, with an excess of aristocratic and military pride, but not without some sense of true honor and generosity. I have lately read a defence of Bertram's character, written with much elegance and plausibility. "The young count," says this critic, "comes before us possessed of a good heart, and of no mean capacity, but with a haughtiness which threatens to dull the kinder passions, and to cloud the intellect. This is the inevitable consequence of an illustrious education. The glare of his birthright has dazzled his young faculties. Perhaps the first words he could distinguish were from the important nurse, giving elaborate directions about his lordship's pap. As soon as he could walk, a crowd of submissive vassals doffed their caps, and hailed his first appearance on his legs. His spelling book had the arms of the family emblazoned on the cover. He had been accustomed to hear himself called the great, the mighty son of Roussillon, ever since he was a helpless child. A succession of complacent tutors would by no means destroy the illusion; and it is from their hands that Shakspeare receives him while yet in his minority. An overweening pride of birth is Bertram's great foible. To cure him of this, Shakspeare sends him to the wars, that he may win fame for himself, and thus exchange a shadow for reality. There the great dignity that his valor acquired for him places him on an equality with any one of his ancestors, and he is no longer beholden to them alone for the world's observance. Thus in his own person he discovers there is something better than mere hereditary honors; and his heart is prepared to acknowledge that the entire devotion of a Helen's love is of more worth than the court-bred smiles of a princess."*

It is not extraordinary that in the first instance, his spirit should revolt at the idea of marrying his mother's "waiting gentlewoman," or that he should refuse her; yet when the king, his feudal lord, whose despotic authority was in this case legal and indisputable, threatens him with the extremity of his wrath and vengeance, that he should submit himself to a hard necessity, was too consistent with the manners of the time to be called *cowardice*. Such forced marriages were not uncommon even in our own country, when the right of wardship, now vested in the Lord Chancellor, was exercised with uncontrolled, and often cruel despotism by the sovereign.

There is an old ballad, in which the king bestows a maid of low degree on a noble of his court, and the undisguised scorn and reluctance of the knight, and the pertinacity of the lady are in point.

* New Monthly Magazine, vol. iv.

He brought her down full forty pound
  Tyed up within a glove,
"Fair maid, I'll give the same to thee,
  Go seek another love."

"O I'll have none of your gold," she said,
  "Nor I'll have none of your fee;
But your fair bodye I must have,
  The king hath granted me."

Sir William ran and fetched her then,
  Five hundred pounds in gold,
Saying, "Fair maid, take this to thee,
  My fault will ne'er be told."

"'Tis not the gold that shall me tempt,"
  These words then answered she;
"But your own body I must have,
  The king hath granted me."

"Would I had drank the water clear,
  When I did drink the wine,
Rather than any shepherd's brat,
  Should be a ladye of mine.',*

Bertram's disgust at the tyranny which has given away his freedom in payment of another's debt,—which has united him to a woman whose merits are not towards him —whose secret love, and long enduring faith, are yet unknown and untried—might well make his bride distasteful to him. He flies her on the very day of their marriage, most like a wilful, haughty, angry boy, but not like a profligate. On other points he is not so easily defended, and Shakspeare, we see, has not defended but corrected him. The latter part of the play is more perplexing than pleasing. We do not indeed repine with Dr. Johnson, that Bertram, after all his misdemeanors, is "dismissed to hap-

* Percy's Reliques.

piness;" but notwithstanding the clever defence that has been made for him, he has our pardon rather than our sympathy; and for mine own part, I could find it easier to love Bertram as Helena does, than to excuse him; her love for him is his best excuse.

PERDITA. VIOLA. OPHELIA.

In Viola and Perdita the distinguishing traits are the same—sentiment and elegance: thus we associate them together, though nothing can be more distinct to the fancy than the Doric grace of Perdita, compared to the romantic sweetness of Viola. They are created out of the same materials, and are equal to each other in the tenderness, delicacy, and poetical beauty of the conception. They are both more imaginative than passionate; but Perdita is the more imaginative of the two. She is the union of the pastoral and romantic with the classical and poetical, as if a dryad of the woods had turned shepherdess. The perfections with which the poet has so lavishly endowed her, sit upon her with a certain careless and picturesque grace, "as though they had fallen upon her unawares." Thus Belphœbe, in the Fairy Queen, issues from the flowering forest with hair and garments all besprinkled with the leaves and blossoms they had entangled in her flight: and so arrayed by chance and "heedless hap" takes all hearts with "stately presence and with princely port," most like to Perdita!

The story of Florizel and Perdita is but an episode in the "Winter's Tale;" and the character of Perdita is properly kept subordinate to that of her mother, Hermione: yet the picture is perfectly finished in every part; Juliet herself is not more firmly and distinctly drawn. But the coloring in Perdita is more silvery light and delicate; the pervading sentiment more touched with the ideal; compared with Juliet, she is like a Guido hung beside a Georgione, or one of Paesiello's airs heard after one of Mozart's.

The qualities which impart to Perdita her distinct individuality, are the beautiful combination of the pastoral with the elegant—of simplicity with elevation—of spirit with sweetness. The exquisite delicacy of the picture is apparent. To understand and appreciate its effective truth and nature, we should place Perdita beside some of the nymphs of Arcadia, or the Italian pastorals, who, however graceful in themselves, when opposed to Perdita, seem to melt away into mere poetical abstractions;—As, in Spencer, the fair but fictitious Florimel, which the subtle enchantress had moulded out of snow, "vermeil tinctured," and informed with an airy spirit, that knew "all wiles of woman's wits," fades and dissolves away, when placed next to the real Florimel, in her warm, breathing, human loveliness.

Perdita does not appear till the fourth act, and the whole of the character is developed in the course of a single scene, (the third,) with a completeness of effect which leaves nothing to be required—nothing to be supplied. She is first introduced in the dialogue between herself and Florizel, where she compares her own lowly state to his princely rank, and expresses her fears of the issue of their unequal attachment. With all her timidity, and her sense of the distance which separates her from her lover, she breathes not a single word which could lead us to impugn either her delicacy or her dignity.

FLORIZEL.

These your unusual weeds to each part of you
Do give a life—no shepherdess, but Flora
Peering in April's front; this your sheep-shearing

Is as a meeting of the petty gods,
And thou the queen on't.

PERDITA.

Sir, my gracious lord,
To chide at your extremes it not becomes me;
O pardon that I name them; your high self,
The gracious mark o' the land, you have obscured
With a swain's bearing; and me, poor lowly maid,
Most goddess-like prank'd up;—but that our feasts
In every mess have folly, and the feeders
Digest it with a custom, I should blush
To see you so attired; sworn, I think,
To show myself a glass.

The impression of her perfect beauty and airy elegance of demeanour, is conveyed in two exquisite passages;

What you do
Still betters what is done. When you speak, sweet,
I'd have you do it ever. When you sing,
I'd have you buy and sell so; so give alms,
Pray so, and for the ordering your affairs
To sing them too. When you do dance, I wish you
A wave o' the sea, that you might ever do
Nothing but that; move still, still so, and own
No other function.

I take thy hand; this hand
As soft as dove's down, and as white as it;
Or Ethiopian's tooth, or the fann'd snow,
That's bolted by the northern blasts twice o'er.

The artless manner in which her innate nobility of soul shines forth through her pastoral disguise, is thus brought before us at once:

This is the prettiest low-born lass that ever
Ran on the green sward: nothing she does, or seems,
But smacks of something greater than herself,
Too noble for this place.

Her natural loftiness of spirit breaks out where she is menaced and reviled by the king as one whom his son has degraded himself by merely looking on; she bears the royal frown without quailing; but the moment he is gone, the immediate recollection of herself, and of her humble state, of her hapless love, is full of beauty, tenderness, and nature:

Even here undone!
I was not much afeard: for once, or twice,
I was about to speak; and tell him plainly
The self-same sun that shines upon his court
Hides not his visage from our cottage, but
Looks on alike.

Will't please you, Sir, begone?
I told you what would come of this. Beseech you,
Of your own state take care: this dream of mine—
Being now awake—I'll queen it no inch further,
But milk my ewes, and weep.

How often have I told you 'twould be thus!
How often said, my dignity would last
But till 'twere known.

FLORIZEL.

It cannot fail, but by
The violation of my faith; and then
Let nature crush the sides o' the earth together
And mar the seeds within! Lift up thy looks.
* * * * * *
Not for Bohemia, nor the pomp that may
Be thereat glean'd; for all the sun sees, or
The close earth wombs, or the profound seas hide
In unknown fathoms, will I break mine oath
To thee, my fair beloved!

Perdita has another characteristic, which lends to the poetical delicacy of the delineation a certain strength and moral elevation, which is peculiarly striking. It is that sense of truth and rectitude, that upright simplicity of mind, which disdains all crooked and indirect means, which would not stoop for an instant to dissemblance, and is mingled with a noble confidence in her love and in her lover. In this spirit is her answer to Camillo, who says, courtier-like,

> Besides, you know
> Prosperity's the very bond of love;
> Whose fresh complexion, and whose heart together,
> Affliction alters.

To which she replies,

> One of these is true;
> I think, affliction may subdue the cheek,
> But not take in the mind.

In that elegant scene where she receives the guests at the sheep-shearing, and distributes the flowers, there is in the full flow of the poetry a most beautiful and striking touch of individual character: but here it is impossible to mutilate the dialogue.

> Reverend sirs,
> For you there's rosemary and rue; these keep
> Seeming and savor all the winter long—
> Grace and remembrance be to you both,
> And welcome to our shearing!

POLIXENES.

> Shepherdess,
> (A fair one are you,) well you fit our ages
> With flowers of winter.

PERDITA.

> Sir, the year growing ancient,
> Not yet on summer's death, nor on the birth
> Of trembling winter, the fairest flowers o' the season
> Are our carnations, and streaked gilliflowers,
> Which some call nature's bastards—of that kind
> Our rustic garden's barren; and I care not
> To get slips of them.

POLIXENES.

Wherefore, gentle maiden,
Do you neglect them?

PERDITA.

For I have heard it said,
There is an art, which in their piedness, shares
With great creating nature.

POLIXENES.

Say there be;
Yet nature is made better by no mean,
But nature makes that mean; so o'er that art
Which, you say, adds to nature, is an art
That nature makes. You see, sweet maid, we marry,
A gentle scion to the wildest stock;
And make conceive a bark of baser kind
By bud of nobler race. This is an art
Which does mend nature, change it rather; but
The art itself is nature.

PERDITA.

So it is.

POLIXENES.

Then make your garden rich in gilliflowers
And do not call them bastards.

PERDITA.

I'll not put
The dibble in earth to set one slip of them—
No more than were I painted, I would wish
This youth should say 'twere well.

It has been well remarked of this passage, that Perdita does not attempt to answer the reasoning of Polixenes: she gives up the argument, but, woman-like, retains her own opinion, or rather, her sense of right, unshaken by his sophistry. She goes on in a strain of poetry, which comes over the soul like music and fragrance mingled: we seem to inhale the blended odors of a thousand flowers, till the sense faints with their sweetness: and she concludes with a touch of passionate sentiment, which melts into the very heart:

O Proserpina!
For the flowers now that frighted, thou let'st fall
From Dis's wagon! daffodils,
That come before the swallow dares, and take
The winds of March with beauty—violets dim,
But sweeter than the lids of Juno's eyes,
Or Cytherea's breath; pale primroses,
That die unmarried, ere they can behold
Bright Phœbus in his strength, a malady
Most incident to maids; bold oxlips, and
The crown imperial; lilies of all kinds,
The flower-de-luce being one! O, these I lack
To make you garlands of; and my sweet friend
To strew him o'er and o'er.

FLORIZEL.
What! like a corse!

PERDITA.
No, like a bank, for love to lie and play on;
Not like a corse; or if,—not to be buried,
But quick and in mine arms!

This love of truth, this *conscientiousness*, which forms so distinct a feature in the character of Perdita, and mingles with its picturesque delicacy a certain firmness and dignity, is maintained consistently to the last. When the two lovers fly together from Bohemia, and take refuge in the court of Leontes, the real father of Perdita, Florizel presents himself before the king with a feigned tale, in which he has been artfully instructed by the old counsellor Camillo. During this scene, Perdita does not utter a word. In the strait in which they are placed, she cannot deny the story which Florizel relates; she will not confirm it. Her silence, in spite of all the compliments and greetings of Leontes, has a peculiar and characteristic grace; and at the conclusion of the scene, when they are betrayed, the truth bursts from her as if instinctively, and she exclaims with emotion,

> The heavens set spies upon us--will not have
> Our contract celebrated.

After this scene, Perdita says very little. The description of her grief, while listening to the relation of her mother's death—"One of the prettiest touches of all was when at the relation of the queen's death, with the manner how she came by it, how attentiveness wounded her daughter: till, from one sign of color to another, she did, with an Alas! I would *fain* say, shed tears!"—her deportment as she stands gazing on the statue of Hermione, fixed in wonder, admiration and sorrow, as if she too were marble—

> O royal piece!
> There's magic in thy majesty, which has
> From thy admiring daughter ta'en the spirits,
> Standing like stone beside thee!

are touches of character conveyed indirectly, and which serve to give a more finished effect to this beautiful picture.

As the innate dignity of Perdita pierces through her rustic disguise,—so the exquisite refinement of Viola triumphs over her masculine attire. Viola is, perhaps, in a degree less elevated and ideal than Perdita, but with a touch of sentiment more profound and heart-stirring; she is "deep-learned in the lore of love,"—at least theoretically,—and speaks as masterly on the subject as Perdita, does of flowers.

DUKE.

How dost thou like this tune?

VIOLA.
It gives a very echo to the seat
Where love is thron'd.

And again,

If I did love you in my master's flame,
With such a suffering, such a deadly life—
In your denial I would find no sense,
I would not understand it.

OLIVIA.
Why, what would you do?

VIOLA.
Make me a willow cabin at your gate,
And call upon my soul within the house;
Write loyal cantons* of contemned love,
And sing them loud even in the dead of night.
Holla your name to the reverberate hills,
And make the babbling gossip of the air
Cry out, Olivia! O you should not rest
Between the elements of air and earth,
But you should pity me.

OLIVIA.
You might do much.

The situation and the character of Viola have been censured for the want of consistency and probability; it is therefore worth while to examine how far this criticism is true. As for her situation in the drama, (of which she is properly the heroine,) it is shortly this. She is shipwrecked on the coast of Illyria: she is alone and without protection in a strange country. She wishes to enter into the service of the Countess Olivia; but she is assured that this is impossible; "for the lady having recently lost an only and beloved brother, has abjured the sight of men, has

* i. e. *canzons*, songs.

shut herself up in her palace, and will admit no kind of suit." In this perplexity, Viola remembers to have heard her father speak with praise and admiration of Orsino, the duke of the country; and having ascertained that he is not married, and that therefore his court is not a proper asylum for her in her feminine character, she attires herself in the disguise of a page, as the best protection against uncivil comments, till she can gain some tidings of her brother.

If we carry our thoughts back to a romantic and chivalrous age, there is surely sufficient probability here for all the purposes of poetry. To pursue the thread of Viola's destiny:—she is engaged in the service of the duke, whom she finds "fancy sick" for the love of Olivia. We are left to infer, (for so it is hinted in the first scene,) that this duke,—who with his accomplishments, and his personal attractions; his taste for music, his chivalrous tenderness, and his unrequited love, is really a very fascinating and poetical personage, though a little passionate and fantastic —had already made some impression on Viola's imagination; and when she comes to play the confidante, and to be loaded with favors and kindness in her assumed character, that she should be touched by a passion made up of pity, admiration, gratitude, and tenderness, does not, I think, in any way detract from the genuine sweetness and delicacy of her character, for "*she never told her love.*"

Now all this, as the critic wisely observes, may not present a very just picture of life; and it may also fail to impart any moral lesson for the especial profit of well-bred young ladies; but is it not in truth and in nature? Did it ever fail to charm or to interest, to seize on the coldest fancy, to touch the most insensible heart?

Viola, then, is the chosen favorite of the enamored duke, and becomes his messenger to Olivia, and the interpreter of his sufferings to that inaccessible beauty. In her character of a youthful page, she attracts the favor of Olivia, and excites the jealousy of her lord. The situation is critical and delicate; but how exquisitely is the character of Viola fitted to her part, carrying her through the ordeal with all the inward and spiritual grace of modesty! What beautiful propriety in the distinction drawn between Rosalind and Viola! The wild sweetness, the frolic humor, which sports free and unblamed amid the shades of Ardennes, would ill become Viola, whose playfulness is assumed as part of her disguise as a court-page, and is guarded by the strictest delicacy. She has not like Rosalind, a saucy enjoyment in her own incognito; her disguise does not sit so easily upon her; her heart does not beat freely under it. As in the old ballad, where "Sweet William" is detected weeping in secret over her "man's array,"* so in Viola, a sweet consciousness of her feminine nature is for ever breaking through her masquerade:

> And on her cheek is ready with a blush,
> Modest as morning, when she coldly eyes
> The youthful Phœbus.

She plays her part well, but never forgets nor allows us to forget, that she is playing a part.

OLIVIA.

Are you a comedian?

VIOLA.

No, my profound heart! and yet by the very fangs of malice I swear, I am not that I play!

And thus she comments on it:

> Disguise, I see thou art wickedness,
> Wherein the pregnant enemy does much;

* Percy's Reliques, vol. iii.—in the ballad of the "Lady turned Serving Man."

How easy is it for the proper false
In women's waxen hearts to set their forms!
Alas! our frailty is the cause, not we.

The feminine cowardice of Viola, which will not allow her even to affect a courage becoming her attire,—her horror at the idea of drawing a sword, is very natural and characteristic; and produces a most humorous effect, even at the very moment it charms and interests us.

Contrasted with the deep, silent, patient love of Viola for the duke, we have the lady-like wilfulness of Olivia; and her sudden passion, or rather fancy, for the disguised page, takes so beautiful a coloring of poetry and sentiment, that we do not think her forward. Olivia is like a princess of romance, and has all the privileges of one; she is like Portia, high born and high bred, mistress over her servants,—but not like Portia, "queen o'er herself." She has never in her life been opposed; the first contradiction, therefore, rouses all the woman in her, and turns a caprice into a headlong passion; yet she apologizes for herself:

I have said too much unto a heart of stone,
And laid mine honor to unchary out;
There is something in me that reproves my fault;
But such a headstrong potent fault it is,
That it but mocks reproof!

And in the midst of her self-abandonment, never allows us to condemn, even while we pity her:

What shall you ask of me that I'll deny,
That honor, saved, may upon asking give?

The distance of rank which separates the countess from the youthful page—the real sex of Viola—the dignified elegance of Olivia's deportment, except where passion gets the better of her pride—her consistent coldness towards the duke—the description of that "smooth, discreet and stable bearing" with which she rules her household—her generous care for her steward Malvolio, in the midst of her own distress,—all these circumstances raise Olivia in our fancy, and render her caprice for the page a source of amusement and interest, not a subject of reproach. *Twelfth Night* is a genuine comedy;—a perpetual spring of the gayest and the sweetest fancies. In artificial society men and women are divided into castes and classes, and it is rarely that extremes in character or manners can approximate. To blend into one harmonious picture the utmost grace and refinement of sentiment, and the broadest effects of humor; the most poignant wit, and the most indulgent benignity;—in short, to bring before us in the same scene, Viola and Olivia, with Malvolio and Sir Toby, belonged only to Nature and to Shakspeare.

A woman's affections, however strong, are sentiments, when they run smooth; and become passions only when opposed.

In Juliet and Helena, love is depicted as a passion, properly so called; that is a natural impulse, throbbing in the heart's blood, and mingling with the very sources of life;—a sentiment more or less modified by the imagination; a strong abiding principle and motive, excited by resistance, acting upon the will, animating all the other faculties, and again influenced by them. This is the most complex aspect of love, and in these two characters it is depicted in colors at once the most various, the most intense, and the most brilliant.

In Viola and Perdita, love, being less complex, appears more refined; more a sentiment than a passion—a compound of impulse and fancy, while the reflective powers and moral energies are more faintly developed. The same remark applies also to Julia and Silvia, in the two

Gentlemen of Verona, and in a greater degree to Hermia and Helen in the Midsummer Night's Dream. In the two latter, though perfectly discriminated, love takes the visionary, fanciful cast, which belongs to the whole piece; it is scarcely a passion or a sentiment, but a dreamy enchantment, a reverie, which a fairy spell dissolves or rivets at pleasure.

But there was yet another possible modification of the sentiment, as combined with female nature; and this Shakspeare has shown to us. He has portrayed two beings in whom all intellectual and moral energy is in a manner latent, if existing; in whom love is an unconscious impulse, and imagination lends the external charm and hue, not the internal power; in whom the feminine character appears resolved into its very elementary principles—as modesty, grace,* tenderness. *Without* these, a woman, is no woman, but a thing which, luckily, wants a name yet; *with* these, though every other faculty were passive or deficient, she might still be herself. These are the inherent qualities with which God sent us into the world: they may be perverted by bad education—they may be obscured by harsh and evil destinies—they may be overpowered by the development of some particular mental power, the predominance of some passion; but they are never wholly crushed out of the woman's soul while it retains those faculties which render it reponsible to its Creator. Shakspeare then has shown us that these elemental feminine qualities, modesty, grace, tenderness, when expanded under genial

* By this word, as used here, I would be understood to mean that inexpressible something within the soul, which tends to the good, the beautiful, the true, and is the antipodes to the vulgar, the violent, and the false;—that which we see diffused externally over the form and movements, where there is perfect innocence and unconsciousness as in children.

influences, suffice to constitute a perfect and happy human creature; such is Miranda. When thrown alone amid harsh and adverse destinies, and amid the trammels and corruptions of society, without energy to resist, or will to act, or strength to endure, the end must needs be desolation.

Ophelia—poor Ophelia! O far too soft, too good, too fair, to be cast among the briars of this working-day world, and fall and bleed upon the thorns of life! What shall be said of her? for eloquence is mute before her! Like a strain of sad sweet music, which comes floating by us on the wings of night and silence, and which we rather feel than hear—like the exhalation of the violet dying even upon the sense it charms—like the snow-flake dissolved in air before it has caught a stain of earth—like the light surf severed from the billow, which a breath disperses—such is the character of Ophelia: so exquisitely delicate, it seems as if a touch would profane it; so sanctified in our thoughts by the last and worst of human woes, that we scarcely dare to consider it too deeply. The love of Ophelia, which she never once confesses, is like a secret which we have stolen from her, and which ought to die upon our hearts as upon her own. Her sorrow asks not words but tears; and her madness has precisely the same effect that would be produced by the spectacle of real insanity, if brought before us: we feel inclined to turn away and veil our eyes in reverential pity, and too painful sympathy.

Beyond every character that Shakspeare has drawn, (Hamlet alone excepted,) that of Ophelia makes us forget the poet in his own creation. Whenever we bring it to mind, it is with the same exclusive sense of her real existence, without reference to the wondrous power which called her into life. The effect (and what an effect!) is produced by means so simple, by strokes so few, and so unobtrusive, that we take no thought of them. It is so purely natural and unsophisticated, yet so profound in its pathos, that, Hazlitt observes, it takes us back to the old ballads—we forget that, in its perfect artlessness, it is the supreme and consummate triumph of art,

The situation of Ophelia in the story,* is that of a young girl who, at an early age, is brought from a life of privacy into the circle of the court—a court such as we read of in those early times, at once rude, magnificent, and corrupted. She is placed immediately about the person of the queen, and is apparently her favorite attendant. The affection of the wicked queen for this gentle and innocent creature, is one of those beautiful redeeming touches, one of those penetrating glances into the secret springs of natural and feminine feeling, which we find only in Shakspeare. Gertrude, who is not so wholly abandoned but that there remains within her heart some sense of the virtues he has forfeited, seems to look with a kind yet melancholy complacency on the lovely being she has destined for the bride of her son; and the scene in which she is introduced as scattering flowers on the grave of Ophelia, is one of those effects of contrast in poetry, in character, and in feeling, at once natural and unexpected, which fill the eye and make the heart swell and tremble within itself:—like the nightingales singing in the grove of the Furies, in Sophocles †

Again, in the father of Ophelia, the Lord Chamberlain

* In the story of the drama; for in the original "History of Amleth the Dane," from which Shakspeare drew his mate.ials, there is a woman introduced who is employed as an instrument to seduce Amleth, but not even the germ of the character of Ophelia.

* In the Œdipus Coloneus.

Polonius—the shrewd, wary, subtle, pompous, garrulous old courtier—have we not the very man who would send his son into the world to see all, learn all it could teach of good and evil, but keep his only daughter as far as possible from every taint of that world he knew so well? So that when she is brought to the court, she seems in her loveliness and perfect purity, like a seraph that had wandered out of bounds, and yet breathed on earth the air of paradise. When her father and her brother find it necessary to warn her simplicity, give her lessons of worldly wisdom, and instruct her "to be scanter of her maiden presence;" for that Hamlet's vows of love "but breathe like sanctified and pious bonds, the better to beguile;" we feel at once that it comes too late: for from the moment she appears on the scene amid the dark conflict of crime and vengeance, and supernatural terrors, we know what must be her destiny. Once at Murano, I saw a dove caught in a tempest; perhaps it was young, and either lacked strength of wing to reach its home, or the instinct which teaches to shun the brooding storm; but so it was—and I watched it, pitying, as it flitted, poor bird! hither and thither, with its silver pinions shining against the black thunder cloud, till, after a few giddy whirls, it fell blinded, affrighted, and bewildered into the turbid wave beneath, and was swallowed up for ever. It reminded me then of the fate of Ophelia; and now when I think of her, I see again before me that poor dove, beating with weary wing, bewildered amid the storm. It is the helplessness of Ophelia, arising merely from her innocence, and pictured without any indication of weakness, which melts us with such profound pity. She is so young, that neither her mind nor her person have attained maturity; she is not aware of the nature of her own feelings; they are prematurely developed in their full force before she has strength to bear them, and love and grief together rend and shatter the frail texture of her existence, like the burning fluid poured into a crystal vase. She says very little, and what she does say seems rather intended to hide than to reveal the emotions of her heart; yet in those few words we are made as perfectly acquainted with her character, and with what is passing in her mind, as if she had thrown forth her soul with all the glowing eloquence of Juliet. Passion with Juliet seems innate, a part of her being, "as dwells the gathered lightning in the cloud;" and we never fancy her but with the dark splendid eyes and Titian like complexion of the south. While in Ophelia we recognize as distinctly the pensive, fair-haired, blue eyed daughter of the north, whose heart seems to vibrate to the passion she has inspired, more conscious of being loved than of loving; and yet, alas! loving in the silent depths of her young heart, far more than she is loved.

When her brother warns her against Hamlet's importunities—

> For Hamlet and the trifling of his favor,
> Hold it a fashion and a toy of blood,
> A violet in the youth of primy nature,
> Forward not permanent, sweet not lasting,
> The perfume and the suppliance of a minute—
> No more!

she replies with a kind of half consciousness—

> No more but so?

LAERTES.

> Think it no more.

He concludes his admonition with that most beautiful passage, in which the soundest sense, the most excellent advice, is conveyed in a strain of the most exquisite poetry.

The chariest maid is prodigal enough,
If she unmask her beauty to the moon—
Virtue itself 'scapes not calumnious strokes;
The canker galls the infants of the spring
Too oft before their buttons be disclos'd;
And in the morn and liquid dew of youth,
Contagious blastments are most imminent.

She answers with the same modesty, yet with a kind of involuntary avowal, that his fears are not altogether without cause:

I shall the effect of this good lesson keep
As watchman to my heart. But, good my brother,
Do not, as some ungracious pastors do,
Show me the steep and thorny way to heaven;
Whilst like the puff'd and reckless libertine,
Himself the primrose path of dalliance treads,
And recks not his own read.*

When her father immediately afterwards catechises her on the same subject, he extorts from her, in short sentences, uttered with bashful reluctance, the confession of Hamlet's love for her, but not a word of her love for him. The whole scene is managed with inexpressible delicacy; it is one of those instances common in Shakspeare, in which we are allowed to perceive what is passing in the minds of a person without any consciousness on their part; only Ophelia herself is unaware that while she is admitting the extent of Hamlet's courtship, she is also betraying how deep is the impression it has made, how entire the love with which it is returned.

POLONIUS.

What is between you? give me up the truth.

OPHELIA.

He hath, my lord, of late, made many tenders
Of his affection to me.

* "And recks not his own read," i. e. heeds not his own lesson

POLONIUS.

Affection! poh! you speak like a green girl,
Unsifted in such perilous circumstances.
Do you believe his tenders, as you call them?

OPHELIA.

I do not know, my lord, what I should think.

POLONIUS.

Marry, I'll teach you: think yourself a baby;
That you have ta'en these tenders for true pay
Which are not sterling. Tender yourself more dearly;
Or, (not to crack the wind of the poor phrase,
Wronging it thus) you'll tender me a fool.

OPHELIA.

My lord, he hath importun'd me with love
In honorable fashion.

POLONIUS.

Ay, fashion you may call it; go to, go to.

OPHELIA.

And hath given countenance to his speech, my lord,
With almost all the holy vows of heaven.

POLONIUS.

Ay, springes to catch woodcocks.
———This is for all:
I would not, in plain terms, from this time forth
Have you so slander any moment's leisure
As to give words or talk with the Lord Hamlet.
Look to't, I charge you; come your ways.

OPHELIA.

I shall obey, my lord.

Besides its intrinsic loveliness, the character of Ophelia has a relative beauty and delicacy, when considered in relation to that of Hamlet, which is the delineation of a man of genius in contest with the powers of this world. The weakness of volition, the instability of purpose, the contemplative sensibility the subtlety of thought, always shrinking from action, and always occupied in "thinking too precisely on the event," united to immense intellectual power, render him unspeakably interesting; and yet I doubt whether any woman, who would have been capable of understanding and appreciating such a man, would have passionately loved him. Let us for a moment imagine any one of Shakspeare's most beautiful and striking female characters in immediate connexion with Hamlet; the gentle Desdemona would never have despatched her household cares in haste, to listen to his philosophical speculations, his dark conflicts with his own spirit. Such a woman as Portia would have studied him; Juliet would have pitied him; Rosalind would have turned him over with a smile to the melancholy Jacques; Beatrice would have laughed at him outright; Isabel would have reasoned with him; Miranda could have but wondered at him: but Ophelia loves him. Ophelia, the young, fair, inexperienced girl, facile to every impression, fond in her simplicity, and credulous in her innocence, loves Hamlet; not from what he is in himself, but for that which he appears to her—the gentle, accomplished prince, upon whom she has been accustomed to see all eyes fixed in hope and admiration, "the expectancy and rose of the fair state," the star of the court in which she moves, the first who has ever whispered soft vows in her ear; and what can be more natural?

But is it not singular, that while no one entertains a doubt of Ophelia's love for Hamlet—though never once expressed by herself, or asserted by others, in the whole course of the drama—yet it is a subject of dispute whether Hamlet loves Ophelia, though she herself allows that he had importuned her with love, and "had given countenance to his suit with almost all the holy vows of heaven;" although in the letter which Polonius intercepted, Hamlet declares that he loves her "best, O most best!"—though he asserts himself, with the wildest vehemence,

> I lov'd Ophelia; forty thousand brothers
> Could not, with all their quantity of love,
> Make up my sum.

—still I have heard the question canvassed; I have even heard it denied, that Hamlet did love Ophelia. The author of the finest remarks I have yet seen on the play and character of Hamlet, leans to this opinion. As the observations I allude to are contained in a periodical publication, and may not be at hand for immediate reference, I shall indulge myself (and the reader no less) by quoting the opening paragraphs of this noble piece of criticism, upon the principle, and for the reason I have already stated in the introduction.

"We take up a play, and ideas come rolling in upon us, like waves impelled by a strong wind. There is in the ebb and flow of Shakspeare's soul all the grandeur of a mighty operation of nature; and when we think or speak of him, it should be with humility where we do not understand, and a conviction that it is rather to the narrowness of our own mind than to any failing in the art of the great magician, that we ought to attribute any sense of weakness which may assail us during the contemplation of his created worlds.

"Shakspeare himself, had he even been as great a critic as a poet, could not have written a regular dissertation upon Hamlet. So ideal and yet so real an existence, could have been shadowed out only in the colors of poetry. When a character deals solely or chiefly with this world and its events, when it acts and is acted upon by objects that have a palpable existence, we see it distinctly, as if it were cast in a material mould, as if it partook of the fixed and settled lineaments of the things on which it lavishes its sensibilities and its passions. We see, in such cases, the vision of an individual soul, as we see the vision of an individual countenance. We can describe both, and can let a stranger into our knowledge. But how tell in words, so pure, so fine, so ideal an abstraction as Hamlet? We can, indeed, figure to ourselves generally his princely form, that outshone all others in manly beauty, and adorn it with the consummation of all liberal accomplishment. We can behold in every look, every gesture, every motion, the future king,

> The courtier's, soldier's, scholar's, eye—tongue—sword,—
> Th' expectancy and rose of the fair state;
> The glass of fashion, and the mould of form,
> Th' observ'd of all observers!

" But when we would penetrate into his spirit, meditate on those things on which he meditates, accompany him even unto the brink of eternity, fluctuate with him on the ghastly sea of despair, soar with him into the purest and serenest regions of human thought, feel with him the curse of beholding iniquity, and the troubled delight of thinking on innocence, and gentleness, and beauty; come with him, from all the glorious dreams cherished by a noble spirit in the halls of wisdom and philosophy, of a sudden into the gloomy courts of sin, and incest, and murder; shudder with him over the broken and shattered fragments of all the fairest creations of his fancy,—be borne with him at once from calm, and lofty, and delighted speculations, into the very heart of fear, and horror, and tribulations,—have the agonies and guilt of our mortal world brought into immediate contact with the world beyond the grave, and the influence of an awful shadow hanging forever on our thoughts—be present at a fearful combat between all the stirred-up passions of humanity in the soul of man, a combat in which one and all of these passions are alternalely victorious and overcome: I say, that when we are thus placed and acted upon, how is it possible to draw a character of this sublime drama, or of the mysterious being who is its moving spirit? In him, his character and situation, there is a concentration of all the interests that belong to humanity. There is scarcely a trait of frailty or of grandeur, which may have endeared to us our most beloved friends in real life, that is not to be found in Hamlet. Undoubtedly Shakspeare loved him beyond all his other creations. Soon as he appears on the stage, we are satisfied: when absent we long for his return. This is the only play which exists almost altogether in the character of one single person. Who ever knew a Hamlet in real life? yet who, ideal as the character is, feels not its reality? This is the wonder. We love him not, we think of him, not because he was witty, because he was melancholy, because he was filial; but we love him because he existed and was himself. This is the sum total of the impression. I believe that, of every other character, either in tragic or epic poetry, the story makes part of the conception; but of Hamlet, the deep and permanent interest is the conception of himself. This seems to belong, not to the character being more perfectly drawn, but to there being a more intense conception of individual human life than perhaps in any other human composition. Here is a being with springs of thought, and feeling, and action, deeper than we can search. These springs rise from an unknown depth, and in that depth there seems to be a oneness of being which we cannot distinctly behold, but which we believe to be there; and thus irreconcilable circumstances, floating on the surface of his actions, have not the effect of making us doubt the truth of the general picture."*

This is all most admirable, most eloquent, most true! but the critic subsequently declares, that "there is nothing in Ophelia which could make her the object of an engrossing passion to so majestic a spirit as Hamlet."

Now, though it be with reluctance, and even considerable mistrust of myself, that I differ from a critic who can thus feel and write, I do not think so—I do think, with submission, that the love of Hamlet for Ophelia is deep, is real, and is precisely the kind of love which such a man as Hamlet would feel for such a woman as Ophelia.

When the heathens would represent their Jove as clothed in all his Olympian terrors, they mounted him on the back of an eagle, and armed him with the lightnings; but when in Holy Writ the Supreme Being is described as coming in his glory, He is up-borne on the wings of cherubim, and his emblem is the dove. Even so our blessed religion, which has revealed deeper mysteries in the human soul than ever were dreamt of by philosophy till she went hand-in-hand with faith, has taught us to pay that worship to the symbols of purity and innocence which in darker times was paid to the manifestations of power; and therefore do I think that the mighty intellect, the capacious, soaring, penetrating genius of Hamlet, may be represented without detracting from its grandeur, as reposing upon the tender virgin innocence of Ophelia, with all that deep delight with which a superior nature contemplates the goodness which is at once perfect in itself, and of itself unconscious. That Hamlet regards Ophelia with this kind of tenderness,—that he loves her with a love as instense as can belong to a nature in which there is (I think) much more of contemplation and sensibility than action or pas-

* Blackwood's Magazine, vol. ii.

sion,—is the feeling and conviction with which I have always read the play of Hamlet.

As to whether the mind of Hamlet be, or be not, touched with madness—this is another point at issue among critics, philosophers, aye, and physicians. To me it seems that he is not so far disordered as to cease to be a responsible human being; that were too pitiable: but rather that his mind is shaken from its equilibrium, and bewildered by the horrors of his situation—horrors, which his fine and subtle intellect, his strong imagination, and his tendency to melancholy, at once exaggerate, and take from him the power either to endure, or "by opposing, end them." We do not see him as a lover, nor as Ophelia first beheld him; for the days when he importuned her with love, were before the opening of the drama—before his father's spirit revisited the earth; but we behold him at once in a sea of troubles, of perplexities, of agonies, of terrors; without remorse, he endures all its horrors, without guilt, he endures all its shame. A loathing of the crime he is called on to revenge, which revenge is again abhorrent to his nature, has set him at strife with himself; the supernatural visitation has perturbed his soul to its inmost depths; all things else, all interests, all hopes, all affections, appear as futile, when the majestic shadow comes lamenting from its place of torment "to shake him with thoughts beyond the reaches of his soul!" His love for Ophelia is then ranked by himself among those trivial, fond records which he has deeply sworn to erase from his heart and brain. He has no thought to link his terrible destiny with hers; he cannot marry her; he cannot reveal to her, young, gentle, innocent as she is, the terrific influences which have changed the whole current of his life and purposes. In his distraction, he overacts the painful part to which he had tasked himself; he is like that judge of the Areopagus who, being occupied with graver matters, flung from him the little bird which had sought refuge in his bosom, and with such angry violence, that unwittingly he killed it.

In the scene with Hamlet,* in which he madly outrages and upbraids himself, Ophelia says very little; there are two short sentences in which she replies to his wild, abrupt discourse—

HAMLET.

I did love you once.

OPHELIA.

Indeed, my lord, you made me believe so.

HAMLET.

You should not have believed me: for virtue cannot so inoculate our old stock, but we shall relish of it. I loved you not.

OPHELIA.

I was the more deceived.

Those who ever heard Mrs. Siddons read the play of Hamlet, cannot forget the world of meaning, of love, of sorrow, of despair, conveyed in these two simple phrases. Here, and in the soliloquy afterwards, where she says,

And I of ladies most deject and wretched,
That sucked the honey of his music vows,

are the only allusions to herself and her own feelings in the course of the play; and these, uttered almost without consciousness on her own part, contain the revelation of a life of love, and disclose the secret burthen of a heart bursting with its own unuttered grief. She believes Hamlet crazed: she is repulsed, she is forsaken, she is outraged, where she had bestowed her young heart, with all its hopes and wishes; her father is slain by the hand of her lo as itver,

* Act iii. Scene 1.

is supposed, in a paroxysm of insanity; she is entangled inextricably in a web of horrors which she cannot even comprehend, and the result seems inevitable.

Of her subsequent madness what can be said? What an affecting—what an astonishing picture of a mind utterly, hopelessly wrecked!—past hope—past cure! There is the fernzy of excited passions—there is the madness caused by intense and continued thought—there is the delirium of fevered nerves: but Ophelia's madness is distinct from these: it is not the suspension, but the utter destruction of the reasoning powers: it is the total imbecility which, as medical people well know, too frequently follows some terrible shock to the spirits. Constance is frantic; Lear is mad; Ophelia is *insane*. Her sweet mind lies in fragments before us—a pitiful spectacle! Her wild, rambling fancies; her aimless, broken speeches; her quick transitions from gayety to sadness—each equally purposeless and causeless; her snatches of old ballads, such as perhaps her nurse sang her to sleep with in her infancy—are all so true to the life, that we forget to wonder, and can only weep. It belonged to Shakspeare alone so to temper such a picture that we can endure to dwell upon it—

> Thought and affliction, passion, hell itself,
> She turns to favor and to prettiness.

That in her madness she should exchange her bashful silence for empty babbling, her sweet maidenly demeanor for the impatient restlessness that spurns at straws, and say and sing precisely what she never would or could have uttered had she been in possession of her reason, is so far from being an impropriety, that it is an additional stroke of nature. It is one of the symptoms of this species of insanity, as we are assured by physicians. I have myself known one instance in the case of a young Quaker girl, whose character resembled that of Ophelia, and whose malady arose from a similar cause.

The whole action of this play sweeps past us like a torrent which hurries along in its dark and resistless course all the personages of the drama towards a catastrophe which is not brought about by human will, but seems like an abyss ready dug to receive them, where the good and wicked are whelmed together.* As the character of Hamlet has been compared, or rather contrasted with the Greek Orestes, being, like him, called on to avenge a crime by a crime, tormented by remorseful doubts, and pursued by distraction; so, to me the character of Ophelia bears a certain relation to that of the Greek Iphigenia,† with the same strong distinction between the classical and the romantic conception of the portrait. Iphigenia led forth to sacrifice, with her unresisting tenderness, her mournful sweetness, her virgin innocence, is doomed to perish by that relentless power, which has linked her destiny with crimes and contests in which she has no part but as a sufferer; and even so, poor Ophelia, "divided from herself and her fair judgment," appears here like a spotless victim offered up to the mysterious and inexorable fates.

"For it is the property of crime to extend its mischiefs over innocence, as it is of virtue to extend its blessings over many that deserve them not, while frequently the author of one or the other is not, as far as we can see, either punished or rewarded."‡ But there's a heaven above us!

* Goethe. See the analysis of Hamlet in Wilhelm Meister.

† The Iphigenia in Aulis of Euripides.

‡ Goethe.

MIRANDA.

We might have deemed it impossible to go beyond Viola, Perdita, and Ophelia, as pictures of feminine beauty; to exceed the one in tender delicacy, the other in ideal grace, and the last in simplicity,—if Shakspeare had not done this, and he alone could have done it. Had he never created a Miranda, we should never have been made to feel how completely the purely natural and the purely ideal can blend into each other.

The character of Miranda resolves itself into the very elements of womanhood. She is beautiful, modest, and tender, and she is these only; they comprise her whole being, external and internal. She is so perfectly unsophisticated, so delicately refined, that she is all but ethereal. Let us imagine any other woman placed beside Miranda—even one of Shakspeare's own loveliest and sweetest creations—there is not one of them that could sustain the comparison for a moment, not one that would not appear somewhat coarse or artificial when brought into immediate contact with this pure child of nature, this "Eve of an enchanted Paradise."

What then has Shakspeare done?—"O wondrous skill and sweet wit of the man!"—he has removed Miranda far from all comparison with her own sex; he has placed her between the demi-demon of earth and the delicate spirit of air. The next step is into the ideal and supernatural; and the only being who approaches Miranda, with whom she can be contrasted, is Ariel. Besides the subtle essence of this ethereal sprite, this creature of elemental light and air, that "ran upon the winds, rode the curl'd clouds, and in the colors of the rainbow lived"—Miranda herself appears a palpable reality, a woman, " breathing thoughtful-breath;" a woman, walking the earth in her mortal loveliness, with a heart as frail-strung as passion-touched, as ever fluttered in a female bosom.

I have said that Miranda possesses merely the elementary attributes of womanhood, but each of these stand in her with a distinct and peculiar grace. She resembles nothing upon the earth; but do we therefore compare her, in our own minds, with any of those fabled beings with which the fancy of ancient poets peopled the forest depths, the fountain, or the ocean?—oread or dryad fleet, sea-maid, or naiad of the stream? We cannot think of them together. Miranda is a consistent, natural human being. Our impression of her nymph-like beauty, her peerless grace, and purity of soul, has a distinct and individual character. Not only she is exquisitely lovely, being what she is, but we are made to feel that she *could* not possibly be otherwise than as she is portrayed. She has never beheld one of her own sex; she has never caught from society one imitated or artificial grace. The impulses which have come to her, in her enchanted solitude, are of heaven and nature, not of the world and its vanities. She has sprung up into beauty beneath the eye of her father, the princely magician; her companions have been the rocks and woods, the many-shaped, many-tinted clouds, and the silent stars; her playmates the ocean billows, that stooped their foamy crests, and ran rippling to kiss her feet. Ariel and his attendant sprites hovered over her head, ministered duteous to her every wish, and presented before her pageants of beauty and grandeur. The very air, made vocal by her father's art, floated in music around her. If we can pre-suppose such a situation with all its circumstances, do we not behold in the character of Miranda not only the credible, but the natural, the necessary results of such a situation? She retains her woman's heart, for that is unalterable and inalienable, as a part of her being; but her deportment, her looks, her language, her thoughts—all these, from the supernatural and poetical circumstances around her, assume a cast of the pure ideal; and to us, who are in the secret of her human and pitying nature, nothing can be more charming and consistent than the effect which she produces upon others, who never having beheld any thing resembling her, approach her as "a wonder," as something celestial.

> Be sure! the goddess on whom these airs attend!

And again—

> What is this maid?
> Is she the goddess who hath severed us,
> And brought us thus together?

And Ferdinand exclaims, while gazing on her,

> My spirits as in a dream are all bound up!
> My father's loss, the weakness that I feel,
> The wreck of all my friends, or this man's threats,
> To whom I am subdued, are but light to me
> Might I but thro' my prison once a day
> Behold this maid: all corners else o' the earth
> Let liberty make use, of, space enough
> Have I in such a prison.

Contrasted with the impression of her refined and dignified beauty, and its effect on all beholders, is Miranda's own soft simplicity, her virgin innocence, her total ignorance of the conventional forms and language of society. It is most natural that in a being thus constituted, the first tears should spring from compassion, "suffering with those that she saw suffer;"

> O the cry did knock
> Against my very heart. Poor souls! they perished.
> Had I been any god of power, I would
> Have sunk the sea within the earth, or e'er
> It should the good ship so have swallowed,
> And the freighting souls within her!

and that her first sigh should be offered to a love at once fearless and submissive, delicate and fond. She has no taught scruples of honor like Juliet; no coy concealments like Viola; no assumed dignity standing in its own defence. Her bashfulness is less a quality than an instinct; it is like the self-folding of a flower, spontaneous and unconscious. I suppose there is nothing of the kind in poetry, equal to the scene between Ferdinand and Miranda. In Ferdinand, who is a noble creature, we have all the chivalrous magnanimity with which man, in a high state of civilization, disguises his real superiority, and does humble homage to the being of whose destiny he disposes; while Miranda, the mere child of nature, is struck with wonder at her own new emotions. Only conscious of her own weakness as a woman, and ignorant of those usages of society which teach us to dissemble the real passions and assume (and sometimes abuse) an unreal and transient power, she is equally ready to place her life, her love, her service beneath his feet.

MIRANDA.

> Alas, now! Pray you,
> Work not so hard: I would the lightning had
> Burnt up those logs, that you are enjoin'd to pile!
> Pray set it down, and rest you: when this burns,

'Twill weep for having wearied you. My father
Is hard at study; pray now, rest yourself:
He's safe for these three hours.

FERDINAND.

O most dear mistress,
The sun will set before I shall discharge
What I must strive to do.

MIRANDA.

If you'll sit down,
I'll bear your logs the while. Pray give me that,
I'll carry it to the pile.

FERDINAND.

No, precious creature;
I had rather crack my sinews, break my back,
Than you should such dishonor undergo,
While I sit lazy by.

MIRANDA.

It would become me
As well as you: and I should do it
With much more ease; for my good will is to it,
And yours against.

MIRANDA.

You look wearily.

FERDINAND.

No, noble mistress; 'tis fresh morning with me
When you are by at night. I do beseech you,
(Chiefly that I might set it in my prayers,)
What is your name?

MIRANDA.

Miranda. O, my father,
I have broke your hest to say so!

FERDINAND.

Admir'd Miranda!
Indeed the top of admiration; worth
What's dearest in the world; Full many a lady

I have eyed with best regard: and many a time
The harmony of their tongues hath into bondage
Brought my too diligent ear; for several virtues
Have I liked several women; never any
With so full soul, but some defect in her
Did quarrel with the noblest grace she ow'd,
And put it to the foil. But you, O you,
So perfect and so peerless, are created
Of every creature's best.

MIRANDA.

I do not know
One of my sex: no woman's face remember,
Save from my glass, mine own; nor have I seen
More that I may call man, than you, good friend,
And my dear father. How features are abroad
I am skill-less of; but, by my modesty,
(The jewel in my dower,) I would not wish
Any companion in the world but you;
Nor can imagination form a shape,
Besides yourself, to like of. But I prattle
Something too wildly, and my father's precepts
Therein forget.

FERDINAND.

I am, in my condition,
A prince, Miranda—I do think a king—
I would not so! and would no more endure
This wooden slavery, than I would suffer
The flesh-fly blow my mouth. Hear my soul speak:
The very instant that I saw you, did
My heart fly to your service; there resides
To make me slave to it; and, for your sake,
Am I this patient log-man.

MIRANDA.

Do you love me?

FERDINAND.

O heavens! O earth! bear witness to this sound,

And crown what I profess with kind event,
If I speak true; if hollowly, invert
What best is boded me to mischief! I,
Beyond all limit of what else in the world,
Do love, prize, honor you.

MIRANDA.

I am a fool,
To weep at what I am glad of.

FERDINAND.

Wherefore weep you?

MIDANDA.

At my unworthiness, that dare not offer
What I desire to give; and much less take,
What I shall die to want. But this is trifling:
And all the morn it seeks to hide itself,
The bigger bulk it shows. Hence, bashful cunning;
And prompt me, plain and holy innocence!
I am your wife, if you will marry me;
If not I'll die your maid: to be your fellow
You may deny me; but I'll be your servant
Whether you will or no!

FERDINAND.

My mistress, dearest!
And I thus humble ever.

MIRANDA.

My husband, then?

FERDINAND.

Ay, with a heart as willing,
As bondage e'er of freedom. Here's my hand.

MIRANDA.

And mine with my heart in it. And now farewell,
Till half an hour hence.

As Miranda, being what she is, could only have had a Ferdinand for her lover, and an Ariel for her attendant, so she could have had with propriety no other father than the majestic and gifted being, who fondly claims her as "a thread of his own life—nay, that for which he lives." Prospero, with his magical powers, his superhuman wisdom, his moral worth and grandeur, and his kingly dignity, is one of the most sublime visions that ever swept with ample robes, pale brow, and sceptred hand, before the eye of fancy. He controls the invisible world, and works through the agency of spirits: not by any evil and forbidden compact, but solely by superior might and intellect—by potent spells gathered from the lore of ages, and abjured when he mingles again as a man with his fellow men. He is as distinct a being from the necromancers and astrologers celebrated in Shakspeare's age, as can well be imagined:* and all the wizards of poetry and fiction, even Faust and St. Leon, sink into common places before the princely, the philosophic, the benevolent Prospero.

The Bermuda Isles in which Shakspeare has placed the scene of the Tempest, were discovered in his time; Sir George Somers and his companions having been wrecked there in a terrible storm,† brought back a most fearful account of these unknown islands, which they described as a land of devils—a most prodigious and enchanted place, subject to continual tempests and supernatural visitings." Such was the idea entertained of the "still-vext Bermoothes" in Shakspeare's age; but later travellers describe them as perfect regions of enchantment in a far different sense: as so many fairy Edens, clustered like a knot of gems upon the bosom of the Atlantic, deck-

* Such as Cornelius Agrippa, Michael Scott, Dr. Dee; the last was the cotemporary of Shakspeare.

† In 1609, about three years before Shakspeare produced the Tempest, which, though placed first in all the editions of his works, was one of the last of his dramas.

ed out in all the lavish luxuriance of nature, with shades of myrtle and cedar, fringed round with groves of coral; in short, each island a tiny paradise, rich with perpetual blossoms, in which Ariel might have slumbered, and ever-verdant bowers, in which Ferdinand and Miranda might have strayed. So that Shakspeare, in blending the wild relations of the shipwrecked mariners with his own inspired fancies, has produced nothing, however lovely in nature and sublime in magical power, which does not harmonize with the beautiful and wondrous reality.

There is another circumstance connected with the Tempest, which is rather interesting. It was produced and acted for the first time upon the occasion of the nuptials of the Princess Elizabeth, the eldest daughter of James I, with Frederic, the elector palatine. It is hardly necessary to remind the reader of the fate of this amiable but most unhappy woman, whose life, almost from the period of her marriage, was one long tempestuous scene of trouble and adversity.

* * * * * * * *

The characters which I have here classed together, as principally distinguished by the predominance of passion and fancy, appear to me to rise, in the scale of ideality, and simplicity, from Juliet to Miranda;—the last being in comparison so refined, so elevated above all stain of earth, that we can only acknowledge her in connexion with it through the emotions of sympathy she feels and inspires.

I remember, when I was in Italy, standing "at evening on the top of Fesole," and at my feet I beheld the city of Florence and the Val d'Arno, with its villas, its luxuriant gardens, groves, and olive grounds, all bathed in crimson light. A transparent vapor or exhalation, which in its tint was almost as rich as the pomegranate flower, moving with soft undulation, rolled through the valley, and the very earth seemed to pant with warm life beneath its rosy veil. A dark purple shade, the forerunner of night, was already stealing over the east; in the western sky still lingered the blaze of the sunset, while the faint perfume of trees, and flowers, and now and then a strain of music wafted upwards, completed the intoxication of the senses. But I looked from the earth to the sky, and immediately above this scene hung the soft crescent moon—alone, with all the bright heaven to herself: and as that sweet moon to the glowing landscape beneath it, such is the character of Miranda compared to that of Juliet.

CHARACTERS OF THE AFFECTIONS.

HERMIONE.

CHARACTERS in which the affections and the moral qualities predominate over fancy and all that bears the name of passion, are not, when we meet with them in real life, the most striking and interesting, nor the easiest to be understood and appreciated; but they are those on which, in the long run, we repose with increasing confidence and ever-new delight. Such characters are not easily exhibited in the colors of poetry, and when we meet with them there, we are reminded of the effect of Raffaelle's pictures. Sir Joshua Reynolds assures us that it took him three weeks to discover the beauty of the frescos in the Vatican; and many if they spoke truth, would prefer one of Titian's or Murillo's Virgins to one of Raffaelle's heavenly Madonnas. The less there is of marked expression or vivid color in a countenance or character, the more difficult to delineate it in such a manner as to captivate and interest us: but when this is done, and done to perfection, it is the miracle of poetry in painting, and of painting in poetry. Only Raffaelle and Correggio have achieved it in one case, and only Shakspeare in the other.

When, by the presence or the agency of some predominant and exciting power, the feelings and affections are upturned from the depths of the heart, and flung to the surface, the painter or the poet has but to watch the workings of the passions, thus in a manner made visible, and transfer them to his page or his canvas in colors more or less vigorous: but where all is calm without, and around, to dive into the profoundest abysses of character, trace the affections where they lie hidden like the ocean springs, wind into the most intricate involutions of the heart, patiently unravel its most delicate fibres, and in a few graceful touches place before us the distinct and visible result, —to do this demanded power of another and a rarer kind.

There are several of Shakspeare's characters which are especially distinguished by this profound feeling, in the conception and subdued harmony of tone in the delineation. To them may be particularly applied the ingenious simile which Goëthe has used to illustrate generally all Shakspeare's characters, when he compares them to the old-fashioned watches in glass cases, which not only showed the index pointing to the hour, but the wheels and springs within, which set that index in motion.

Imogen, Desdemona, and Hermione, are three women placed in situations nearly similar, and equally endowed with all the qualities which can render that situation striking and interesting. They are all gentle, beautiful, and innocent; all are models of conjugal submission, truth and tenderness; and all are victims of the unfounded jealousy of their husbands. So far the parallel is close, but here the resemblance ceases; the circumstances of each situation are varied with wonderful skill, and the characters which are as different as it is possible to imagine, conceived and discriminated with a power of truth, and a delicacy of feeling, yet more astonishing.

Critically speaking, the character of Hermione is the most simple in point of dramatic effect, that of Imogen the most varied and complex. Hermione is most distinguished by her magnanimity and her fortitude, Desdemona by her gentleness and refined grace, while Imogen combines all the best qualities of both, with others which they do not possess; consequently she is, as a character, superior to either; but considered as women I suppose the preference would depend on individual taste.

Hermione is the heroine of the three first acts of the Winter's Tale. She is the wife of Leontes, King of Sicilia, and though in the prime of beauty and womanhood, is not represented in the first bloom of youth. Her husband on slight grounds, suspects her of infidelity with his friend Polixenes, King of Bohemia; the suspicion once admitted, and working on a jealous, passionate, and vindictive mind, become a settled and confirmed opinion. Hermione is thrown into a dungeon; her new-born infant is taken from her, and by the order of her husband, frantic with jealousy, exposed to death on a desert shore; she is herself brought to a public trial for treason and incontinency, defends herself nobly, and is pronounced innocent by the oracle. But at the very moment that she is acquitted, she learns the death of the prince her son, who,

> Conceiving the dishonor of his mother ;
> And strait declined, drooped, took it deeply,
> Fastened and fixed, the shame on't in himself,
> Threw off his spirit, appetite, and sleep,
> And downright languished.

She swoons away with grief, and her supposed death concludes the third act. The two last acts are occupied with the adventures of her daughter Perdita ; and with the restoration of Perdita to the arms of her mother, and the reconciliation of Hermione and Leontes, the piece concludes.

Such, in few words, is the dramatic situation. The character of Hermione exhibits what is never found in the other sex, but rarely in our own—yet sometimes ;—dignity without pride, love without passion, and tenderness without weakness. To conceive a character, in which there enters so much of the negative, required perhaps no rare and astonishing effort of genius, such as created a Juliet, a Miranda, or a Lady Macbeth ; but to delineate such a character in the poetical form, to develope it through the medium of action and dialogue, without the aid of description ; to preserve its tranquil, mild, and serious beauty, its unimpassioned dignity, and at the same time keep the strongest hold upon our sympathy and our imagination ; and out of this exterior calm, produce the most profound pathos, the most vivid impression of life and internal power ; it is this which renders the character of Hermione one of Shakspeare's master-pieces.

Hermione is a queen, a matron, and a mother : she is good and beautiful, and royally descended. A majestic sweetness, a grand and gracious simplicity, an easy, unforced, yet dignified self-possession, are in all her deportment and in every word she utters. She is one of those characters, of whom it has been said proverbially, that "still waters run deep." Her passions are not vehement, but in her settled mind the sources of pain or pleasure, love or resentment, are like the springs that feed the mountain lakes, impenetrable, unfathomable, and inexhaustible.

Shakspeare has conveyed (as is his custom) a part of the character of Hermione in scattered touches, and through the impressions which she produces on all around her. Her surpassing beauty is alluded to in few but strong terms:

This jealousy
Is for a precious creature: as she is rare,
Must it be great.
Praise her but for this her out-door form,
(Which on my faith, deserves high speech.)

If one by one you wedded all the world,
Or from the all that are, took something good
To make a perfect woman; she you killed
Would be unparelleled.

I might have looked upon my queen's full eyes,
Have taken treasure from her lips—
————and left them
More rich for what they yielded.

The expressions "most sacred lady," "dread mistress," "sovereign," with which she she is addressed or alluded to, the boundless devotion and respect of those around her, and their confidence in her goodness and innocence, are so many additional strokes in the portrait.

For her my lord,
I dare my life lay down, and will do't sir,
Please you t' accept it, that the queen is spotless
I' the eyes of heaven, and to you.

Every inch of woman in the world,
Ay, every dram of woman's flesh, is false,
If she be so.

I would not be a stander-by to hear
My sovereign mistress clouded so, without
My present vengeance taken!

The mixture of playful courtesy, queenly dignity, and lady-like sweetness, with which she prevails on Polixenes to prolong his visit, is charming.

HERMIONE.
You'll stay?

POLIXENES.
No, madam.

HERMIONE.
Nay, but you will.

POLIXENES.
I may not, verily.

HERMIONE.
Verily!
You put me off with limber vows: but I,
Tho' you would seek t' unsphere the stars with oaths,
Should still say, "Sir, no going!" Verily,
You shall *not* go! A lady's verily is
As potent as a lord's. Will you go yet?
Force me to keep you as a prisoner,
Not like a guest?

And though the situation of Hermione admits of but few general reflections, one little speech, inimitably beautiful and characteristic, has become almost proverbial from its truth. She says

One good deed, dying tongueless,
Slaughters a thousand, waiting upon that.

Our praises are our wages; you may ride us
With one soft kiss a thousand furlongs, ere
With spur we heat an acre.

She receives the first intimation of her husband's jealous suspicions with incredulous astonishment. It is not that, like Desdemona, she does not, or cannot understand; but she *will* not. When he accuses her more plainly, she replies with a calm dignity—

Should a villain say so—
The most replenished villain in the world—
He were as much more villain: you, my lord,
Do but mistake.

This characteristic composure of temper never forsakes her; and yet it is so delineated that the impression is that of grandeur, and never borders upon pride or coldness: it is the fortitude of a gentle but a strong mind, conscious of its own innocence. Nothing can be more affecting than her calm reply to Leontes, who, in his jealous rage, heaps insult upon insult, and accuses her before her own attendants, as no better "than one of those to whom the vulgar give bold titles."

How will this grieve you,
When you shall come to clearer knolwedge
That you have thus published me! Gentle, my lord,
You scarce can right me thoroughly then,
To say you *did* mistake.

Her mild dignity and saint-like patience, combined as they are with the strongest sense of the cruel injustice of her husband, thrill us with admiration as well as pity; and we cannot but see and feel that for Hermione to give way to tears and feminine complaints under such a blow, would be quite incompatible with the character. Thus she says of herself, as she is led to prison:

There's some ill planet reigns:
I must be patient till the heavens look

With an aspect more favorable. Good, my lords,
I am not prone to weeping, as our sex
Commonly are; the want of which vain dew
Perchance shall dry your pities; but I have
That honorable grief lodged here, that burns
Worse than tears drown. Beseech you all, my lords,
With thoughts so qualified as your charities
Shall best instruct you, measure me: and so
The king's will be performed.

When she is brought to trial for supposed crimes, called on to defend herself, "standing to prate and talk for life and honor, before who please to come and hear," the sense of her ignominious situation—all its shame and all its horror press upon her, and would apparently crush even *her* magnanimous spirit, but for the consciousness of her own worth and innocence, and the necessity that exists for asserting and defending both.

If powers divine
Behold our human actions, (as they do,)
I doubt not, then, but innocence shall make
False accusation blush, and tyranny
Tremble at patience
* * * * * *
For life, I prize it,
As I weigh grief, which I would spare. For honor—
'Tis a derivative from me to mine,
And only, that I stand for.

Her earnest, eloquent justification of herself, and her lofty sense of female honor, are rendered more affecting and impressive by that chilling despair, that contempt for a life which has been made bitter to her through unkindness, which is betrayed in every word of her speech, though so calmly characteristic. When she enumerates the unmerited insults which have been heaped upon her, it is without asperity or reproach, yet in a tone which shows how completely the iron has entered her soul. Thus when Leontes threatens her with death:

Sir, spare your threats:
The bug which you would fright me with I seek:
To me can life be no commodity;
The crown and comfort of my life, your favor,
I do give lost; for I do feel it gone,
But know not how it went. My second joy,
The first fruits of my body, from his presence
I am barr'd, like one infectious. My third comfort—
Starr'd most unluckily?—is from my breast,
The innocent milk in its most innocent mouth
Haled out to murder. Myself on every post
Proclaimed a strumpet; with immodest hatred,
The child-bed privilege denied, which 'longs
To women of all fashion. Lastly, hurried
Here to this place, 'i the open air, before
I have got strength of limit. Now, my liege,
Tell me what blessings I have here alive,
That I should fear to die? Therefore, proceed,
But yet hear this; mistake me not. No! life,
I prize it not a straw; but for mine honor,
(Which I would free,) if I shall be condemn'd
Upon surmises; all proofs sleeping else,
But what your jealousies awake; I tell you,
'Tis rigor, and not law.

The character of Hermione is considered open to criticism on one point. I have heard it remarked, that when she secludes herself from the world for sixteen years, during which time she is mourned as dead by her repentant husband, and is not won to relent from her resolve by his sorrow, his remorse, his constancy to her memory; such conduct, argues the critic, is unfeeling as it is inconceivable in a tender and virtuous woman. Would Imogen have done so, who is so generously ready to grant a pardon before it be asked? or Desdemona, who does not forgive because she cannot even resent? No, assuredly; but this is only another proof of the wonderful delicacy and consistency with which Shakspeare has discriminated the characters of all three. The incident of Hermione's supposed death and concealment for sixteen years, is not indeed very probable in itself, nor very likely to occur in every day life. But besides all the probability necessary for the purposes of poetry, it has all the likelihood it can derive from the peculiar character of Hermione, who is precisely the woman who could and would have acted in this manner. In such a mind as hers, the sense of a cruel injury, inflicted by one she had loved and trusted, without awakening any violent anger or any desire of vengeance, would sink deep—almost incurably and lastingly deep. So far she is most unlike either Imogen or Desdemona, who are portrayed as much more flexible in temper; but then the circumstances under which she is wronged are very different, and far more unpardonable. The self-created, frantic jealousy of Leontes is very distinct from that of Othello, writhing under the arts of Iago; or that of Posthumus, whose understanding has been cheated by the most damning evidence of his wife's infidelity. The jealousy which in Othello and Posthumus is an error of judgment, in Leontes is a vice of the blood: he suspects without cause, condemns without proof; he is without excuse,—unless the mixture of pride, passion, and imagination, and the predisposition to jealousy with which Shakspeare has portrayed him, be considered as an excuse. Hermione has been openly insulted: he to whom she gave herself, her heart, her soul, has stooped to the weakness and baseness of suspicion, has doubted her truth, has wronged her love, has sunk in her esteem and forfeited her confidence; she has been branded with vile names: her son, her eldest hope, is dead—dead through the false accusation which has stuck infamy on his mother's name; and her innocent babe, stained with illegitimacy, disowned and rejected, has been exposed to a cruel death. Can we believe that the mere tardy acknowledgment of her innocence could make amends for wrongs and agonies such as these? or heal a heart which must have bled inwardly, consumed by that untold grief, "which burns worse than tears drown?" Keeping in view the peculiar character of Hermione, such as she is delineated, is she one either to forgive hastily or forget quickly? and though she might, in her solitude, mourn over her repentant husband, would his repentance suffice to restore him at once to his place in her heart? to efface from her strong and reflecting mind the recollection of his miserable weakness? or can we fancy this high-souled woman left childless through the injury which has been inflicted on her, widowed in heart by the unworthiness of him she loved, a spectacle of grief to all—to her husband a continual reproach and humiliation—walking through the parade of royalty in the court which had witnessed her anguish, her shame, her degradation, and her despair? Methinks that the want of feeling, nature, delicacy, and consistency, would lie in such an exhibition as this. In a mind like Hermione's, where the strength of feeling is founded in the power of thought, and where there is little of impulse or imagination,—"the depth, but not the tumult of the soul,"*—there are but two influences which predominate over the will,—time and religion. And what then remained, but that wounded in heart and spirit, she should retire from the world?—not to brood over her wrongs, but to study forgiveness, and wait the fulfilment of the oracle which had promised the termination of her sorrows. Thus

*——The gods approve
The depth, and not the tumult of the soul.

WORDSWORTH.

"Il pouvait y avoir des vagues majestueuses et non de l'orage dans son coeur," was finely observed of Madame de Stael in her maturer years; it would have been true of Hermione at any period of her life.

a premature reconciliation would not only have been painfully inconsistent with the character, it would also have deprived us of that most beautiful scene, in which Hermione is discovered to her husband as the statue or image of herself. And here we have another instance of that admirable art, with which the dramatic character is fitted to the circumstances in which it is placed: that perfect command over her own feelings, that complete self-possession necessary to this extraordinary situation, is consistent with all that we imagine of Hermione; in any other woman it would be so incredible as to shock all our ideas of probability.

This scene, then, is not only one of the most picturesque and striking instances of stage effect to be found in the ancient or modern drama, but, by the skilful manner in which it is prepared, it has, wonderful as it appears, all the merit of consistency and truth. The grief, the love, the remorse, and impatience of Leontes, are finely contrasted with the astonishment and admiration of Perdita, who, gazing on the figure of her mother like one entranced, looks as if she were also turned to marble. There is here one little instance of tender remembrance in Leontes, which adds to the charming impression of Hermione's character.

> Chide me, dear stone! that I may say indeed
> Thou art Hermione; or rather thou art she
> In thy not chiding, for she was as tender
> As infancy and grace.
>
> Thus she stood,
> Even with such life of majesty—warm life—
> As now it coldly stands—when first I woo'd her!

The effect produced on the different persons of the drama by this living statue—an effect which at the same moment is and is *not* illusion—the manner in which the feelings of the spectators become entangled between the conviction of death and the impression of life, the idea of a deception, and the feeling of a reality, and the exquisite coloring of poetry and touches of natural feeling with which the whole is brought up,—till wonder, expectation, and intense pleasure, hold our pulse and breath suspended on the event,—are quite inimitable.

The expressions used here by Leontes,

> Thus she stood,
> Even with such life of majesty—*warm life.*
> The fixture of her eye has motion in't
> And we are mock'd by art.

And by Polixenes,

> The very life seems warm upon her lip,

appear strangely applied to a statue, such as we usually imagine it—of the cold colorless marble; but it is evident that in this scene Hermione personates one of those images or effigies, such as we may see in the old Gothic cathedrals, in which the stone, or marble, was colored after nature. I remember coming suddenly upon one of these effigies, either at Basle or at Fribourg, which made me start; the figure was as large as life; the drapery of crimson, powdered with stars of gold; the face and eyes, and hair tinted after nature, though faded by time. It stood in a Gothic niche, over a tomb as I think, and in a kind of dim uncertain light. It would have been very easy for a living person to represent such an effigy, particularly if it had been painted by that "rare Italian master, Julio Romano,"* who as we are informed was the reputed author of this wonderful statue.

The moment when Hermione descends from her pedestal to the sound of soft music, and throws herself without

* Winter's Tale, Act v. Scene ii.

speaking into her husband's arms, is one of inexpressible interest. It appears to me that her silence during the whole of this scene (except where she invokes a blessing on her daughter's head) is in the finest taste as a poetical beauty, besides being an admirable trait of character. The misfortunes of Hermione, her long religious seclusion, the wonderful and almost supernatural part she has just enacted have invested her with such a sacred and awful charm, that any words put into her mouth, must, I think, have injured the solemn and profound pathos of the situation.

There are several among Shakspeare's characters which exercise a far stronger power over our feelings, our fancy, our understanding, than that of Hermione; but not one,—unless perhaps Cordelia,—constructed upon so high and pure a principle. It is the union of gentleness with power which constitutes the perfection of mental grace. Thus, among the ancients, with whom the *graces* were also the *charities*,* one and the same word signified equally *strength* and *virtue*. This feeling, carried into the fine arts, was the secret of the antique grace—the grace of repose. The same eternal nature—the same sense of immutable truth and beauty, which revealed this sublime principle of art to the ancient Greeks, revealed it to the genius of Shakspeare; and the character of Hermione, in which we have the same largeness of conception and delicacy of execution,—the same effect of suffering without passion, and grandeur without effort, is an instance, I think that he felt within himself, and by intuition, what we study all our lives in the remains of ancient art. The calm, regular, classical beauty of Hermione's character is the more impressive from the wild and Gothic accompaniments of her story, and the beautiful relief afforded

* To show, perhaps, that while form alone may constitute beauty, sentiment is necessary to grace.

by the pastoral and romantic grace which is thrown around her daughter Perdita.

The character of Paulina, in the Winter's Tale, though it has obtained but little notice and no critical remark, (that I have seen,) is yet one of the striking beauties of the play: and it has its moral too. As we see running through the whole universe that principle of contrast which may be called the life of nature, so we behold it every where illustrated in Shakspeare: upon this principle he has placed Emilia beside Desdemona, the nurse beside Juliet; the clowns and dairymaids, and the merry pedlar thief Autolycus round Florizel and Perdita;—and made Paulina the friend of Hermione.

Paulina does not fill any ostensible office near the person of the queen but is a lady of high rank in the court—the wife of the Lord Antigones. She is a character strongly drawn from real and common life—a clever, generous, strong-minded, warm-hearted woman, fearless in asserting the truth, firm in her sense of right, enthusiastic in all her affections; quick in thought, resolute in word, and energetic in action; but heedless, hot-tempered, impatient, loud, bold, voluble, and turbulent of tongue; regardless of the feelings of those for whom she would sacrifice her life, and injuring from excess of zeal those whom she most wishes to serve. How many such are there in the world! But Paulina, though a very termagant, is yet a poetical termagant in her way; and the manner in which all the evil and dangerous tendencies of such a temper are placed before us, even while the individual character preserves the strongest hold upon our respect and admiration, forms an impressive lesson, as well as a natural and delightful portrait.

In the scene, for instance, where she brings the infant before Leontes with the hope of softening him to a sense of his injustice—" an office which," as she observes, "becomes a woman best"—her want of self-government, her bitter, inconsiderate reproaches, only add, as we might easily suppose, to his fury.

PAULINA.

I say I come
From your good queen!

LEONTES.

Good queen!

PAULINA.

Good queen, my lord, good queen—I say good queen;
And would by combat make her good, so were I
A man, the worst about you.

LEONTES.

Force her hence.

PAULINA.

Let him that makes but trifles of his eyes,
First hand me—on mine own accord, I'll off;
But first I'll do my errand. The good queen
(For she is good) hath brought you forth a daughter;
Here 'tis; commends it to your blessing.

LEONTES.

Traitors!
Will you not push her out? Give her the bastard.

PAULINA.

For ever.
Unvenerable be thy hands, if thou
Tak'st up the princess by that forced baseness
Which he has put upon 't!

LEONTES.

He dreads his wife.

PAULINA.

So, I would *you* did; then, 'twere past all doubt
You'd call your children yours.

LEONTES.

A callat,
Of boundless tongue, who late hath beat her husband,
And now baits me!—This brat is none of mine.

PAULINA.

It is yours,
And might we lay the old proverb to your charge,
So like you, 'tis the worse.

* * * * * * * *

LEONTES.

A gross hag!
And Lozel, thou art worthy to be hang'd,
That will not stay her tongue.

ANTIGONES.

Hang all the husbands
That cannot do that feat, you'll leave yourself
Hardly one subject.

LEONTES.

Once more, take her hence.

PAULINA.

A most unworthy and unnatural lord
Can do no more.

LEONTES.

I'll have thee burned

PAULINA.

I care not:
It is an heretic that makes the fire
Not she which burns in 't.

Here, while we honor her courage and her affection, we cannot help regretting her violence. We see, too, in Paulina, what we so often see in real life, that it is not those who are most susceptible in their own temper and feelings, who are most delicate and forbearing towards the feelings of others. She does not comprehend, or will not allow for, the sensitive weakness of a mind less firmly tempered than her own. There is a reply of Leontes to one of her cutting speeches which is full of feeling, and a lesson to those who with the best intentions in the world force the painful truth, like a knife, into the already lacerated heart.

PAULINA.

If, one by one, you wedded all the world,
Or, from the all that are took something good
To make a perfect woman, she you killed
Would be unparallel'd

LEONTES.

I think so. Kill'd!
She I kill'd? I did so; but thou strik'st me
Sorely, to say I did; it is as bitter
Upon thy tongue, as in my thought. Now good now,
Say so but seldom.

CLEOMENES.

Not at all, good lady;
You might have spoken a thousand things that would
Have done the time more benefit, and grac'd
Your kindness better.

We can only excuse Paulina by recollecting that it is a part of her purpose to keep alive in the heart of Leontes the remembrance of his queen's perfections, and of his own cruel injustice. It is admirable, too, that Hermione and Paulina, while sufficiently approximated to afford all the pleasure of contrast, are never brought too nearly in contact on the scene or in the dialogue;* for this would have been a fault in taste, and have necessarily weakened the effect of both characters:—either the serene grandeur of Hermione would have subdued and overawed the fiery spirit of Paulina, or the impetuous temper of the latter.

* Only in the last scene, when with solemnity befitting the occasion, Paulina invokes the majestic figure to "descend, and be stone no more," and where she presents her daughter to her, "Turn, good lady! our Perdita is found."

must have disturbed, in some respect, our impression of the calm, majestic, and somewhat melancholy beauty of Hermione.

DESDEMONA.

The character of Hermione is addressed more to the imagination ;—that of Desdemona to the feelings. All that can render sorrow majestic is gathered round Hermione ;—all that can render misery heart-breaking is assembled round Desdemona. The wronged but self-sustained virtue of Hermione commands our veneration ; the injured and defenceless innocence of Desdemona so wrings the soul, " that all for pity we could die."

Desdemona, as a character, comes nearest to Miranda, both in herself as a woman, and in the perfect simplicity and unity of the delineation ; the figures are differently draped —the proportions are the same. There is the same modesty, tenderness, and grace ; the same artless devotion in the affections, the same predisposition to wonder, to pity, to admire ; the same almost ethereal refinement and delicacy ; but all is pure poetic nature within Miranda and around her ; Desdemona is more associated with the palpable realities of every-day existence, and we see the forms and habits of society tinting her language and deportment ; no two beings can be more alike in character —nor more distinct as individuals.

The love of Desdemona for Othello, appears at first such a violation of all probabilities, that her father at once imputes it to magic, " to spells and mixtures powerful o'er the blood."

> She in spite of nature,
> Of years, of country, credit, every thing,
> To fall in love with what she feared to look on !

And the devilish malignity of Iago, whose coarse mind cannot conceive an affection founded purely in sentiment, derives from her love itself a strong argument against her.

> Aye, there's the point, as to be bold with you,
> Not to affect many proposed matches
> Of her own clime, complexion, and degree,
> Whereto, we see, in all things nature tends, &c.*

Notwithstanding this disparity of age, character, country, complexion, we, who are admitted into the secret, see her love rise naturally, and neccessarily out of the leading propensities of her nature.

At the period of the story a spirit of wild adventure had seized all Europe. The discovery of both Indies was yet recent; over the shores of the western hemisphere still fable and mystery hung, with all their dim enchantments, visionary terrors, and golden promises; perilous expeditions and distant voyages were every day undertaken from hope of plunder, or mere love of enterprise; and from these the adventurers returned with tales of "Antres vast and deserts wild—of cannibals that did each other eat—of Anthropophagi, and men whose heads did grow beneath their shoulders." With just such stories did Raleigh and Clifford, and their followers, return from the new world: and thus by their splendid or fearful exaggerations, which the imperfect knowledge of those times could not refute, was the passion for the romantic and marvellous nourished at home, particularly among the women. A cavalier of those days had no nearer, no surer way to his mistress' heart, than by entertaining her with these wondrous narratives. What was a general feature of his time, Shakspeare seized and adapted to his purpose with the most exquisite felicity of effect. Desdemona, leaving her household cares

* Act iii. Scene 3.

in haste, to hang breathless on Othello's tales, was doubtless a picture from the life; and her inexperience and her quick imagination lend it an added propriety; then her compassionate disposition is interested by all the disastrous chances, hair-breadth 'scapes, and moving accidents by flood and field, of which he has to tell; and her exceeding gentleness and timidity, and her domestic turn of mind, render her more easily captivated by the military renown, the valor, and lofty bearing of the noble Moor—

> And to his honors and his valiant parts
> Does she her soul and fortunes consecrate.

The confession and the excuse for her love is well placed in the mouth of Desdemona, while the history of the rise of that love, and of his course of wooing, is, with the most graceful propriety, as far as she is concerned, spoken by Othello, and in her absence. The last two lines summing up the whole—

> She loved me for the dangers I had passed,
> And I loved her that she did pity them—

comprise whole volumes of sentiment and metaphysics.

Desdemona displays at times a transient energy, arising from the power of affection, but gentleness gives the prevailing tone to the character—gentleness in its excess—gentleness verging on passiveness—gentleness which not only cannot resent, but cannot resist.

OTHELLO.
Then of so gentle a condition.

IAGO.
Aye! too gentle.

OTHELLO.
Nay, that's certain.

Here the exceeding softness of Desdemona's temper is turned against her by Iago, so that it suddenly strikes Othello in a new point of view, as the inability to resist temptation; but to us who perceive the character as a whole, this extreme gentleness of nature is yet delineated with such exceeding refinement, that the effect never approaches to feebleness. It is true that *once* her extreme timidity leads her in a moment of confusion and terror to prevaricate about the fatal handkerchief. This handkerchief, in the original story of Cynthio, is merely one of those embroidered handkerchiefs which were as fashionable in Shakspeare's time as in our own; but the minute description of it as "lavorato alla morisco sottilissimamente,"* suggested to the poetical fancy of Shakspeare one of the most exquisite and characteristic passages in the whole play. Othello makes poor Desdemona believe that the handkerchief was a talisman.

There's magic in the web of it.
A sybil, that had numbered in the world
The sun to make two hundred compasses,
In her prophetic fury sew'd the work:
The worms were hallow'd that did breed the silk,
And it was dyed in mummy, which the skilful
Conserv'd of maiden's hearts.

DESDEMONA.

Indeed! is't true?

OTHELLO.

Most veritable, therefore look to't well.

DESDEMONA.

Then would to heaven that I had never seen it!

OTHELLO.

Ha!—wherefore?

* Which being interpreted into modern English, means, I believe, nothing more than that the pattern was what we now call *arabesque.*

DESDEMONA.

Why do you speak so startingly and rash?

OTHELLO.

Is't lost?—Is't gone? Speak, is it out of the way?

DESDEMONA.

Heavens bless us!

OTHELLO.

Say you?

DESDEMONA.

It is not lost—but what an' if it were?

OTHELLO.

Ha!

DESDEMONA.

I say it is not lost.

OTHELLO.

Fetch it, let me see it.

DESDEMONA.

Why so I can, sir, but I will not now, &c.

Desdemona, whose soft credulity, whose turn for the marvellous, whose susceptible imagination had first directed her thoughts and affections to Othello, is precisely the woman to be frightened out of her senses by such a tale as this, and betrayed by her fears into a momentary tergiversation. It is most natural in such a being, and shows us that even in the sweetest natures there can be no completeness and consistency without moral energy.*

* There is an incident in the original tale, "Il Moro di Venezia," which could not well be transferred to the drama, but which is very effective, and adds, I think, to the circumstantial horrors of the story. Desdemona does not accidentally drop the handkerchief; it is stolen from her by Iago's little child, an infant of three years old, whom he trains or bribes to the theft. The love of Desdemona for this child, her little playfellow—the pretty description of her taking it in her arms and caressing it, while it profits by its situation to steal the handkerchief from her bosom, are well imagined, and beautifully told; and

With the most perfect artlessness, she has something of the instinctive, unsconscious address of her sex; as when she appeals to her father—

> So much duty has my mother show'd
> To you, preferring you before her father,
> So much I challenge, that I may profess
> Due to the Moor, my lord.

And when she is pleading for Cassio—

> What! Michael Cassio!
> That came a wooing with you; and many a time,
> When I have spoken of you disparagingly,
> Hath ta'en your part?

In persons who unite great sensibility and lively fancy, I have often observed this particular species of address, which is always unconscious of itself, and consists in the power of placing ourselves in the position of another, and imagining, rather than perceiving, what is in their hearts. We women have this *address* (if so it can be called) naturally, but I have seldom met with it in men. It is not inconsistent with extreme simplicity of character, and quite distinct from that kind of art which is the result of natural acuteness and habits of observation—quick to perceive the foibles of others, and as quick to turn them to its own purposes; which is always conscious of itself, and if united with strong intellect, seldom perceptible to others. In the mention of her mother, and the appeal to Othello's self-love, Desdemona has no design formed on conclusions previously drawn; but her intuitive quickness of feeling, added to her imagination, lead her more safely to the same

the circumstance of Iago employing his own innocent child, as the instrument of his infernal villainy, adds a deeper, and, in truth, an unneccessary touch of the fiend to his fiendish character.

results, and the distinction is as truly as it is delicately drawn.

When Othello first outrages her in a manner which appears inexplicable, she seeks and finds excuses for him. She is so innocent, that not only she cannot believe herself suspected, but she cannot conceive the existence of guilt in others.

> Something, sure, of state,
> Either from Venice, or some unhatch'd practice
> Made demonstrable here in Cyprus to him,
> Hath puddled his clear spirit.
> 'Tis even so—
> Nay, we must think, men are not gods,
> Nor of them look for such observances
> As fit the bridal.

And when the direct accusation of crime is flung on her in the vilest terms, it does not anger but stun her, as if it transfixed her whole being: she attempts no reply, no defence; and reproach or resistance never enter her thought.

> Good friend, go to him—for by this light of heaven
> I know not how I lost him: here I kneel:—
> If e'er my will did tresspass 'gainst his love,
> Either in discourse of thought or actual deed;
> Or that my eyes, mine ears, or any sense,
> Delighted them in any other form;
> Or that I do not yet, and ever did,
> And ever will, though he do shake me off
> To beggarly divorcement, love him dearly,
> Comfort forswear me! Unkindness may do much,
> And his unkindness may defeat my life,
> But never taint my love.

And there is one stroke of consummate delicacy, surprising, when we remember the latitude of expression prevailing in Shakspeare's time, and which he allowed to his other women generally; she says, on recovering from her stupefaction—

Am I that name, Iago?

IAGO.
What name, sweet lady?

DESDEMONA.
That, which she says my lord did say I was.

So completely did Shakspeare enter into the angelic refinement of the character.

Endued with that temper which is the origin of superstition, in love as in religion,—which, in fact, makes love itself a religion,—she not only does not utter an upbraiding, but nothing that Othello does or says, no outrage, no injustice, can tear away the charm with which her imagination had invested him, or impair her faith in his honor; "Would you had never seen him!" exclaims Emilia.

DESDEMONA.
So would not I!—my love doth so approve him,
That even his stubborness, his checks and frowns,
Have grace and favor in them.

There is another peculiarity, which, in reading the play of Othello, we rather feel than perceive: through the whole of the dialogue appropriated to Desdemona, there is not one general observation. Words are with her the vehicle of sentiment, and never of reflection; so that I cannot find throughout a sentence of general application. The same remark applies to Miranda; and to no other female character of any importance or interest; not even to Ophelia.

The rest of what I wished to say of Desdemona, has been anticipated by an anonymous critic, and so beautifully, so justly, so eloquently expressed, that I with pleasure erase my own page to make room for his:

"Othello," observes this writer, "is no love story; all that is below tragedy in the passion of love, is taken away at once, by the awful character of Othello; for such he seems to us to be designed to be. He appears never as a lover, but at once as a husband: and the relation of his love made dignified as it is a husband's justification of his marriage, is also dignified, as it is a soldier's relation of his stern and perilous life. His love itself, as long as it is happy is perfectly calm and serene—the protecting tenderness of a husband. It is not till it is disordered, that it appears as a passion; then is shown a power in contention with itself—a mighty being struck with death, and bringing up from all the depths of life convulsions and agonies. It is no exhibition of the power and the passion of love, but of the passion of life vitally wounded, and self-overmastering. If Desdemona had been really guilty, the greatness would have been destroyed, because his love would have been unworthy, false. But she is good, and his love is most perfect, just, and good. That a man should place his perfect love on a wretched thing, is miserably debasing, and shocking to thought; but that loving perfectly and well, he should by hellish human circumvention be brought to distrust and dread, and abjure his own perfect love, is most mournful indeed—it is the infirmity of our good nature wrestling in vain with the strong powers of evil. Moreover he would, had Desdemona been false, have been the mere victim of fate; whereas he is now in a manner his own victim. His happy love was heroic tenderness; his injured love is terrible passion; and disordered power, engendered within itself to its own destruction, is the height of all tragedy.

"The character of Othello is perhaps the most greatly drawn, the most heroic of any of Shakspeare's actors; but it is, perhaps, that one also of which his reader last acquires the intelligence. The intellectual and warlike energy of his mind—his tenderness of affection—his loftiness of spirit—his frank, generous magnanimity—impetuosity like a thunderbolt—and that dark fierce flood of boiling passion, polluting even his imagination,—compose a character entirely original, most difficult to delineate, but perfectly delineated."

Emilia in this play is a perfect portrait from common life, a masterpiece in the Flemish style: and though not necessary as a contrast, it cannot be but that the thorough vulgarity, the low cunning, the loose principles of this plebeian woman united to high degree of spirit, energetic feeling, and strong good sense, serve to place in brighter relief the exquisite refinement, the moral grace, the unblemished truth, and the soft submission of Desdemona.

On the other perfections of this tragedy, considered as a production of genius—on the wonderful characters of Othello and Iago—on the skill with which the plot is conducted, and its simplicity which a word unravels,* and on the overpowering horror of the catastrophe—eloquence and analytical criticism have been exhausted: I will only add, that the chief source of the pathos throughout—of that pathos which at once softens and deepens to tragic effect—lies in the character of Desdemona. No woman differently constituted could have excited the same intense and painful compassion, without losing something of that exalted charm, which invests her from beginning to end, which we are apt to impute to the interest of the situation and to the poetical coloring, but which lies, in fact, in the very essence of the character. Desdemona, with all her timid flexibility and soft acquiesence, is not weak; for the nega-

* Consequences are so linked together, that the exclamation of Emilia,

> O thou dull Moor!—That handkerchief thou speakest of
> I found by fortune, and did give my husband!

Is sufficient to reveal to Othello the whole history of his ruin.

tive alone is weak, and the mere presence of goodness and affection implies in itself a species of power;—power without consciousness, power without effort, power with repose —that soul of grace!

I know a Desdemona in real life, one in whom the absence of intellectual power is never felt as a deficiency, nor the absence of energy of will as impairing the dignity, nor the most imperturbable serenity, as a want of feeling: one in whom thoughts appear mere instincts, the sentiment of rectitude supplies the principle, and virtue itself seems rather a necessary state of being, rather than an imposed law. No shade of sin or vanity has yet stolen over that bright innocence. No discord within has marred the loveliness without—no strife of the factitious world without has disturbed the harmony within. The comprehension of evil appears for ever shut out, as if goodness had converted all things to itself; and all to the pure in heart must necessarily be pure. The impression produced is exactly that of the character of Desdemona: genius is a rare thing, but abstract goodness is rarer. In Desdemona, we cannot but feel that the slightest manifestation of intellectual power or active will would have injured the dramatic effect. She is a victim consecrated from the first,—"an offering without blemish," alone worthy of the grand final sacrifice; all harmony, all grace, all purity, all tenderness, all truth! But alas! to see her fluttering like a cherub, in the talons of a fiend! —to see her——O poor Desdemona!

IMOGEN.

We come now to Imogen. Others of Shakspeare's characters are, as dramatic and poetical conceptions, more striking, more brilliant, more powerful; but of all his women, considered as individuals rather than as heroines, Imogen is the most perfect. Portia and Juliet are pictured to the fancy with more force of contrast, more depth of light and shade; Viola and Miranda, with more aerial delicacy of outline; but there is no female portrait that can be compared to Imogen as a woman—none in which so great a variety of tints are mingled together into such perfect harmony. In her we have all the fervor of youthful tenderness, all the romance of youthful fancy, all the enchantment of ideal grace,—the bloom of beauty, the brightness of intellect, and the dignity of rank, taking a peculiar hue from the conjugal character which is shed over all, like a consecration and a holy charm. In Othello and the Winter's Tale, the interest excited for Desdemona and Hermione is divided with others; but in Cymbeline, Imogen is the angel of light, whose lovely presence pervades and animates the whole piece. The character altogether may be pronounced finer, more complex in its elements, and more fully developed in all its parts, than those of Hermione and Desdemona; but the position in which she is placed is not, I think, so fine—at least, not so effective, as a tragic situation.

Shakspeare has borrowed the chief circumstances of Imogen's story from one of Boccaccio's tales.*

A company of Italian merchants who are assembled in a tavern at Paris, are represented as conversing on the subject of their wives: all of them express themselves with levity, or scepticism, or scorn, on the virtue of women, except a young Genoese merchant named Bernabo, who maintains, that by the especial favor of heaven he possesses a wife no less chaste than beautiful. Heated by the wine, and excited by the arguments and the coarse raillery

* Decamerone. Novella, 9mo. Giornata, 2do.

of another young merchant, Ambrogiolo, Bernabo proceeds to enumerate the various perfections and accomplishments of his Zinevra. He praises her loveliness, her submission, and her discretion—her skill in embroidery, her graceful service, in which the best trained page of the court could not exceed her; and he adds, as rarer accomplishments, that she could mount a horse, fly a hawk, write and read, and cast up accounts, as well as any merchant of them all. His enthusiasm only excites the laughter and mockery of his companions, particularly of Ambrogiolo, who, by the most artful mixture of contradiction and argument, rouses the anger of Bernabo, and he at length exclaims, that he would willingly stake his life, his head, on the virtue of his wife. This leads to the wager which forms so important an incident in the drama. Ambrogiolo bets one thousand florins of gold against five thousand, that Zinevra, like the rest of her sex, is accessible to temptation—that, in less than three months she will undermine her virtue, and bring her husband the most undeniable proofs of her falsehood. He sets off for Genoa, in order to accomplish his purpose; but on his arrival, all that he learns, and all that he beholds with his own eyes of the discreet and noble character of the lady, make him despair of success by fair means; he therefore has recourse to the basest treachery. By bribing an old woman in the service of Zinevra, he is conveyed to her sleeping apartment, concealed in a trunk, from which he issues in the dead of the night; he takes note of the furniture of the chamber, makes himself master of her purse, her morning robe, or cymar, and her girdle, and of a certain mark on her person. He repeats these observations for two nights, and, furnished with these evidences of Zinevra's guilt, he returns to Paris, and lays them before the wretched husband. Bernabo rejects every proof of his wife's infidelity, except that which finally convinces Posthumus. When Ambrogiolo mentions the "mole, cinquespotted," he stands like one who has received a poniard in his heart; without further dispute he pays down the forfeit, and filled with rage and despair, both at the loss of his money and the falsehood of his wife, he returns towards Genoa; he retires to his country-house, and sends a messenger to the city with letters to Zinevra, desiring that she would come and meet him, but with secrer orders to the man to despatch her by the way. The servant prepares to execute his master's command, but overcome by her entreaties for mercy, and his own remorse, he spares her life, on condition that she will fly from the country for ever. He then disguises her in his own cloak and cap, and brings back to her husband the assurance that she is killed, and that her body has been devoured by the wolves. In the disguise of a mariner, Zinevra then embarks on board a vessel bound to the Levant, and on her arrival at Alexandria she is taken into the service of the Sultan of Egypt, under the name of Sicurano: she gains the confidence of her master, who, not suspecting her sex, sends her as captain of the guard which was appointed for the protection of the merchants at the fair of Acre. Here she accidently meets Ambrogiolo, and sees in his possession the purse and girdle, which she immediately recognises as her own. In reply to her inquiries, he relates with fiendish exultation the manner in which he had obtained possession of them, and she persuades him to go back with her to Alexandria. She then sends a messenger to Genoa in the name of the Sultan, and induces her husband to come and settle in Alexandria. At a proper opportunity, she summons both to the presence of the Sultan, obliges Ambrogiolo to make a full confession of his treachery, and wrings from her husband the avowal of his supposed murder of herself; then falling at the feet of the Sultan, discovers her real name and sex, to the great amazement of all. Bernabo is pardoned at the prayer of his wife, and Ambrogiolo is condemned to be fastened to a stake, smeered with honey, and left to be devoured by the flies and locusts, this horrible sentence is executed ; while Zinevra, enriched by the presents of the Sultan, and the forfeit wealth of Ambrogiolo, returns with her husband to Genoa, where she lives in great honor and happiness, and maintains her reputation for virtue to the end of her life.

These are the materials from which Shakspeare has drawn the dramatic situation of Imogen. He has also endowed her with several of the qualities which are attributed to Zinevra ; but for the essential truth and beauty of the individual character, for the sweet coloring of pathos, and sentiment, and poetry, interfused through the whole, he is indebted only to nature and himself.

It would be a waste of words to refute certain critics who have accused Shakspeare of a want of judgment in the adoption of the story ; of having transferred the manners of a set of intoxicated merchants and a merchant's wife to heroes and princesses, and of having entirely destroyed the interest of the catastrophe.* The truth is, that Shakspeare has wrought out the materials before him with the most luxuriant fancy and the most wonderful skill. As for the various anachronisms, and the confusion of names, dates, and manners, over which Dr. Johnson exults in no measured terms, the confusion is no where but in his own heavy obtuseness of sentiment and perception, and his want of poetical faith. Look into the old Italian poets, whom we read continually with still increasing pleasure ; does any one think of sitting down to disprove the existence of Ariodante, king of Scotland ? or to prove that the mention of Proteus and Pluto, baptism and the Virgin Mary,

* Vide Dr. Johnson, and Dunlap's History of Fiction.

in a breath, amounts to an anachronism? Shakspeare, by throwing his story far back into a remote and uncertain age, has blended, by his "own omnipotent will," the heroic, the ideal, and the classical—the extreme of refinement and the extreme of simplicity, into one of the loveliest fictions of romantic poetry, and, to use Schlegel's expression, "has made the social manners of the latest times harmonize with heroic deeds, and even with the appearance of the gods."*

But admirable as is the conduct of the whole play, rich in variety of character and in picturesque incident, its chief beauty and interest is derived from Imogen.

When Ferdinand tells Miranda that she was "created of every creatures best," he speaks like a lover, or refers only to her personal charms: the same expression might be applied critically to the character of Imogen; for as the portrait of Miranda is produced by resolving the female character into its original elements, so that of Imogen unites the greatest number of those qualities which we imagine to constitute excellence in woman.

Imogen, like Juliet, conveys to our mind the impression of extreme simplicity in the midst of the most wonderful complexity. To conceive her aright, we must take some peculiar tint from many characters, and so mingle them, that, like the combination of hues in a sun-beam, the effect shall be as one to the eye. We must imagine something of the romantic enthusiasm of Juliet, of the truth and constancy of Helen, of the dignified purity of Isabel, of the tender sweetness of Viola, of the self-possession and intellect of Portia—combined together so equally and so harmoniously, that we can scarcely say that one quality predominates over the other. But Imogen is less imaginative than Juliet, less spirited and intellectual than Portia,

* See Hazlitt and Schlegel on the catastrophe of Cymbeline.

less serious than Helen and Isabel; her dignity is not so imposing as that of Hermione, it stands more on the defensive; her submission, though unbounded, is not so passive as that of Desdemona;—and thus while she resembles each of these characters individually, she stands wholly distinct from all.

It is true, that the conjugal tenderness of Imogen is at once the chief subject of the drama, and the pervading charm of her character; but it is not true, I think, that she is merely interesting from her tenderness and constancy to her husband. We are so completely let into the essence of Imogen's nature, that we feel as if we had known and loved her before she was married to Posthumus, and that her conjugal virtues are a charm superadded, like the color laid upon a beautiful groundwork. Neither does it appear to me that Posthumus is unworthy of Imogen, or only interesting on Imogen's account. His character, like those of all the other persons of the drama, is kept subordinate to hers: but this could not be otherwise, for she is the proper subject—the heroine of thepoem. Every thing is done to ennoble Posthumus, and justify her love for him; and though we certainly approve him more for her sake than for his own, we are early prepared to view him with Imogen's eyes; and not only excuse, but sympathize in her admiration of one

> Who sat 'mongst men like a descended god,
> *　*　*　*　*
> Who liv'd in court, which it is rare to do,
> Most praised, most loved:
> A sample to the youngest; to the more mature
> A glass that feated them.

And with what beauty and delicacy is her conjugal and matronly character discriminated! Her love for her husband is as deep as Juliet's for her lover, but without any of that headlong vehemence, that fluttering amid hope, fear and transport—that giddy intoxication of heart and sense, which belongs to the novelty of passion, which we feel once, and but once, in our lives. We see her love for Posthumus acting upon her mind, with the force of an habitual feeling, heightened by enthusiastic passion, and hallowed by the sense of duty. She asserts and justifies her affection with energy indeed, but with a calm and wife-like dignity—

CYMBELINE.

Thou took'st a beggar, wouldst have made my throne
A seat for baseness.

IMOGEN.

No, I rather added a lustre to it.

CYMBELINE.

O thou vile one.

IMOGEN.

Sir,
It is your fault that I have loved Posthumus;
You bred him as my playfellow, and he is
A man worth any woman: Overbuys me
Almost the sum he pays.

Compare also, as examples of the most delicate discrimination of character and feeling, the parting scene between Imogen and Posthumus, that between Romeo and Juliet, and that between Troilus and Cressida:—compare the confiding matronly tenderness, the deep but resigned sorrow of Imogen, with the despairing agony of Juliet, and the petulant grief of Cressida.

When Posthumus is driven into exile, he comes to take a last farewell of his wife:

IMOGEN.

My dearest husband,
I something fear my father's wrath, but nothing
(Always reserv'd my holy duty) what
His rage can do on me. You must be gone,
And I shall here abide the hourly shot
Of angry eyes: not comforted to live
But that there is this jewel in the world
That I may see again.

POSTHUMUS.

My queen! my mistress!
O lady, weep no more! lest I give cause
To be suspected of more tenderness
Than doth become a man. I will remain
The loyal'st husband that did e'er plight troth.
* * * * *
Should we be taking leave
As long a term as yet we have to live,
The loathness to depart would grow—Adieu!

IMOGEN.

Nay, stay a little:
Were you but riding forth to air yourself,
Such parting were too petty.
Look here, love,
This diamond was my mother's: take it heart;
But keep it till you woo another wife,
When Imogen is dead!

Imogen, in whose tenderness there is nothing jealous or fantastic, does not seriously apprehend that her husband will woo another wife when she is dead. It is one of those fond fancies which women are apt to express in moments of feeling, merely for the pleasure of hearing a protestation to the contrary. When Posthumus leaves her, she does not burst forth in eloquent lamentation, but that silent, stunning, overwhelming sorrow, which renders the mind insensible to all things else, is represented with equal force and simplicity.

IMOGEN.

There cannot be a pinch in death
More sharp than this is.

CYMBELINE.

O disloyal thing,
That shouldst repair my youth! thou heapst
A year's age on me.

IMOGEN.

I beseech you, sir,
Harm not yourslf with your vexation; I
Am senseless of your wrath; a touch more rare*
Subdues all pangs, all fears.

CYMBELINE

Past grace? obedience?

IMOGEN.

Past hope, and in despair—that way past grace.

In the same circumstances the impetuous excited feelings of Juliet, and her vivid imagination, lend something far more widely agitated, more intensely poetical and passionate to her grief.

JULIET.

Art thou gone so? My love, my lord, my friend!
I must hear from thee every day i' the hour,
For in a minute there are many days—
O by this count I shall be much in years,
Ere I again behold my Romeo!

ROMEO.

Farewell! I will omit no opportunity
That may convey my greetings, love, to thee.

JULIET.

O think'st thou we shall ever meet again?

ROMEO.

I doubt it not, and all these woes shall serve
For sweet discourses in our time to come.

* More rare—*i. e.* more exquisitely poignant.

JULIET.
O God! I have an ill-divining soul:
Methinks I see thee, now thou art below,
As one dead in the bottom of a tomb;
Either my eye-sight fails; or thou look'st pale.

We have no sympathy with the pouting disappointment of Cressida, which is just like that of a spoiled child which has lost its sugar-plum, without tenderness, passion, or poetry; and, in short, perfectly characteristic of that vain fickle, dissolute, heartless woman,—"unstable as water."—

CRESSIDA.
And is it true, that I must go from Troy?

TROILUS.
A hateful truth.

CRESSIDA.
What, and from Troilus too?

TROILUS.
From Troy and Troilus.

CRESSIDA.
Is it possible?

TROILUS.
And suddenly.

CRESSIDA.
I must then to the Greeks?

TROILUS.
No remedy.

CRESSIDA.
A woful Cressid 'mongst the merry Greeks!
When shall we see again?

TROILUS.
Hear me, my love. Be thou but true of heart—

CRESSIDA.
I true! How now? what wicked deem is this?

TROILUS.
Nay, we must use expostulation kindly,
For it is parting from us:

I speak not, be thou true, as fearing thee;
For I will throw my glove to death himself,
That there's no maculation in thy heart:
But be thou true, say I, to fashion in
My sequent protestations. Be thou true,
And I will see thee.

CRESSIDA.

O heavens! be true again—
O heavens! you love me not.

TROILUS.

Die I a villain, then!
In this I do not call your faith in question,
So mainly as my merit.——
——But be not tempted.

CRESSIDA.

Do you think I will?

*　　*　　*　　*　　*

In the eagerness of Imogen to meet her husband, there is all a wife's fondness, mixed up with the breathless hurry arising from a sudden and joyful surprise; but nothing of the picturesque eloquence, the ardent, exuberant, Italian imagination of Juliet, who, to gratify her impatience, would have "her heralds, thoughts;"—press into her service the nimble-pinioned doves and wind-swift, Cupids, —change the course of nature, and "lash the steeds of Phœbus to the west." Imogen only thinks "one score of miles, 'twixt sun and sun," slow travelling for a lover and wishes for a horse with wings—

O for a horse with wings! Hear'st thou, Pisanio?
He is at Milford Haven. Read, and tell me
How far 'tis thither. If one of mean affairs
May plod it in a week, why may not I
Glide thither in a day? Then, true Pisanio,
(Who long'st, like me, to see thy lord—who long'st—
O let me bate, but not like me—yet long'st,
But in a fainter kind—O not like me,
For mine's beyond, beyond) say and speak thick—

(Love's counsellor should fill the bores of hearing
To the smothering of the sense) how far is it
To this same blessed Milford? And, by the way,
Tell me how Wales was made so happy, as
To inherit such a haven. But, first of all,
How we may steal from hence and for the gap
That we shall make in time, from our hence going
And our return to excuse. But first, how get hence:
Why should excuse be born or e'er begot?
We'll talk of that hereafter. Prithee speak,
How many score of miles may we well ride
'Twixt hour and hour?

PISANIO.

One score, 'twixt sun and sun,
Madam, 's enough for you: and too much, too.

IMOGEN.

Why one that rode to his execution, man,
Could never go so slow!

There are two or three other passages bearing on the conjugal tenderness of Imogen, which must be noted for the extreme intensity of the feeling, and the unadorned elegance of the expression.

I would thou grew'st unto the shores o' the haven,
And question'dst every sail. If he should write
And I not have it, 'twere a paper lost
As offer'd mercy is. What was the last
That he spake to thee?

PISANIO.

'Twas, His queen! his queen!

IMOGEN.

Then waved his handkerchief?

PISANIO.

And kiss'd it, madam.

IMOGEN.

Senseless linen! happier therein than I!
And that was all?

PISANIO.

No, madam; for so long
As he could make me with this eye or ear

Distinguish him from others, he did keep
The deck, with glove, or hat, or handkerchief
Still waving, as the fits and stirs of his mind
Could best express how slow his soul sail'd on,
How swift his ship.

IMOGEN.

Thou shouldst have made him
As little as a crow, or less, ere left
To after eye him.

PISANIO.

Madam, so I did.

IMOGEN.

I would have broke mine eye-strings; crack'd them, but
To look upon him; till the dimunition
Of space had pointed him sharp as my needle:
Nay, followed him, till he had melted from
The smallness of a gnat to air; and then
Have turn'd mine eye, and wept.

Two little incidents, which are introduced with the most unobtrusive simplicity, convey the strongest impression of her tenderness for her husband, and with that perfect unconsciousness on her part, which adds to the effect. Thus, when she has lost her bracelet—

Go, bid my woman
Search for a jewel, that too casually
Hath left mine arm. It was thy master's; 'shrew me
If I would lose it for a revenue
Of any king in Europe. I do think
I saw't this morning; confident I am,
Last night 'twas on my arm—*I kissed it.*
I hope it has not gone to tell my lord
That I kiss aught but he.

It has been well observed that our consciousness that the bracelet is really gone to bear false witness against her, adds an inexpressibly touching effect to the simplicity and tenderness of the sentiment.

When she opens her bosom to meet the death to which her husband has doomed her, she finds his lettors preserved next her heart.

> What's here?
> The letters of the loyal Leonatus?—
> Soft, we'll no defence.

The scene in which Posthumus stakes his ring on the virtue of his wife, and gives Iachimo permission to tempt her, is taken from the story. The baseness and folly of such conduct have been justly censured; but Shakspeare, feeling that Posthumus needed every excuse, has managed the quarrelling scene between him and Iachimo with the most admirable skill. The manner in which his high spirit is gradually worked up by the taunts of this Italian fiend, is contrived with far more probability, and much less coarseness, than in the original tale. In the end he is not the challenger, but the challenged; and could hardly, except on a moral principle, much too renfied for those rude times) have declined the wager without compromising his own courage, and his faith in the honor of Imogen.

IACHIMO.

I durst attempt it against any lady in the world.

POSTHUMUS.

You are a great deal abused in too bold a persuasion; and I doubt not you sustain what you're worthy of by your attempt.

IACHIMO.

What's that?

POSTHUMUS.

A repulse: though your *attempt*, as you call it, deserved more—a punishment too.

PHILARIO.

Gentlemen, enough of this. It came in too suddenly; let it die as it was born, and I pray you be better acquainted.

IACHIMO.

Would I had put my estate and my neighbor's on the approbation of what I have said!

POSTHUMUS.

What lady would you choose to assail?

IACHIMO.

Yours, whom in constancy you think stands so safe.

In the interview between Imogen and Iachimo, he does not begin his attack on her virtue by a direct accusation against Posthumus; but by dark hints and half uttered insinuations, such as Iago uses to madden Othello, he intimates that her husband, in his absence from her, has betrayed her love and truth, and forgotten her in the arms of another. All that Imogen says in this scene is comprised in a few lines—a brief question or a more brief remark. The proud and delicate reserve with which she veils the anguish she suffers, is inimitably beautiful. The strongest expression of reproach he can draw from her, is only, "My lord, I fear, has forgot Britain." When he continues in the same strain, she exclaims in an agony, "Let me hear no more!" When he urges her to revenge, she asks, with all the simplicity of virtue, "How should I be revenged?" And when he explains to her how she is to be avenged, her sudden burst of indignation, and her immediate perception of his treachery, and the motive for it, are powerfully fine: it is not only the anger of a woman whose delicacy has been shocked, but the spirit of a princess insulted in her court.

Away! I do condemn mine ears, that have
So long attended thee. If thou wert honorable,
Thou wouldst have told this tale for virtue, not
For such an end thou seek'st, as base as strange.
Thou wrong'st a gentleman, who is as far
From thy report, as thou from honor; and

Solicit'st here a lady that disdains
Thee and the devil alike.

It has been remarked that "her readiness to pardon Iachimo's false imputation, and his designs against herself, is a good lesson to prudes, and may show that where there is a real attachment to virtue, there is no need of an outrageous antipathy to vice."*

This is true: but can we fail to perceive that the instant and ready forgiveness of Imogen is accounted for, and rendered more graceful and characteristic by the very means which Iachimo employs to win it? He pours forth the most enthusiastic praises of her husband, professes that he merely made this trial of her out of his exceeding love for Posthumus, and she is pacified at once; but with exceeding delicacy of feeling she is represented as maintaining her dignified reserve and her brevity of speech to the end of the scene.†

We must also observe how beautifully the character of Imogen is distinguished from those of Desdemona and Hermione. When she is made acquainted with her husband's cruel suspicions, we see in her deportment neither the meek submission of the former, nor the calm resolute dignity of the latter. The first effect produced on her by her husband's letter is conveyed to the fancy by the exclamation of Pisanio, who is gazing on her as she reads:

What shall I need to draw my sword? The paper
Has cut her throat already! No, 'tis slander,
Whose edge is sharper than the sword!

And her first exclamations we trace besides astonishment, and anguish, and the acute sense of the injustice inflicted on her, a flash of indignant spirit which we do not find in Desdemona nor Hermione.

* Characters of Shakspeare's Plays.

† Vide act i. Scene 7.

False to his bed!—What is 't to be false?
To lie in watch there, and to think of him?
To weep 'twixt clock and clock? If sleep charge nature,
To break it with a fearful dream of him.
And cry myself awake?—that's false to his bed,
Is it?

This is followed by that affecting lamentation over the falsehood and injustice of her husband, in which she betrays no atom of jealousy or wounded self-love, but observes, in the extremity of her anguish, that after *his* lapse from truth, "all good seeming would be discredited," and she then resigns herself to his will with the most entire submission.

In the original story, Zinevra prevails on the servant to spare her, by her exclamations and entreaties for mercy. "The lady, seeing the poniard, and hearing those words, exclaimed in terror, 'Alas! have pity on me for the love of heaven! do not become the slayer of one who never offended thee, only to pleasure another. God, who knows all things, knows that I have never done that which could merit such a reward from my husband's hand.'"

Now let us turn to Shakspeare. Imogen says,

Come, fellow, be thou honest;
Do thou thy master's bidding; when thou seest him,
A little witness my obedience. Look!
I draw the sword myself; take it, and hit
The inocent mansion of my love, my heart.
Fear not; 'tis empty of all things but grief:
Thy master is not there, who was, indeed,
The riches of it. Do his bidding; strike!

The devoted attachment of Pisanio to his royal mistress, all through the piece, is one of those side touches by which Shakspeare knew how to give additional effect to his characters.

Cloten is odious:* but we must not overlook the peculiar fitness and propriety of his character, in connexion with that of Imogen. He is precisely the kind of man who would be most intolerable to such a woman. He is a fool,—so is Slender, and Sir Andrew Ague cheek: but the folly of Cloten is not only ridiculous, but hateful; it arises not so much from a want of understanding as a total want of heart; it is the perversion of sentiment, rather than the deficiency of intellect; he has occasional gleams of sense, but never a touch of feeling. Imogen describes herself not only as "sprighted with a fool," but as "frighted and anger'd worse." No other fool but Cloten—a compound of the booby and the villain—could excite in such a mind as Imogen's the same mixture of terror, contempt, and abhorrence. The stupid, obstinate maglignity of Cloten, and the wicked machinations of the queen—

> A father cruel and a step-dame false,
> A foolish suitor to a wedded lady—

justify whatever might need excuse in the conduct of Imogen—as her concealed marriage and her flight from her father's court—and serve to call out several of the most beautiful and striking parts of her character:—particularly

* The character of Cloten has been pronounced by some unnatural, by others inconsistent, and by others obsolete. The following passage occurs in one of Miss Seward's letters, vol. iii. p. 246:—"It is curious that Shakspeare should, in so singular a character as Cloten, have given the exact prototype of a being whom I once knew. The unmeaning frown of countenance, the shuffling gait, the burst of voice, the bustling insignificance, the fever and ague fits of valor, the froward tetchiness, the unprincipled malice, and, what is more curious, those occasional gleams of good sense amidst the floating clouds of folly which generally darkened and confused the man's brain, and which, in the character of Cloten, we are apt to impute to a violation of unity in character; but in the some-time Captain C———, I saw that the portrait of Cloten was not cut of nature."

that decision and vivacity of temper, which in her harmonize so beautifully with exceeding delicacy, sweetness, and submission.

In the scene with her detested suitor, there is at first a careless majesty of disdain, which is admirable.

I am much sorry, sir,
You put me to forget a lady's manners,
By being so verbal;* and learn now, for all,
That I, which know my heart, do here pronounce,
By the very truth of it, I care not for you,
And am so near the lack of charity,
(T' accuse myself,) I hate you; which I had rather
You felt, than make my boast.

But when he dares to provoke her by reviling the absent Posthumus, her indignation heightens her scorn, and her scorn sets a keener edge on her indignation.

CLOTEN.
For the contract you pretend with that base wretch,
One bred of alms, and fostered with cold dishes,
With scraps o' the court: it is no contract, none.

IMOGEN.
Profane fellow!
Wert thou the son of Jupiter, and no more,
But what thou art, besides, thou wert too base
To be his groom; thou wert dignified enough,
Even to the point of envy, if 'twere made
Comparative for your virtues, to be styl'd
The under hangman of his kingdom; and hated
For being prefer'd so well.

He never can meet more mischance than come
To be but named of thee. His meanest garment
That ever hath but clipp'd his body, is dearer
In my respect, than all the hairs above thee,
Were they all made such men.

* i. e. *full of words.*

One thing more must be particularly remarked, because it serves to individualize the character from the beginning to the end of the poem. We are constantly sensible that Imogen, besides being a tender and devoted woman, is a princess and a beauty, at the same time that she is ever superior to her position and her external charms. There is, for instance, a certain airy majesty of deportment—a spirit of accustomed command breaking out every now and then—the dignity, without the assumption of rank and royal birth, which is apparent in the scene with Cloten and elsewhere; and we have not only a general impression that Imogen, like other heroines, is beautiful, but the peculiar style and character of her beauty is placed before us: we have an image of the most luxuriant loveliness, combined with exceeding delicacy, and even fragility of person—of the most refined elegance, and the most exquisite modesty, set forth in one or two passages of description, as when Iachimo is contemplating her asleep.

> Cytherea,
> How bravely thou becom'st thy bed! fresh lily,
> And whiter than the sheets.
> 'Tis her breathing that
> Perfumes the chamber thus. The flame o' the taper
> Bows toward her; and would underpeep her lids
> To see the enclos'd lights, now canopied
> Under those windows, white and azure, lac'd
> With blue of heaven's own tinct!

The preservation of her feminine character under her masculine attire; her delicacy, her modesty, and her timidity, are managed with the same perfect consistency and unconscious grace as in Viola. And we must not forget that her "neat cookery," which is so prettily eulogized by Guiderius—

> He cut our roots in characters,
> And sauc'd our broths, as Juno had been sick,
> And he her dieter,

formed part of the education of a princess in those remote times.

Few reflections of a general nature are put into the mouth of Imogen, and what she says is more remarkable for sense, truth, and tender feeling, than for wit, or wisdom, or power of imagination. The following little touch of poetry reminds us of Juliet—

> Ere I could
> Give him that parting kiss, which I had set
> Between two charming words, comes in my father,
> And like the tyrannous breathing of the north
> Shakes all our buds from growing.

Her exclamation on opening her husband's letter, reminds us of the profound and thoughtful tenderness of Helen.

> O learned indeed were that astronomer
> That knew the stars, as I his characters!
> He'd lay the future open.

The following are more in the manner of Isabel—

> Most miserable
> Is the desire that's glorious: bless'd be those,
> How mean soe'er, that have their honest wills,
> That seasons comfort.
> Against self-slaughter
> There is a prohibition so divine
> That cravens my weak hand.
> Thus may poor fools
> Believe false teachers; though those that are betray'd
> Do feel the reason sharply, yet the traitor
> Stands in worse case of wo.
> Are we not brothers?
> So man and man should be;
> But clay and clay differs in dignity,
> Whose dust is both alike.
> Will poor folks lie
> That have afflictions on them, knowing 'tis
> A punishment or trial? Yes: no wonder,
> When rich ones scarce tell true: to lapse in fulness

Is sorer than to lie for need; and falsehood
Is worse in kings than beggars.

The sentence which follows, and which, I believe, has become proverbial, has much of the manner of Portia, both in the thought and the expression:

Hath Britain all the sun that shines? Day, night,
Are they not but in Britain? I' the world's volume
Our Britain seems as of it, but not in it;
In a great pool, a swan's nest; prithee, think
There's livers out of Britain.

* * * *

The catastrophe of this play has been much admired for the peculiar skill with which all the various threads of interest are gathered together at last, and entwined with the destiny of Imogen. It may be added, that one of its chief beauties is the manner in which the character of Imogen is not only preserved, but rises upon us to the conclusion with added grace: her instantaneous forgiveness of her husband, before he even asks it, when she flings herself at once into his arms,

Why did you throw your wedded lady from you?

and her magnanimous reply to her father, when he tells her, that by the discovery of her two brothers she has lost a kingdom—

No—I have gained two worlds by it—

clothing a noble sentiment in a noble image,—give the finishing touches of excellence to this most enchanting portrait.

On the whole Imogen is a lovely compound of goodness, truth and affection, with just so much of passion, and intellect, and poetry, as serve to lend to the picture that power and glowing richness of effect which it would otherwise have wanted; and of her it might be said, if we could condescend to quote from any other poet with Shakspeare open before us, that her person was a paradise, and her soul the cherub to guard it."*

* Dryden.

CORDELIA.

There is in the beauty of Cordelia's character an effect too sacred for words, and almost too deep for tears: within her heart is a fathomless well of purest affection, but its waters sleep in silence and obscurity—never failing in their depth and never overflowing in their fulness. Every thing in her seems to lie beyond our view, and affects us in a manner which we feel rather than perceive. The character appears to have no surface, no salient points upon which the fancy can readily seize: there is little external development of intellect, less of passion and still less of imagination. It is completely made out in the course of a few scenes, and we are surprised to find that in those few scenes there is matter for a life of reflection, and materials enough for twenty heroines. If Lear be the grandest of Shakspeare's tragedies, Cordelia in herself, as a human being, governed by the purest and holiest impulses and motives, the most refined from all dross of selfishness and passion, approaches near to perfection; and in her adaptation, as a dramatic personage, to a determinate plan of action, be pronounced altogether perfect. The character, speak of it critically as a poetical conception, is not, however to be comprehended at once, or easily; and in the same manner Cordelia, as a woman, is one whom we must have loved before we could have known her, and known her long before we could have known her truly.

Most people, I believe, have heard the story of the young German artist Müller, who, while employed in copying and graving Raffaelle's Madonna del Sisto, was so penerated by its celestial beauty, so distrusted his own power to do justice to it, that between admiration and despair he fell into a sadness, thence through the usual gradations, into a melancholy, thence into madness, and died just as he had put the finishing stroke to his own matchless work, which had occupied him for eight years. With some slight tinge of this concentrated kind of enthusiasm I have learned to contemplate the character of Cordelia; I have looked into it till the revelation of its hidden beauty and an intense feeling of the wonderful genius which created it, have filled me at once with delight and despair. Like poor Müller, but with more reason, I *do* despair of ever conveying, through a different and inferior medium, the impression made on my own mind to the mind of another.

Schlegel, the most eloquent of critics, concludes his remarks on King Lear with these words: "Of the heavenly beauty of soul of Cordelia, I will not venture to speak." Now if I attempt what Schlegel and others have left undone, it is because I feel that this general acknowledgment of her excellence can neither satisfy those who have studied the character, nor convey a just conception of it to the mere reader. Amid the awful, the overpowering interest of the story, amid the terrible convulsions of passion and suffering, and pictures of moral and physical wretchedness which harrow up the soul, the tender influence of Cordelia, like that of a celestial visitant, is felt and acknowledged without being quite understood. Like a soft star that shines for a moment from behind a stormy cloud, and the next is swallowed up in tempest and darkness, the impression it leaves is beautiful and deep,—but vague. Speak of Cordelia, to a critic or to a general reader, all agree in the beauty of the portrait, for all must feel it; but when we come to details, I have heard more various and opposite opinions relative to her than any other of Shakspeare's characters—a proof of what I have advanced in the first instance, that from the simplicity with which the character is dramatically treated, and the small space it occupies, few are aware of its internal power or its wonderful depth of purpose.

It appears to me that the whole character rests upon the two sublimest principles of human action—the love of truth and the sense of duty; but these, when they stand alone, (as in the Antigone,) are apt to strike us as severe and cold. Shakspeare has, therefore, wreathed them round with the dearest attributes of our feminine nature, the power of feeling and inspiring affection. The first part of the play shows us how Cordelia is loved, the second part how she can love. To her father she is the object of a secret preference; his agony at her supposed unkindness draws from him the confession, that he had loved her most, and "thought to set his rest on her kind nursery." Till then she had been "his best object, the argument of his praise, balm of his age, most best, most dearest!" The faithful and worthy Kent is ready to brave death or exile in her defence; and afterwards a farther impression of her benign sweetness is conveyed in a simple and beautiful manner, when we are told that "since the lady Cordelia went to France, her father's poor fool had much pined away." We have her sensibility "when patience and sorrow strove which should express her goodliest:" and all her filial tenderness when she commits her poor father to the care of the physician, when she hangs over him as he is sleeping, and kisses him as she contemplates the wreck of grief and majesty.

> O my dear father! restoration hang
> Its medicine on my lips; and let this kiss
> Repair those violent harms that my two sisters
> Have in thy reverence made!
> Had you not been their father, these white flakes

Had challenged pity of them! Was this a face
To be exposed against the warring winds,
To stand against the deep dread-bolted thunder,
In the most terrible and nimble stroke
Of quick cross-lightening? to watch, (poor perdu!)
With thin helm? mine enemy's dog,
Though he bit me, should have stood that night
Against my fire.

Her mild magnanimity shines out in her farewell to her sisters, of whose real character she is perfectly aware:

Ye jewels of our father! with washed eyes
Cordelia leaves you! I know ye what ye are,
And like a sist [illegible] am most loth to call
Your faults as they are nam'd. Use well our father,
To your professed bosoms I commit him.
But yet, alas! stood I within his grace,
I would commend him to a better place;
So farewell to you both.

GONERIL.

Prescribe us not our duties!

The modest pride with which she replies to the Duke of Burgundy is admirable: this whole passage is too illustrative of the peculiar character of Cordelia, as well as too exquisite, to be mutilated.

I yet beseech your majesty,
If, for I want that glib and oily art,
To speak and propose not, (since what I well intend
I'll do't before I speak,) that you make known,
It is no vicious blot, murder, or foulness,
No unchaste action, or dishonored step
That hath deprived me of your grace and favor;
But even for want of that, for which I am richer,
A still soliciting eye, and such a tongue
I am glad I have not, tho' not to have it
Hath lost me in your liking.

LEAR.

Better thou hadst not been born
Than not to have pleased me better.

FRANCE.

Is it but this?—a tardiness of nature,
That often leaves the history unspoke
Which it intends to do?—My lord of Burgundy,
What say you to the lady? love is not love
When it is mingled with respects that stand
Aloof from th' entire point. Will you have her?
She is herself a dowry.

BURGUNDY.

Royal Lear,
Give but that portion which yourself proposed,
And here I take Cordelia by the hand
Duchess of Burgundy.

LEAR.

Nothing. I have sworn; I am firm.

BURGUNDY.

I am sorry, then, you have so lost a father
That you must lose a husband.

CORDELIA.

Peace be with Burgundy?
Since that respects of fortune are his love,
I shall not be his wife.

FRANCE.

Fairest Cordelia! thou art more rich, being poor,
Most choice forsaken, and most lov'd despised!
Thee and thy virtues here I seize upon.

She takes up arms, "not for ambition, but a dear father's right." In her speech after her defeat, we have a calm fortitude and elevation of soul, arising from the consciousness of duty, and lifting her above all consideration of self: she observes,

> We are not the first
> Who with best meaning have incurred the worst!

She thinks and fears only for her father.

> For, thee, oppressed king, am I cast down;
> Myself would else out-frown false fortune's frown.

To complete the picture, her very voice is characteristic, "ever soft, gentle, and low, an excellent thing in woman."

But it will be said that the qualities here exemplified—as sensibility, gentleness, magnanimity, fortitude, generous affection—are qualities which belong, in their perfection, to others of Shakspeare's characters—to Imogen for instance, who unites them all; and yet Imogen and Cordelia are wholly unlike each other. Even though we should reverse their situations, and give to Imogen the filial devotion of Cordelia, and to Cordelia the conjugal virtues of Imogen, still they would remain perfectly distinct as women. What is it, then, which lends to Cordelia that peculiar and individual truth of character which distinguishes her from every other human being?

It is a natural reserve, a tardiness of disposition "which often leaves the history unspoke which it intends to do,"—a subdued quietness of deportment and expression—aveiled shyness thrown over all her emotions,—her language and her manner,—making the outward demonstration invariably fall short of what we know to be the feeling within. Not only is the portrait singularly beautiful and interesting in itself, but the conduct of Cordelia, and the part which she bears in the beginning of the story, is rendered consistent and natural by the wonderful truth and delicacy with which this peculiar disposition is sustained throughout the play.

In early youth, and more particularly if we are gifted with a lively imagination, such a character as that of Cordelia is calculated above every other to impress and captivate us. Any thing like mystery, any thing withheld or withdrawn from our notice, seizes on our fancy by awakening our curiosity. Then we are won more by what we half perceive and half create, than by what is openly expressed and freely bestowed. But this feeling is a part of our young life: when time and years have chilled us, when we can no longer afford to send our souls abroad, nor from our own superfluity of life and sensibility spare the materials out of which we build a shrine for our idol—then do we seek, we ask, we thirst for that warmth of frank, confiding tenderness, which revives in us the withered affections and feelings, buried but not dead. Then the excess of love is welcomed, not repelled—it is gracious to us as the sun and dew to the seared and riven trunk, with its few green leaves. Lear is old—"fourscore and upward"—but we see what he has been in former days: the ardent passions of youth have turned to rashness and wilfulness; he is long passed that age when we are more blessed in what we bestow than in what we receive. When he says to his daughters "I gave ye all!" we feel that he requires all in return, with a jealous, restless, exacting affection which defeats its own wishes. How many such are there in the world! How many to sympathize with the fiery, fond old man, when he shrinks as if petrified from Cordelia's quiet calm reply!

LEAR.

Now our joy,
Although the last not least—
What can you say to draw
A third more opulent than your sisters? Speak!

CORDELIA.

Nothing, my lord.

LEAR.

Nothing!

CORDELIA.

Nothing.

LEAR.

Nothing can come of nothing—speak again!

CORDELIA.

Unhappy that I am! I cannot heave
My heart into my mouth. I love your majesty
According to my bond; nor more, nor less.

Now this is perfectly natural. Cordelia has penetrated the vile characters of her sisters. Is it not obvious that in proportion as her own mind is pure and guileless, she must be disgusted with their gross hypocrisy and exaggeration, their empty protestations, their "plaited cunning;" and would retire from all competition with what she so disdains and abhors,—even into the opposite extreme? In such a case, as she says herself—

What should Cordelia do?—love and be silent?

For the very expressions of Lear—

What can you say to draw
A third more opulent than your sisters?

are enough to strike dumb forever a generous, delicate, but shy disposition such as is Cordelia's, by holding out a bribe for professions.

If Cordelia were not thus portrayed, this deliberate coolness would strike us as verging on harshness or obstinacy; but it is beautifully represented as a certain modification of character, the necessary result of feelings habitually, if not naturally, repressed! and through the whole play we trace the same peculiar and individual disposition—the same absence of all display—the same sobriety of speech veiling the most profound affections—the same quiet steadiness of purpose—the same shrinking from all exhibition of emotion.

"Tous les sentimens naturels ont leur pudeur," was a *viva voce* observation of Madame de Staël, when disgusted by the sentimental affectation of her imitators. This "pudeur," carried to an excess, appears to me the peculiar characteristic of Cordelia. Thus, in the description of her deportment when she receives the letter of the Earl of Kent, informing her of the cruelty of her sisters and the wretched condition of Lear, we seem to have her before us.

KENT.

Did your letters pierce the queen to any demonstration of grief?

GENTLEMAN.

Ay, sir, she took them, and read them in my presence;
And now and then an ample tear stole down
Her delicate cheek. It seemed she was a queen
Over her passion; who, most rebel-like,
Sought to be king over her.

KENT.

O then it moved her!

GENTLEMAN.

Not to a rage,
Faith, once or twice she heaved the name of father
Pantingly forth, as if it pressed her heart,
Cried, *Sisters! Sisters! Shame of ladies—Sisters!*
What, in the storm! in the night!
Let pity not be believed! Then she shook
The holy water from her heavenly eyes;
* * * * *
Then away she started, to deal with grief alone.

Here the last line—the image brought before us of Cordelia starting away from observation "to deal with grief alone," is as exquisitely beautiful as it is characteristic.

But all the passages hitherto quoted must yield in beauty and power to that scene, in which her poor father recognises her, and in the intervals of distraction asks forgiveness of his wronged child. The subdued pathos and simplicity of Cordelia's character, her quiet but intense feeling, the misery and humiliation of the bewildered old man, are brought before us in so few words, and at the same time sustained with such a deep intuitive knowledge of the innermost workings of the human heart, that as there is nothing surpassing this scene in Shakspeare himself, so there is nothing that can be compared to it in any other writer.

CORDELIA.

How does my royal lord? How fares your majesty?

LEAR.

You do me wrong to take me out of the grave.
Thou art a soul in bliss; but I am bound
Upon a wheel of fire, that mine own tears
Do scald like molten lead.

CORDELIA.

Sir, do you know me?

LEAR.

You are a spirit, I know: when did you die?

CORDELIA.

Still, still far wide!

PHYSICIAN.

He's scarce awake. let him alone awhile.

LEAR.

Where have I been? Where am I? Fair day-light?
I am mightily abused. I should even die with pity
To see another thus. I know not what to say.
I will not swear these are my hands. Let's see;
I feel this pin prick. Would I were assured
Of my condition.

CORDELIA.

O look upon me, sir,

And hold your hands in benediction o'er me!
No, sir, you must not kneel.

LEAR.

Pray do not mock me:
I am a very foolish, fond old man,
Four score and upwards, and to deal plainly with you,
I fear I am not in my perfect mind.
Methinks I should know you, and know this man,
Yet I am doubtful: for I am mainly ignorant
What place this is; and all the skill I have
Remembers not these garments, nor I know not
Where I did lodge last night. Do not laugh at me;
For as I am a man, I think this lady
To be my child Cordelia.

CORDELIA.

And so I am, I am!

LEAR.

Be your tears wet? Yes, faith; I pray you weep not.
If you have poison for me I will drink it,
I know you do not love me; for your sisters
Have, as I do remember, done me wrong—
You have some cause, they have not.

CORDELIA.

No cause, no cause!

As we do not estimate Cordelia's affection for her father by the coldness of her language, so neither should we measure her indignation against her sisters by the mildness of her expressions. What, in fact, can be more eloquently significant, and at the same time more characteristic of Cordelia, than the single line when she and her father are conveyed to their prison—

Shall we not see these *daughters* and these *sisters*?

The irony here is so bitter and intense, and at the same time so quiet, so feminine, so dignified in the expression, that who but Cordelia would have uttered it in the same manner, or would have condensed such ample meaning into so few and simple words?

We lose sight of Cordelia during the whole of the second and third, and great part of the fourth act; but towards the conclusion she reappears. Just as our sense of human misery and wickedness, being carried to its extreme height, becomes nearly intolerable, "like an engine wrenching our frame of nature from its fixed place," then, like a redeeming angel, she descends to mingle in the scene, "loosening the springs of pity in our eyes," and relieving the impressions of pain and terror by those of admiration and a tender pleasure. For the catastrophe, it is indeed terrible! wondrous terrible! When Lear enters with Cordelia dead in his arms, compassion and awe so seize on all our faculties, that we are left only to silence and to tears. But if I might judge from my own sensations, the catastrophe of Lear is not so overwhelming as the catastrophe of Othello. We do not turn away with the same feeling of absolute unmitigated despair. Cordelia is a saint ready prepared for heaven—our earth is not good enough for her: and Lear!—O who, after sufferings and tortures such as his, would wish to see his life prolonged? What! replace a sceptre in that shaking hand?— a crown upon that old gray head, on which the tempest had poured in its wrath?—on which the deep dread-bolted thunders and the winged lightnings had spent their fury?—O never, never!

> Let him pass! he hates him
> That would upon the rack of this rough world
> Stretch him out longer.

In the story of King Leyr and his three daughters, as it is related in the "delectable and mellifluous" romance of Perceforest, and in the chronicle of Geoffrey of Monmouth, the conclusion is fortunate. Cordelia defeats her sisters, and replaces her father on his throne. Spencer, in his version of the story, has followed these authorities. Shakspeare has preferred the catastrophe of the old ballad, founded apparently on some lost tradition. I suppose it is by way of amending his errors, and bringing back this daring innovator to sober history, that it has been thought fit to alter the play of Lear for the stage, as they have altered Romeo and Juliet: they have converted the seraph-like Cordelia into a puling love-heroine, and sent her off victorious at the end of the play—exit with drums and colors flying—to be married to Edgar. Now any thing more absurd, more discordant with all our previous impressions, and with the characters as unfolded to us, can hardly be imagined, "I cannot conceive," says Schlegel, "what ideas of art and dramatic connexion those persons have, who suppose we can at pleasure tack a double conclusion to a tragedy—a melancholy one for hardhearted spectators, and a merry one for those of softer mould." The fierce manners depicted in this play, the extremes of virtue and vice in the persons, belong to the remote period of the story.* There is no attempt at character in the old narratives; Regan and Goneril are monsters of ingratitude, and Cordelia merely distinguished by her filial piety; whereas, in Shakspeare, this filial piety is an affection quite distinct from the qualities which serve to individualize the human being; we have a perception of innate character apart from all accidental circumstance; we see that if Cordelia had never known her father, had never been re-

* King Lear may be supposed to have lived about one thousand years before the Christian era, being the fourth or fifth in descent from King Brut, the great-grandson of Eneas, and the fabulous founder of the kingdom of Britain.

jected from his love, had never been born a princess or a crowned queen, she would not have been less Cordelia,—less distinctly *herself;* that is, a woman of a steady mind, of calm but deep affections, of inflexible truth, of few words, and of reserved deportment.

As to Regan and Goneril—"tigers, not daughters"—we might wish to regard them as mere hateful chimeras, impossible as they are detestable, but unfortunately there was once a Tullia. I know not where to look for the prototype of Cordelia; there was a Julia Alpinula, the young priestess of Aventicum,* who, unable to save her father's life by the sacrifice of her own, died with him—"*infelix patris, infelix proles*"—but this is all we know of her. There was the Roman daughter, too: I remember seeing at Genoa, Guido's "Pietta Romana," in which the expression of the female bending over the aged parent, who feeds from her bosom, is perfect,—but it is not a Cordelia; only Raffaelle could have painted Cordelia.

But the character which at once suggests itself in comparison with Cordelia, as the heroine of filial tenderness and piety, is certainly the Antigone of Sophocles. As poetical conceptions, they rest on the same basis—they are both pure abstractions of truth, piety, and natural affection; and in both, love, as a passion, is kept entirely out of sight—for though the womanly character is sustained, by making them the objects of devoted attachment; yet to have portrayed them as influenced by passion, would have destroyed that unity of purpose and feeling which is one source of power; and, besides, have disturbed that serene purity and grandeur of soul, which equally distinguishes both heroines. The spirit, however, in which the two characters are conceived, is as different as possible, and we

* She is commemorated by Lord Byron. Vide Childe Harold, Canto iii.

must not fail to remark, that Antigone, who plays a principal part in two fine tragedies, and is distinctly and completely made out, is considered as a masterpiece—the very triumph of the ancient classical drama: whereas, there are many among Shakspeare's characters which are equal to Cordelia as dramatic conceptions, and superior to her in finishing of outline, as well as in the richness of the poetical coloring.

When Œdipus, pursued by the vengeance of the gods, deprived of sight by his own mad act, and driven from Thebes by his subjects and his sons, wanders forth, abject and forlorn, he is supported by his daughter Antigone, who leads him from city to city, begs for him, and pleads for him against the harsh, rude men, who, struck more by his guilt than his misery would drive him from his last asylum. In the opening of the "Œdipus Coloneus," where the wretched old man appears leaning on his child, and seats himself in the consecrated Grove of the Furies, the picture presented to us is wonderfully solemn and beautiful. The patient, duteous tenderness of Antigone; the scene in which she pleads for her brother Polynices, and supplicates her father to receive his offending son; her remonstrance to Polynices, when she entreats him not to carry the threatened war into his native country, are finely and powerfully delineated; and in her lamentation over Œdipus, when he perishes in the mysterious grove, there is a pathetic beauty, apparent even through the stiffness of the translation.

> Alas! I only wished I might have died
> With my poor father; wherefore should I ask
> For longer life?
> O I was fond of misery with him;
> E'en what was most unlovely grew beloved
> When he was with me. O my dearest father,
> Beneath the earth now in deep darkness hid,

Worn as thou wert with age, to me thou still
Wert dear, and shalt be ever.
—Even as he wished he died,
In a strange land—for such was his desire—
A shady turf covered his lifeless limbs,
Nor unlamented fell! for O these eyes,
My father, still shall weep for thee, nor time
E'er blot thee from my memory.

The filial pity of Antigone is the most affecting part of the tragedy of "Œdipus Coloneus:" her sisterly affection, and her heroic self devotion to a religious duty, form the plot of the tragedy called by her name. When her two brothers, Eteocles and Polynices, had slain each other before the walls of Thebes, Creon issued an edict forbidding the rites of sepulture to Polynices, (as the invader of his country,) and awarding instant death to those who should dare to bury him. We know the importance, which the ancients attached to the funeral obsequies, as alone securing their admission into the Elysian fields. Antigone, upon hearing the law of Creon, which thus carried vengeance beyond the grave, enters in the first scene, announcing her fixed resolution to brave the threatened punishment: her sister Ismene shrinks from sharing the peril of such an undertaking, and endeavors to dissuade her from it, on which Antigone replies—

Wert thou to proffer what I do not ask—
Thy poor assistance—I would scorn it now;
Act as thou wilt, I'll bury him myself;
Let me perform but that, and death is welcome.
I'll do the pious deed, and lay me down
By my dear brother; loving and beloved,
We'll rest together.

She proceeds to execute her generous purpose: she covers with earth the mangled corse of Polynices; pours over it the accustomed libations; is detected in her pious office, and after nobly defending her conduct, is led to death by command of the tyrant. Her sister Ismene, struck with shame and remorse, now comes forward to accuse herself as a partaker in the offence, and share her sister's punishment, but Antigone sternly and scornfully rejects her; and after pouring forth a beautiful lamentation on the misery of perishing "without the nuptial song—a virgin and a slave," she dies *a l' antique*—she strangles herself to avoid a lingering death.

Hemon, the son of Creon, unable to save her life, kills himself upon her grave: but throughout the whole tragedy, we are left in doubt whether Antigone does or does not return the affection of this devoted lover.

Thus it will be seen that in the Antigone, there is a great deal of what may be called the effect of situation, as well as a great deal of poetry and character: she says the most beautiful things in the world, performs the most heroic actions, and all her words and actions are so placed before us as to *command* our admiration. According to the classical ideas of virtue and heroism, the character is sublime; and in the delineation, there is a severe simplicity mingled with its Grecian grace—a unity, a grandeur, an elegance which appeal to our taste, and our understanding, while they fill and exalt the imagination: but in Cordelia it is not the external coloring or form—it is not what she says or does, but what she is in herself, what she feels, thinks, and suffers, which continually awaken our sympathy and interest. The heroism of Cordelia is more passive and tender—it melts into our heart; and in the veiled loveliness and unostentatious delicacy of her character there is an effect more profound and artless, if it be less striking and less elaborate than in the Grecian heroine. To Antigone we give our admiration; to Cordelia our tears. Antigone stands before us in her austere and statue-like beauty, like one of the marbles of the Parthenon. If Cordelia remind us of any thing on earth, it is one of the Madonnas in the old Italian pictures—" with downcast eyes beneath th' almighty dove:" and as that heavenly form is connected with our human sympathies only by the expression of maternal tenderness, or maternal sorrow; even so, Cordelia would be almost too angelic, were she not linked to our earthly feelings, bound to our very hearts, by her filial love, her wrongs, her sufferings, and her tears.

HISTORICAL CHARACTERS.

CLEOPATRA.

I **CANNOT** agree with one of the most philosophical of Shakspeare's critics, who has asserted "that the actual truth of particular events, in proportion as we are conscious of it, is a drawback on the pleasure, as well as the dignity of tragedy." If this observation applies at all, it is equally just with regard to characters: and in either case can we admit it? The reverence and the simpleness of heart with which Shakspeare has treated the received and admitted truths of history—I mean according to the imperfect knowledge of his time—is admirable; his inaccuracies are few; his general accuracy, allowing for the distinction between the narrative and the dramatic form, is acknowledged to be wonderful. He did not steal the precious material from the treasury of history, to debase its purity,—new-stamp it arbitrarily with effigies and legends of his own devising, and then attempt to pass it current, like Dryden, Racine, and the rest of those poetical coiners. He only rubbed off the rust, purified and brightened it, so that history herself has been known to receive it back as sterling.

Truth wherever manifested, should be sacred; so Shakspeare deemed, and laid no profane hand upon her altars. But tragedy—majestic tragedy! is worthy to stand before the sanctuary of Truth, and to be the priestess of her oracles. "Whatever in religion is holy and sublime, in virtue amiable or grave; whatsoever hath passion or admiration in all the changes of that which is called fortune from without, or the wily subtleties and refluxes of man's thought from within;"*—whatever is pitiful in the weakness, sublime in the strength, or terrible in the perversion of human intellect, these are the domain of Tragedy. Sibyl and Muse at once, she holds aloft the book of human fate, and is the interpreter of its mysteries. It is not, then, making a mock of the serious sorrows of real life, nor of those human beings who lived, suffered, and acted upon this earth, to array them in her rich and stately robes, and present them before us as powers evoked from dust and darkness, to awaken the generous sympathies, the terror or the pity of mankind. It does not add to the pain, as far as tragedy is a source of emotion, that the wrongs and

* Milton.

sufferings represented, the guilt of Lady Macbeth, the despair of Constance, the arts of Cleopatra, and the distresses of Katharine, had a real existence; but it adds infinitely to the moral effect as a subject of contemplation and a lesson of conduct.*

I shall be able to illustrate these observations more fully in the course of this section, in which we will consider those characters which are drawn from history; and first Cleopatra.

Of all Shakspeare's female characters, Miranda and Cleopatra appear to me the most wonderful. The first, unequalled as a poetical conception; the latter miraculous as a work of art. If we could make a regular classification of his characters, these would form the two extremes of simplicity and complexity; and all his other characters would be found to fill up some shade or gradation between these two.

Great crimes, springing from high passions, grafted on high qualities, are the legitimate source of tragic poetry. But to make the extreme of littleness produce an effect like grandeur—to make the excess of frailty produce an effect like power—to heap up together all that is most unsubstantial, frivolous, vain, contemptible, and variable, till the worthiness be lost in the magnitude, and a sense of the sublime spring from the very elements of littleness,—to do this, belonged only to Shakspeare, that worker of miracles. Cleopatra is a brilliant antitheses—a compound of contradictions—of all that we most hate, with what we

* "That the treachery of King John, the death of Arthur, and the grief of Constance, has a real truth in history, sharpens the sense of pain, while it hangs a leaden weight on the heart and the imagination. Something whispers us that we have no right to make a mock of calamities like these, or to turn the truth of things into the puppet and play-thing of our fancies."—See Characters of Shakspeare's Plays.—To consider *thus* is not to consider *too* deeply, but not deeply *enough*.

most admire. The whole character is the triumph of the external over the innate, and yet, like one of her country's hieroglyphics, though she present at first view a splendid and perplexing anomaly, there is deep meaning and wondrous skill in the apparent enigma, when we come to analyze and decipher it. But how are we to arrive at the solution of this glorious riddle, whose dazzling complexity continually mocks and eludes us? What is most astonishing in the character of Cleopatra is its antithetical construction—its *consistent inconsistency*, if I may use such an expression—which renders it quite impossible to reduce it to any elementary principles. It will, perhaps, be found on the whole, that vanity and the love of power predominate; but I dare not say it *is* so; for these qualities and a hundred others mingle into each other, and shift, and change, and glance away, like the colors in a peacock's train.

In some others of Shakspeare's female characters, also remarkable for their complexity, (Portia and Juliet, for instance,) we are struck with the delightful sense of harmony in the midst of contrast, so that the idea of unity and simplicity of effect is produced in the midst of variety; but in Cleopatra, it is the absence of unity and simplicity which strikes us. The impression is that of perpetual and irreconcilable contrast. The continual approximation of whatever is most opposite in character, in situation, in sentiment, would be fatiguing, were it not so perfectly natural; the woman herself would be distracting, if she were not so enchanting.

I have not the slightest doubt that Shakspeare's Cleopatra is the real historical Cleopatra—the "Rare Egyptian"—individualized and placed before us. Her mental accomplishments, her unequalled grace, her woman's wit and woman's wiles, her irresistible allurements, her starts of irregular grandeur, her bursts of ungovernable temper, her vivacity of imagination, her petulant caprice, her fickleness and her falsehood, her tenderness and her truth, her childish susceptibility to flattery, her magnificent spirit, her royal pride, the gorgeous eastern coloring of the character; all these contradictory elements has Shakspeare seized, mingled them in their extremes, and fused them into one brilliant impersonation of classical elegance, Oriental voluptuousness, and gypsy sorcery.

What better proof can we have of the individual truth of the character, than the admission, that Shakspeare's Cleopatra produces exactly the same effect on us that is recorded of the real Cleopatra?—She dazzles our faculties, perplexes our judgment, bewilders and bewitches our fancy; from the beginning to the end of the drama, we are conscious of a kind of fascination against which our moral sense rebels, but from which there is no escape. The epithets applied to her perpetually by Antony and others confirm this impression: "enchanting queen!"—"witch," —"spell,"—"great fairy,"—"cockatrice,"—"serpent of old Nile,"—"thou grave charm!"*—are only a few of them: and who does not know by heart the famous quotations in which this Egyptian Circes is described with all her infinite seductions?

Fie! wrangling queen!
Whom every thing becomes—to chide, to laugh,
To weep. Whose every passion fully strives
To make itself in thee, fair and admired.

Age cannot wither her, nor custom stale
Her infinite variety:—
For vilest things
Become themselves in her.

* *Grave*, in the sense of mighty or potent.

And the pungent irony of Enobarbus has well exposed her feminine arts, when he says, on the occasion of Antony's intended departure—

Cleopatra, catching but the least noise of this, dies instantly;—I have seen her die twenty times upon far poorer moment.

ANTONY.

She is cunning past man's thought.

ENOBARBUS.

Alack, sir, no! her passions are made of nothing but the finest part of pure love. We cannot call her winds and waters, sighs and tears; they are greater storms and tempests than almanacks can report: this cannot be cunning in her; if it be, she makes a shower of rain as well as Jove.

The whole secret of her absolute dominion over the facile Antony may be found in one little speech.

See where he is—who's with him—what he does—
(I did not send you.) If you find him sad,
Say I am dancing; if in mirth, report
That I am sudden sick! Quick! and return.

CHARMAIN.

Madam, methinks if you did love him dearly,
You do not hold the method to enforce
The like from him.

CLEOPATRA.

What should I do, I do not?

CHARMAIN.

In each thing give him way: cross him in nothing.

CLEOPATRA.

Thou teachest like a fool: the way to lose him.

CHARMAIN.

Tempt him not too far.

But Cleopatra is a mistress of her art, and knows better: and what a picture of her triumphant petulance, her imperious and imperial coquetry, is given in her own words!

That time—O times!
I laughed him out of patience; and that night
I laughed him into patience: and the next morn,
Ere the ninth hour, I drunk him to his bed;
Then put my tires and mantles on him, whilst
I wore his sword, Philippan.

When Antony enters full of some serious purpose which he is about to impart, the woman's perverseness, and the tyrannical waywardness with which she taunts him and plays upon his temper, are admirably depicted.

I know, by that same eye, there's some good news,
What says the married woman?* You may go;
Would she had never given you leave to come!
Let her not say, 'tis I that keep you here;
I have no power upon you; her's you are.

ANTONY.
The gods best know ——

CLEOPATRA.
O, never was there queen
So mightily betrayed! Yet at the first,
I saw the treasons planted.

ANTONY.
Cleopatra!

CLEOPATRA.
Why should I think you can be mine, and true,
Though you in swearing shake the throned gods,
Who have been false to Fulvia? Riotous madness,
To be entangled with those mouth-made vows,
Which break themselves in swearing!

ANTONY.
Most sweet queen!

* Fulvia! The first wife of Antony.

CLEOPATRA.

Nay, pray you seek no color for your going,
But bid farewell, and go.

She recovers her dignity for a moment at the news of Fulvia's death, as if roused by a blow:

Though age from folly could not give me freedom,
It does from childishness—Can Fulvia die?

And then follows the artful mockery with which she tempts and provokes him, in order to discover whether he regrets his wife.

O most false love!
Where be the sacred vials thou shouldst fill
With sorrowful water? Now I see, I see
In Fulvia's death, how mine received shall be.

ANTONY.

Quarrel no more; but be prepared to know
The purposes I bear: which are, or cease,
As you shall give th' advice. Now, by the fire
That quickens Nilus' shrine I go from hence
Thy soldier, servant, making peace or war,
As thou affectest.

CLEOPATRA.

Cut my lace, Charmian, come—
But let it be. I am quickly ill, and well,
So Antony loves.

ANTONY.

My precious queen, forbear;
And give true evidence to his love which stands
An honorable trial.

CLEOPATRA.

So Fulvia told me.
I prithee turn aside, and weep for her;
Then bid adieu to me, and say, the tears

Belong to Egypt. Good now, play one scene
Of excellent dissembling; and let it look
Like perfect honor.

ANTONY.

You'll heat my blood—no more!

CLEOPATRA.

You can do better yet; but this is meetly.

ANTONY.

Now, by my sword—

CLEOPATRA.

And target still—he mends;
But this is not the best. Look, prithee, Charmian,
How this Herculean Roman does become
The carriage of his chafe!

This is, indeed, most "excellent dissembling;" but when she has fooled and chafed the Herculean Roman to the verge of danger, then comes that return to tenderness which secures the power she has tried to the utmost, and we have all the elegant, the poetical Cleopatra in her beautiful farewell.

Forgive me!
Since my becomings kill me when they do not
Eye well to you. Your honor calls you hence,
Therefore be deaf to my unpitied folly,
And all the gods go with you! Upon your sword
Sit laurell'd victory; and smooth success
Be strewed before your feet!

Finer still are the workings of her variable mind and lively imagination, after Antony's departure; her fond repining at his absence, her violent spirit, her right royal wilfulness and impatience, as if it were a wrong to her majesty, an insult to her sceptre, that there should exist in her despite such things as space and time; and high treason to her sovereign power, to dare to remember what she chooses to forget.

Give me to drink mandragora,
That I might sleep out this great gap of time
My Antony is away.
O, Charmian!
Where think'st thou he is now? Stands he, or sits he,
Or does he walk? or is he on his horse?
O, happy horse, to bear the weight of Antony!
Do bravely, horse; for wot'st thou whom thou mov'st?
The demi-Atlas of this earth—the arm
And burgonet of men. He's speaking now,
Or murmuring, Where's my serpent of old Nile?
For so he calls me.
Met'st thou my posts?

ALEXAS.

Ay, madam, twenty several messengers—
Why do you send so thick?

CLEOPATRA.

Who's born that day
When I forget to send to Antony,
Shall die a beggar. Ink and paper, Charmian.
Welcome, my good Alexas. Did I, Charmian,
Ever love Cæsar so?

CHARMIAN.

O that brave Cæsar!

CLEOPATRA.

Be chok'd with such another emphasis!
Say the brave Antony.

CHARMIAN.

The valiant Cæsar!

CLEOPATRA.

By Isis, I will give thee bloody teeth,
If thou with Cæsar paragon again
My man of men!

CHARMIAN.

By your most gracious pardon,
I sing but after you.

CLEOPATRA.

My salad days
When I was green in judgment, cold in blood,

To say as I said then. But, come away—
Get me some ink and paper: he shall have every day
A several greeting, or I'll unpeople Egypt.

We learn from Plutarch, that it was a favorite amusement with Antony and Cleopatra to ramble through the streets at night, and bandy ribald jests with the populace of Alexandria. From the same authority, we know that they were accustomed to live on the most familiar terms with their attendants and the companions of their revels. To these traits we must add, that with all her violence, perverseness, egotism, and caprice, Cleopatra mingled a capability for warm affections and kindly feeling, or rather what we should call in these days, a constitutional *good-nature*—and was lavishly generous to her favorites and dependents. These characteristics we find scattered through the play; they are not only faithfully rendered by Shakspeare, but he has made the finest use of them in his delineation of manners. Hence the occasional freedom of her women and her attendants, in the midst of their fears and flatteries, becomes most natural and consistent; hence, too, their devoted attachment and fidelity, proved even in death. But as illustrative of Cleopatra's disposition, perhaps the finest and most characteristic scene in the whole play, is that in which the messenger arrives from Rome with the tidings of Antony's marriage with Octavia. She perceives at once with quickness that all is not well, and she hastens to anticipate the worst, that she may have the pleasure of being disappointed. Her impatience to know what she fears to learn—the vivacity with which she gradually works herself up into a state of excitement, and at length into fury—is wrought out with a force of truth which makes us recoil.

CLEOPATRA.

Antony is dead!

If thou say so, villain, thou kill'st thy mistress.
But well and free,
If thou so yield him, there is gold, and here
My bluest veins to kiss; a hand that kings
Have lipp'd, and trembled kissing.

MESSENGER.

First, madam, he is well.

CLEOPATRA.

Why there's more gold. But, sirrah, mark! we use
To say, the dead are well: bring it to that,
The gold I give thee will I melt, and pour
Down thy ill-uttering throat.

MESSENGER.

Good Madam, hear me.

CLEOPATRA.

Well, go to, I will.
But there's no goodness in thy face. If Antony
Be free and healthful, why so tart a favor
To trumpet such good tidings? If not well,
Thou should'st come like a fury crown'd with snakes.

MESSENGER.

Will 't please you hear me?

CLEOPATRA.

I have a mind to strike thee ere thou speak'st;
Yet if thou say Antony lives, is well,
Or friends with Cæsar, or not captive to him,
I'll set thee in a shower of gold, and hail
Rich pearls upon thee.

MESSENGER.

Madam, he's well.

CLEOPATRA.

Well said.

MESSENGER.

And friends with Cæsar,

CLEOPATRA.

Thou art an honest man.

MESSENGER.

Cæsar and he are greater friends than ever.

CLEOPATRA.

Make thee a fortune from me.

MESSENGER.

But yet, madam—

CLEOPATRA.

I do not like *but yet*—it does allay
The good precedence. Fie upon *but yet*—
But yet is as a gaoler to bring forth
Some monstrous malefactor. Prithee, friend,
Pour out thy pack of matter to mine ear,
The good and bad together. He's frends with Cæsar;
In state of health, thou say'st; and thou say'st free.

MESSENGER.

Free, madam! No; I made no such report:
He's bound unto Octavia.

CLEOPATRA.

For what good turn?

MESSENGER.

Madam, he's married to Octavia.

CLEOPATRA.

The most infectious pestilence upon thee! [*Strikes him down.*

MESSENGER.

Good madam, patience.

CLEOPATRA.

What say you? [*Strikes him again.*
Hence, horrible villain! or I'll spurn thine eyes
Like balls before me—I'll unhair thine head—
Thou shalt be whipp'd with wire, and stewed in brine,
Smarting in ling'ring pickle.

MESSENGER.
Gracious madam!
I, that do bring the news, made not the match.

CLEOPATRA.
Say 'tis not so, a province I will give thee,
And make thy fortunes proud: the blow thou hadst
Shall make thy peace for moving me to rage!
And I will boot thee with what gift beside
Thy modesty can beg.

MESSENGER.
He's married, madam.

CLEOPATRA.
Rogue, thou hast lived too long. [*Draws a dagger.*

MESSENGER.
Nay, then I'll run.
What mean you madam? I have made no fault. [*Exit.*

CHARMIAN.
Good madam, keep yourself within yourself;
The man is innocent.

CLEOPATRA.
Some innocent 'scape not the thunderbolt.
Melt Egypt into Nile! And kindly creatures
Turn all to serpents! Call the slave again;
Though I am mad, I will not bite him—Call!

CHARMIAN.
He is afraid to come.

CLEOPATRA.
I will not hurt him.
These hands do lack nobility, that they strike
A meaner than myself.

* * * * * * * *

CLEOPATRA.
In praising Antony, I have dispraised Cæsar.

CHARMIAN.

Many times, madam.

CLEOPATRA.

I am paid for't now—
Lead me from hence.
I faint. O Iras, Charmian—'tis no matter:
Go to the fellow, good Alexas; bid him
Report the features of Octavia, her years,
Her inclination—let him not leave out
The color of her hair. Bring me word quickly. *Exit Alex.*
Let him for ever go—let him not!—Charmian,
Though he be painted one way like a Gorgon,
T'other way he's a Mars. Bid you Alexas [*To Mardian.*
Bring me word how tall she is. Pity me, Charmian,
But do not speak to me. Lead me to my chamber.

I have given this scene entire, because I know nothing comparable to it. The pride and arrogance of the Egyptian queen, the blandishment of the woman, the unexpected but natural transitions of temper and feeling, the contest of various passions, and at length,—when the wild hurricane has spent its fury, the melting into tears, faintness, and languishment, are portrayed with the most astonishing power, and truth, and skill in feminine nature. More wonderful still is the splendor and force of coloring which is shed over this extraordinary scene. The mere idea of an angry woman beating her menial presents something ridiculous or disgusting to the mind; in a queen or a tragedy heroine it is still more indecorous;* yet this scene is as far as possible from the vulgar or the comic. Cleopatra seems privileged to "touch the brink of all we hate" with impunity. This imperial termagant, this "wrangling

* The well known violence and coarseness of Queen Elizabeth's manners, in which she was imitated by the women about her, may in Shakspeare's time have rendered the image of a royal virago less offensive and less extraordinary.

queen, whom every thing becomes," becomes even her fury. We know not by what strange power it is, that in the midst of all these unruly passions and childish caprices, the poetry of the character, and the fanciful and sparkling grace of the delineation are sustained, and still rule in the imagination ; but we feel that it is so.

I need hardly observe, that we have historical authority for the excessive violence of Cleopatra's temper. Witness the story of her boxing the ears of her treasurer, in presence of Octavius, as related by Plutarch. Shakspeare has made a fine use of this anecdote also towards the conclusion of the drama, but it is not equal in power to this scene with the messenger.

The man is afterwards brought back, almost by force, to satisfy Cleopatra's jealous anxiety, by a description of Octavia :—but this time made wise by experience, he takes care to adapt his information to the humors of his imperious mistress, and gives her a satirical picture of her rival. The scene which follows, in which Cleopatra—artful, acute, and penetrating as she is—becomes the dupe of her feminine spite and jealousy, nay, assists in duping herself; and after having cuffed the messenger for telling her truths which are offensive, rewards him for the falsehood which flatters her weakness—is not only an admirable exhibition of character, but a fine moral lesson.

She concludes, after dismissing the messenger with gold and thanks,

I repent me much
That I so harry'd him. Why, methinks by him
This creature's no such thing?

CHARMIAN.

O nothing, madam.

CLEOPATRA.

The man hath seen some majesty, and should know!

Do we not fancy Cleopatra drawing herself up with all the vain consciousness of rank and beauty as she pronounces this last line? and is not this the very woman who celebrated her own apotheosis,—who arrayed herself in the robe and diadem of the goddess Isis, and could find no titles magnificent enough for her children but those of *the Sun and the Moon.*

The despotism and insolence of her temper are touched in some other places most admirably. Thus, when she is told that the Romans libel and abuse her, she exclaims,

> Sink Rome, and their tongues rot
> That speak against us!

And when one of her attendants observes, that "Herod of Jewry dared not look upon her but when she were well pleased," she immediately replies, "that Herod's head I'll have."*

When Proculeius surprises her in her monument, and snatches her poniard from her, terror and fury, pride, passion, and disdain, swell in her haughty soul, and seem to shake her very being.

CLEOPATRA.

> Where art thou, death?
> Come hither, come! come, come and take a queen
> Worth many babes and beggars!

PROCULEIUS.

> O temperance, lady!

CLEOPATRA.

> Sir, I will eat no meat; I'll not drink, sir;
> If idle talk will once be necessary;
> I'll not sleep neither; this mortal house I'll ruin,
> Do Cæsar what he can! Know, sir, that I
> Will not wait pinioned at your master's court,

* She was as good as her word. See the life of Antony in Plutarch.

Nor once be chastis'd with the sober eye
Of dull Octavia. Shall they hoist me up,
And show me to the shouting varletry
Of censuring Rome? Rather a ditch in Egypt
Be gentle grave to me! rather on Nilus' mud
Lay me stark naked, and let the water-flies
Blow me into abhorring! rather make
My country's high pyramids my gibbet,
And hang me up in chains!

In the same spirit of royal bravado, but finer still, and worked up with a truly Oriental exuberance of fancy and imagery, is her famous description of Antony, addressed to Dolabella:

Most noble empress, you have heard of me?

CLEOPATRA.

I cannot tell.

DOLABELLA.

Assuredly, you know me.

CLEOPATRA.

No matter, sir, what I have heard or known.
You laugh when boys, or women, tell their dreams;
Is't not your trick?

DOLABELLA.

I understand not, madam.

CLEOPATRA.

I dream'd there was an Antony;
O such another sleep, that I might see
But such another man!

DOLABELLA.

If it might please you—

CLEOPATRA.

His face was as the heavens; and therein stuck
A sun and moon; which kept their course, and lighted
The little O, the earth.

DOLABELLA.

Most sovereign creature—

CLEOPATRA.

His legs bestri'd the ocean ; his reared arm
Crested the world ; his voice was propertied
As all the tuned spheres, and that to friends ;
But when he meant to quail or shake the orb
He was as rattling thunder. For his bounty,
There was no winter in't ; an autumn 'twas,'
That grew the more by reaping. His delights
Were dolphin like ; they show'd his back above
The element they liv'd in. In his livery*
Walk'd crowns and corronets ; realms and islands were
As plates† dropp'd from his pocket.

DOLABELLA.

Cleopatra!

CLEOPATRA.

Think you there was, or might be, such a man
As this I dream'd of?

DOLABELLA.

Gentle madam no.

CLEOPATRA.

You lie,—up to the hearing of the gods!

There was no room left in this amazing picture for the display of that passionate maternal tenderness, which was a strong and redeeming feature in Cleopatra's historical character; but it is not left untouched; for when she is imprecating mischiefs on herself, she wishes, as the last and worst of possible evils, that "thunder may smite Cæsarion!"

In representing the mutual passion of Antony and Cleopatra as real and fervent, Shakspeare has adhered to the truth of history as well as to general nature. On Antony's side it is a species of infatuation, a single and engrossing

* *i. e.* retinue. † *i. e.* silver coins from the Spanish *plata*.

feeling: it is, in short, the love of a man declined in years for a woman very much younger than himself, and who has subjected him by every species of female enchantment. In Cleopatra the passion is of a mixt nature, made up of real attachment, combined with the love of pleasure, the love of power, and the love of self. Not only is the character most complicated, but no one sentiment could have existed pure and unvarying in such a mind as hers; her passion in itself is true, fixed to one centre: but like the pennon streaming from the mast, it flutters and veers with every breath of her variable temper: yet in the midst of all her caprices, follies, and even vices, womanly feeling is still predominant in Cleopatra; and the change which takes place in her deportment towards Antony, when their evil fortune darkens round them, is as beautifnl and interesting in itself as it is striking and natural. Instead of the airy caprice and provoking petulance she displays in the first scenes, we have a mixture of tenderness, and artifice, and fear, and submissive blandishment. Her behavior, for instance, after the battle of Actium, when she quails before the noble and tender rebuke of her lover, is partly female subtlety and partly natural feeling.

CLEOPATRA.

O my lord, my lord,
Forgive my fearful sails! I little thought
You would have follow'd.

ANTONY.

Egypt, thou know'st too well
My heart was to the rudder tied by the strings,
And thou shouldst tow me after. O'er my spirit
Thy full supermacy thou know'st; and that
Thy beck might from the bidding of the gods
Command me.

CLEOPATRA.

O, my pardon!

ANTONY.

Now I must
To the young man send humble treaties, dodge
And palter in the shifts of lowness; who
With half the bulk o' the world play'd as I pleased,
Making and marring fortunes. You did know
How much you were my conqueror; and that
My sword, made weak by my affection would
Obey it on all cause.

CLEOPATRA.

O pardon, pardon!

ANTONY.

Fall not a tear, I say; one of them rates
All that is won and lost. Give me a kiss.
Even this repays me.

It is perfectly in keeping with the individual character that Cleopatra, alike destitute of moral strength and physical courage, should cower terrified and subdued before the masculine spirit of her lover, when once she has fairly roused it. Thus Tasso's Armida, half syren, half sorceress, in the moment of strong feeling, forgets her incantations, and has recourse to persuasion, to prayer, and to tears.

Lascia gl'incanti, e vuol provar se vaga
E supplice belta sia miglior maga.

Though the poet afterwards gives us to understand that even in this relinquishment of art there was a more refined artifice.

- Nella doglia amara
Gia tutte non oblia l' arti e le frodi.

And something like this inspires the conduct of Cleopatra towards Antony in his fallen fortunes. The reader should refer to that fine scene, where Antony surprises Thyreus kissing her hand "that kingly seal and plighter of high hearts," and rages like a thousand hurricanes.

The character of Mark Antony, as delineated by Shakspeare, reminds me of the Farnese Hercules. There is an ostentatious display of power, an exaggerated grandeur, a colossal effect in the whole conception, sustained throughout in the pomp of the language, which seems as it flows along to resound with the clang of arms and the music of the revel. The coarseness and violence of the historic portrait are a little kept down; but every word which Antony utters is characteristic of the arrogant but magnanimous Roman, who, "with half the bulk o' the world played as he pleased," and was himself the sport of a host of mad (and bad) passions, and the slave of a woman.

History is followed closely in all the details of the catastrophe, and there is something wonderfully grand in the hurried march of events towards the conclusion. As disasters hem her round, Cleopatra gathers up her faculties to meet them, not with the calm fortitude of a great soul, but the haughty, tameless spirit of a wilful woman, unused to reverse or contradiction.

Her speech after Antony has expired in her arms, I have always regarded as one of the most wonderful in Shakspeare. Cleopatra is not a woman to grieve silently. The contrast between the violence of her passions and the weakness of her sex, between her regal grandeur and her excess of misery, her impetuous, unavailing struggles with the fearful destiny which has compassed her, and the mixture of wild impatience and pathos in her agony, are really magnificent. She faints on the body of Antony, and is recalled to life by the cries of her women—

IRAS.
Royal Egypt—empress!

CLEOPATRA.

No more, but e'en a woman!* and commanded
By such poor passion as the maid that milks,
And does the meanest chares.—It were for me
To throw my sceptre at the injurious gods;
To tell them that our world did equal theirs
Till they had stolen our jewel. All's but nought;
Patience is sottish, and impatience does
Become a dog that's mad. Then is it sin
To rush into the secret house of death
Ere death dare come to us? How do you, women?
What, what? good cheer! why how now, Charmian?
My noble girls!—ah, women, women! look
Our lamp is spent, is out.
We'll bury him, and then what's brave, what's noble,
Let's do it after the high Roman fashion,
And make death proud to take us.

But although Cleopatra talks of dying "after the high Roman fashion," she fears what she most desires, and cannot perform with simplicity what costs her such an effort. That extreme physical cowardice which was so strong a trait in her historical character, which led to the defeat of Actium, which made her delay the execution of a fatal resolve till she had "tried conclusions infinite of *easy* ways to die," Shakspeare has rendered with the finest possible effect, and in a manner which heightens instead of diminishing our respect and interest. Timid by nature, she is courageous by the mere force of will, and she lashes herself up with high-sounding words into a kind of false daring. Her lively imagination suggests every incentive which can spur her on to the deed she has resolved, yet trembles, to contemplate. She pictures to herself all the degradations which must attend her captivity; and let it be observed, that those which she anticipates are precisely such

* Cleopatra replies to the first word she hears on recovering her senses, "No more *an empress*, but a mere woman!

as a vain, luxurious, and haughty woman would especially dread, and which only true virtue and magnanimity could despise. Cleopatra could have endured the loss of freedom; but to be led in triumph through the streets of Rome is insufferable. She could stoop to Cæsar with dissembling courtesy, and meet duplicity with superior art; but "to be chastised" by the scornful or upbraiding glance of the injured Octavia—"rather a ditch in Egypt!"

If knife, drugs, serpents have
Edge, sting, or operation, I am safe.
Your wife, Octavia, with her modest eyes,
And still conclusion,* shall acquire no honor
Demurring upon me.
Now, Iras, what think'st thou?
Thou, an Egyptian puppet, shalt be shown
In Rome as well as I. Mechanic slaves,
With greasy aprons, rules, and hammers, shall
Uplift us to the view. In their thick breaths,
Rank of gross diet shall we be enclouded,
And forced to drink their vapor.

IRAS.
The gods forbid!

CLEOPATRA.
Nay, 'tis most certain, Iras. Saucy lictors
Will catch at us like strumpets; and scald rhymers
Ballad us out o' tune! The quick comedians
Extemporally will stage us, and present
Our Alexandrian revels. Antony
Shall be brought drunken forth; and I shall see
Some squeaking Cleopatra boy my greatness.

She then calls for her diadem, her robes of state, and attires herself as "if again for Cydnus, to meet Mark Antony." Coquette to the last, she must make Death proud to

* *i. e.* sedate determination.—JOHNSON.

take her, and die, "phœnix-like," as she had lived, with all the pomp of preparation—luxurious in her despair.

The death of Lucretia, of Portia, of Arria, and others, who died " after the high Roman fashion," is sublime according to the Pagan ideas of virtue, and yet none of them so powerfully affect the imagination as the catastrophe of Cleopatra. The idea of this frail, timid, wayward woman, dying with heroism from the mere force of passion and will, takes us by surprise. The attic elegance of her mind, her poetical imagination, the pride of beauty and royalty predominating to the last, and the sumptuous and picturesque accompaniments with which she surrounds herself in death, carry to its extreme height that effect of contrast which prevails through her life and character. No arts, no invention could add to the real circumstances of Cleopatra's closing scene. Shakspeare has shown profound judgment and feeling in adhering closely to the classical authorities; and to say that the language and sentiments worthily fill up the outline, is the most magnificent praise that can be given. The magical play of fancy and the overpowering fascination of the character are kept up to the last; and when Cleopatra, on applying the asp, silences the lamentations of her women—

> Peace! Peace!
> Dost thou not see my baby at my breast,
> That sucks the nurse to sleep?—

These few words—the contrast between the tender beauty of the image and the horror of the situation—produce an effect more intensely mournful than all the ranting in the world. The generous devotion of her women adds the moral charm which alone was wanting; and when Octavius hurries in too late to save his victim, and exclaims, when gazing on her—

> She looks like sleep—
> As she would catch an other Antony
> In her strong toil of grace,

the image of her beauty and her irresistible arts, triumphant even in death, is at once brought before us, and one masterly and comprehensive stroke consummates this most wonderful, most dazzling delineation.

I am not here the apologist of Cleopatra's historical character, nor of such women as resemble her: I am considering her merely as a dramatic portrait of astonishing beauty, spirit, and originality. She has furnished the subject of two Latin, sixteen French, six English, and at least, four Italian, tragedies;* yet Shakspeare alone has availed himself of all the interest of the story, without falsifying the character. He alone has dared to exhibit the Egyptian queen with all her greatness and all her littleness—all her frailties of temper—all her paltry arts and dissolute passions—yet preserved the dramatic propriety and poetical coloring of the character, and awakened our pity for fallen grandeur, without once beguiling us into sympathy with guilt and error. Corneille has represented Cleopatra as a model of chaste propriety, magnanimity, constancy, and every female virtue; and the effect is almost ludicrous. In our own language, we have two very fine tragedies on the story of Cleopatra: in that

* The Cleopatra of Jodelle was the first regular French tragedy; the last French tragedy on the same subject was the Cleopatra of Marmontel. For the representation of this tragedy, Vaucanson, the celebrated French mechanist, invented an automaton asp, which crawled and hissed to the life,—to the great delight of the Parisians. But it appears that neither Vaucanson's asp, nor Clairon, could save Cleopatra from a deserved fate. Of the English tragedies, one was written by the Countess of Pembroke, the sister of Sir Philip Sydney; and is, I believe, the first instance in our language of original dramatic writing by a female.

of Dryden, which is in truth a noble poem, and which he himself considered his master-piece, Cleopatra is a mere common-place "all-for-love" heroine, full of constancy and fine sentiments. For instance—

> My love's so true,
> That I can neither hide it where it is,
> Nor show it where it is not. Nature meant me
> A wife—a silly, harmless, household dove,
> Fond without art, and kind without deceit.
> But fortune, that has made a mistress of me,
> Has thrust me out to the wild world, unfurnished
> Of falsehood to be happy.

Is this Antony's Cleopatra,—the Circe of the Nile,—the Venus of the Cydnus? *She* never uttered any thing half so mawkish in her life.

In Fletcher's "False One," Cleopatra is represented at an earlier period of her history: and to give an idea of the aspect under which the character is exhibited, (and it does not vary throughout the play,) I shall give one scene: if it be considered out of place, its extreme beauty will form its best apology.

Ptolomy and his council having exhibited to Cæsar all the royal treasures in Egypt, he is so astonished and dazzled at the view of the accumulated wealth, that he forgets the presence of Cleopatra, and treats her with negligence. The following scene between her and her sister Arsinoe occurs immediately afterwards.

ARSINOE.

You're so impatient!

CLEOPATRA.

Have I not cause?
Women of common beauties and low births,
When they are slighted are allowed their angers—
Why should not I, a princess, make him know
The baseness of his usage?

ARSINOE.

Yes, 'tis fit:
But then again you know what man——

CLEOPATRA.

He's no man!
The shadow of a greatness hangs upon him,
And not the virtue; he is no conqueror,
Has suffered under the base dross of nature;
Poorly delivered up his power to wealth.
The god of bed-rid men taught his eyes treason;
Against the truth of love he has rais'd rebellion—
Defied his holy flames.

EROS.

He will fall back again,
And satisfy your grace.

CLEOPATRA.

Had I been old,
Or blasted in my bud, he might have show'd
Some shadow of dislike: but to prefer
The lustre of a little trash, Arsinoe,
And the poor glow-worm light of some faint jewels
Before the light of love, and soul of beauty—
Oh how it vexes me! He is no soldier:
All honorable soldiers are love's servants.
He is a merchant, a mere wandering merchant,
Servile to gain: he trades for poor commodities,
And makes his conquests, thefts! Some fortunate captains
That quarter with him and are truly valiant,
Have flung the name of "Happy Cæsar" on him;
Himself ne'er won it. He's so base and covetous
He'll sell his sword for gold.

ARSINOE.

This is too bitter.

CLEOPATRA.

O I could curse myself, that was so foolish,
So fondly childish, to believe his tongue—
His promising tongue—ere I could catch his temper.
I'd trash enough to have cloy'd his eyes withal,
(His covetous eyes,) such as I scorn to tread on,
Richer than e'er he saw yet, and more tempting;

Had I known he'd stoop'd at that, I'd sav'd mine honor—
I had been happy still. But let him take it,
And let him brag how poorly I'm rewarded;
Let him go conquer still weak wretched ladies;
Love has his angry quiver too, his deadly,
And when he finds scorn, arm'd at the strongest—
I am a fool to fret thus for a fool,—
An old blind fool too! I lose my health; I will not,
I will not cry; I will not honor him
With tears diviner than the gods he worships;
I will not take the pains to curse a poor thing.

EROS.

Do not; you shall not need.

CLEOPATRA.

Would I were prisoner
To one I hate, that I might anger him!
I will love any man to break the heart of him!
Any that has the heart and will to kill him!

ARSINOE.

Take some fair truce.

CLEOPATRA.

I will go study mischief,
And put a look on arm'd with all my cunnings,
Shall meet him like a basilisk, and strike him.
Love! put destroying flames into mine eyes,
Into my smiles deceits, that I may torture him—
That I may make him love to death, and laugh at him.

Enter APOLLODORUS.

APOLLODORUS.

Cæsar commends his service to your grace.

CLEOPATRA.

His service? What's his service.

EROS.

Pray you be patient;
The noble Cæsar loves still.

CLEOPATRA.

What's his will?

APOLLODORUS.

He craves access unto your highness.

CLEOPATRA.

No;
Say no; I will have none to trouble me.

ARSINOE.

Good sister!—

CLEOPATRA.

None, I say; I will be private.
Would thou hadst flung me into Nilus, keeper,
When first thou gav'st consent to bring my body,
To this unthankful Cæsar!

APOLLODORUS.

'Twas your will, madam.
Nay more, your charge upon me, as I honor'd you.
You know what danger I endur'd.

CLEOPATRA.

Take this, *(giving a jewel.)*
And carry it to that lordly Cæsar sent thee;
There's a new love, a handsome one, a rich one,
One that will hug his mind: bid him make love to it;
Tell the ambitious broker this will suffer ——

Enter CÆSAR.

APOLLODORUS.

He enters.

CLEOPATRA.

How!

CÆSAR.

I do not use to wait, lady;
Where I am all the doors are free and open.

CLEOPATRA.

I guess so by your rudeness.

CÆSAR.

You're not angry?
Things of your tender mould should be most gentle.
Why should you frown? Good gods, what a set anger
Have you forc'd into your face! Come, I must temper you.
What a coy smile was there, and a disdainful!
How like an ominous flash it broke out from you!
Defend me, love! Sweet who has angered you?

CLEOPATRA.

Show him a glass! That false face has betrayed me—
That base heart wronged me.

CÆSAR.

Be more sweetly angry,
I wronged you fair?

CLEOPATRA.

Away with your foul flatteries;
They are too gross! But that I dare be angry,
And with as great a god as Cæsar is,
To show how poorly I respect his memory,
I would not speak to you.

CÆSAR.

Pray you undo this riddle,
And tell me how I've vexed you?

CLEOPATRA.

Let me think first,
Whether I may put on a patience
That will with honor suffer me. Know, I hate you;
Let that begin the story. Now I'll tell you.

CÆSAR.

But do it mildly; in a noble lady,
Softness of spirit, and a sober nature,
That moves like summer winds, cool, and blows sweetness,
Shows blessed, like herself.

CLEOPATRA.

And that great blessedness
You first reaped of me; till you taught my nature,
Like a rude storm, to talk aloud and thunder,
Sleep was not gentler than my soul, and stiller.
You had the string of my affections,
And my fair fruits I gave you leave to taste of;
You must expect the winter of mine anger.
You flung me off—before the court disgraced me—
When in the pride I appeared of all my beauty—
Appeared your mistress; took unto your eyes
The common strumpet, love of hated lucre—

Courted with covetous heart the slave of nature,—
Gave all your thoughts to gold, that men of glory,
And minds adorned with noble love, would kick at!
Soldiers of royal mark scorn such base purchase;
Beauty and honor are the marks they shoot at.
I spake to you then, I courted you, and woo'd you,
Called you dear Cæsar, hung about you tenderly,
Was proud to appear your friend—

CÆSAR.

You have mistaken me.

CLEOPATRA.

But neither eye, nor favor, not a smile
Was I blessed back withal, but shook off rudely;
And, as you had been sold to sordid infamy,
You fell before the images of treasure,
And in your soul you worshipped. I stood slighted,
Forgotten, and contemned; my soft embraces,
And those sweet kisses which you called Elysium,
As letters writ in sand, no more remembered;
The name and glory of your Cleopatra
Laughed at, and made a story to your captains!
Shall I endure?

CÆSAR.

You are deceived in all this;
Upon my life you are; 'tis your much tenderness.

CLEOPATRA.

No, no; I love not that way; you are cozened;
I love with as much ambition as a conqueror,
And where I love will triumph!

CÆSAR.

So you shall;
My heart shall be the chariot that shall bear you;
All I have won shall wait upon you. By the gods,
The bravery of this woman's mind has fired me!
Dear mistress, shall I but this once——

CLEOPATRA.

How! Cæsar!
Have I let slip a second vanity
That gives the hope?

CÆSAR.

You shall be absolute,
And reign alone as queen; you shall be any thing.

CLEOPATRA.

* * * * *

Farewell, unthankful!

CÆSAR.

Stay!

CLEOPATRA.

I will not.

CÆSAR.

I command!

CLEOPATRA.

Command, and go without, sir.
I do command *thee* be my slave for ever,
And vex, while I laugh at thee!

CÆSAR.

Thus low, beauty——— [*He kneels.*

CLEOPATRA.

It is too late; when I have found thee absolute,
The man that fame reports thee, and to me,
May be I shall think better. Farewell, conqueror. [*Exit.*

Now this is magnificent poetry, but this is not Cleopatra, this is not "the gypsy queen." The sentiment here is too profound, the majesty too real, and too lofty. Cleopatra could be great by fits and starts, but never sustained her dignity upon so high a tone for ten minutes together. The Cleopatra of Fletcher reminds us of the antique colossal statue of her in the Vatican, all grandeur and grace.

Cleopatra, in Dryden's tragedy, is like Guido's dying Cleopatra in the Pitti palace, tenderly beautiful. Shakspeare's Cleopatra is like one of those graceful and fantastic pieces of antique Arabesque, in which all anomalous shapes, and impossible and wild combinations of form, are woven together in regular confusion and most harmonious discord: —and such, we have reason to believe, was the living woman herself, when she existed upon this earth.

I do not understand the observation of a late critic, that in this play "Octavia is only a dull foil to Cleopatra." Cleopatra requires no foil, and Octavia is not dull, though in a moment of jealous spleen, her accomplished rival gives her that epithet.* It is possible that her beautiful character, if brought more forward and colored up to the historic portrait, would still be eclipsed by the dazzling splendor of Cleopatra's; for so I have seen a flight of fireworks blot out for awhile the silver moon and ever-burning stars. But here the subject of the drama being the love of Antony and Cleopatra, Octavia is very properly kept in the background, and far from any competition with her rival: the interest would otherwise have been unpleasantly divided, or rather Cleopatra herself must have served but as a foil to the tender, virtuous, dignified, and generous Octavia, the very *beau-ideal* of a noble Roman lady—

> Admired Octavia, whose beauty claims
> No worse a husband than the best of men;
> Whose virtue and whose general graces speak
> That which none else can utter.

Dryden has committed a great mistake in bringing Octavia and her children on the scene, and in immediate contact with Cleopatra. To have thus violated the truth of

* "The sober eye of dull Octavia."—Act v. Scene 2.

history* might have been excusable, but to sacrifice the truth of nature and dramatic propriety, to produce a mere stage effect, was unpardonable. In order to preserve the unity of interest, he has falsified the character of Octavia as well as that of Cleopatra :† he has presented us with a regular scolding match between the rivals, in which they come sweeping up to each other from opposite sides of the stage, with their respective trains, like two pea-hens in a passion. Shakspeare would no more have brought his captivating, brilliant, but meretricious Cleopatra into immediate comparison with the noble and chaste simplicity of Octavia, than a connoiseur in art would have placed Canova's Dansatrice, beautiful as it is, beside the Athenian Melpomene, or the Vestal of the Capitol.

The character of Octavia is merely indicated in a few touches, but every stroke tells. We see her with "downcast eyes sedate and sweet, and looks demure," with her modest tenderness and dignified submission—the very antipodes of her rival! Nor should we forget that she has furnished one of the most graceful similes in the whole compass of poetry, where her soft equanimity in the midst of grief is compared to

> The swan's down feather
> That stands upon the swell at flood of tide,
> And neither way inclines.

The fear which seems to haunt the mind of Cleopatra,

* Octavia was never in Egypt.

† "The Octavia of Dryden, is a much more important personage than in the Antony and Cleopatra of Shakspeare. She is, however, more cold and unamiable, for in the very short scenes in which the Octavia of Shakspeare is introduced, she is placed in rather an interesting point of view. But Dryden has himself informed us that he was apprehensive that the justice of a wife's claim would draw the audience to her side, and lessen their interest in the lover and the

lest she should be "chastised by the sober eye" of Octavia, is exceedingly characteristic of the two women: it betrays the jealous pride of her, who was conscious that she had forfeited all real claim to respect: and it places Octavia before us in all the majesty of that virtue which could strike a kind of envying and remorseful awe even into the bosom of Cleopatra. What would she have thought and felt, had some soothsayer foretold to her the fate of her own children whom she so tenderly loved? Captives, and exposed to the rage of the Roman populace, they owed their existence to the generous, admirable Octavia, in whose mind there entered no particle of littleness. She received into her house the children of Antony and Cleopatra, educated them with her own, treated them with truly maternal tenderness, and married them nobly.

Lastly, to complete the contrast, the death of Octavia should be put in comparison with that of Cleopatra.

After spending several years in dignified retirement, respected as the sister of Augustus, but more for her own virtues, Octavia lost her eldest son Marcellus, who was expressively called the "Hope of Rome." Her fortitude gave way under this blow, and she fell into a deep melancholy, which gradually wasted her health. While she was thus declining into death, occurred that beautiful scene, which has never yet, I believe, been made the subject of a picture, but should certainly be added to my gallery, (if I had one,) and I would hang it opposite to the dying Cleopatra. Virgil was commanded by Augustus to read aloud to his sister, that book of the Eneid in which he had

mistress. He seems accordingly to have studiously lowered the character of the injured Octavia, who, in her conduct to her husband, shows much duty and little love." Sir W. Scott (in the same fine piece of criticism prefixed to Dryden's All for Love,) gives the preference to Shakspeare's Cleopatra.

commemorated the virtues and early death of the young Marcellus. When he came to the lines—

> This youth, the blissful vision of a day,
> Shall just be shown on earth, then snatch'd away, &c.

the mother covered her face and burst into tears. But when Virgil mentioned her son by name, ("Tu Marcellus eris,") which he had artfully deferred till the concluding lines, Octavia, unable to control her agitation, fainted away. She afterwards, with a magnificent spirit, ordered the poet a gratuity of ten thousand sesterces for each line of the panegyric.* It is probable that the agitation she suffered on this occasion hastened the effects of her disorder; for she died soon after, (of grief, says the historian,) having survived Antony about twenty years.

Octavia, however, is only a beautiful sketch: while in Volumnia, Shakspeare has given us the portrait of a Roman matron, conceived in the true antique spirit, and finished in every part. Although Coriolanus is the hero of the play, yet much of the interest of the action and the final catastrophe turn upon the character of his mother Volumnia, and the power she exercised over his mind, by which, according to the story, "she saved Rome and lost her son." Her lofty patriotism, her patrician haughtiness; her maternal pride, her eloquence, and her towering spirit, are exhibited with the utmost power of effect, yet the truth of female nature is beautifully preserved, and the portrait, with all its vigor, is without harshness.

I shall begin by illustrating the relative position and feelings of the mother and son, as these are of the greatest importance in the action of the drama, and consequently most prominent in the characters. Though Volumnia is a Roman matron, and though her country owes its salvation

* In all, about two thousand pounds.

to her, it is clear that her maternal pride and affection are stronger even than her patriotism. Thus when her son is exiled, she bursts into an imprecation against Rome and its citizens;

> Now the red pestilence strike all trades in Rome,
> And occupations perish!

Here we have the impulses of individual and feminine nature, overpowering all national and habitual influences. Volumnia would never have exclaimed like the Spartan mother, of her dead son, "Sparta has many others as brave as he;" but in a far different spirit she says to the Romans,

> Ere you go, hear this;
> As far as doth the Capitol exceed
> The meanest house in Rome, so far my son,
> Whom you have banished, does exceed you all.

In the very first scene, and before the introduction of the principal personages, one citizen observes to another that the military exploits of Marcius were performed, not so much for his country's sake "as to please his mother." By this admirable stroke of art, introduced with such simplicity of effect, our attention is aroused, and we are prepared in the very outset of the piece for the important part assigned to Volumnia, and for her share in producing the catastrophe.

In the first act we have a very graceful scene, in which the two Roman ladies, the wife and mother of Coriolanus, are discovered at their needle-work, conversing on his absence and danger, and are visited by Valeria—

> The noble sister of Publicola.
> The moon of Rome: chaste as the icicle,
> That's curded by the frost from purest snow,
> And hangs on Dian's temple!

Over this little scene Shakspeare, without any display of learning, has breathed the very spirit of classical antiquity. The haughty temper of Volumnia, her admiration of the valor and high bearing of her son, and her proud but unselfish love for him, are finely contrasted with the modest sweetness, the conjugal tenderness, and the fond solicitude of his wife Virgilia.

VOLUMNIA.

When yet he was but tender-bodied, and the only son of my womb; when youth with comeliness pluck'd all gaze his way; when, for a day of king's entreaties, a mother should not sell him an hour from her beholding; I,—considering how honor would become such a person; that it was no better than picture-like to hang by the wall, if renown made it not stir,—was pleased to let him seek danger where he was like to find fame. To a cruel war I sent him, from whence he returned, his brows bound with oak. I tell thee, daughter—I sprang not more in joy at first hearing he was a man-child, than now in first seeing he had proved himself a man.

VIRGILIA.

But had he died in the business, madam, how then?

VOLUMNIA.

Then his good report should have been my son; I therein would have found issue. Hear me profess sincerely: had I a dozen sons, each in my love alike, and none less dear than thine and my good Marcius, I had rather had eleven die nobly for their country, than one voluptuously surfeit out of action.

Enter a GENTLEWOMAN.

Madam, the lady Valeria is come to visit you.

VIRGILIA.

Beseech you, give me leave to retire myself.

VOLUMNIA.

Indeed you shall not.
Methinks, I hear hither your husband's drum—
See him pluck Aufidius down by the hair;
As children from a bear, the Volces shunning him
Methinks, I see him stamp thus, and call thus—
"Come on you cowards! you were got in fear,

Though you were born in Rome." His bloody brow
With his mail'd hand then wiping, forth he goes;
Like to a harvest-man, that's tasked to mow
Or all, or lose his hire.

VIRGILIA.

His bloody brow! O Jupiter, no blood!

VOLUMNIA.

Away, you fool! it more becomes a man
Than gilt his trophy. The breasts of Hecuba,
When she did suckle Hector, look'd not lovelier
Than Hector's forehead, when it spit forth blood
At Grecian swords contending. Tell Valeria
We are fit to bid her welcome. [*Exit Gent.*

VIRGILIA.

Heavens bless my lord from fell Aufidius!

VOLUMNIA.

He'll beat Aufidius' head below his knee,
And tread upon his neck.

This distinction between the two females is as interesting and beautiful as it is well sustained: thus when the victory of Coriolanus is proclaimed, Menenius asks "Is he wounded?"

VIRGILIA.

O no, no, no!

VOLUMNIA.

Yes, he is wounded—I thank the gods for it!

And when he returns victorious from the wars, his high-spirited mother receives him with blessings and applause—his gentle wife with gracious silence and with tears.

The resemblance of temper in the mother and the son, modified as it is by the difference of sex, and by her greater age and experience, is exhibited with admirable truth. Volumnia, with all her pride and spirit, has some prudence and self command; in her language and deportment all is matured and matronly. The dignified tone of authority she assumes towards her son, when checking his headlong impetuosity,—her respect and admiration for his noble qualities, and her strong sympathy even with the feelings she combats, are all displayed in the scene in which she prevails on him to soothe the incensed plebeians.

VOLUMNIA.

Pray be counsell'd!
I have a heart as little apt as yours,
But yet a brain that leads my use of anger
To better vantage.

MENENIUS.

Well said, noble woman:
Before he should thus stoop to the herd, but that
The violent fit o' the time craves it as physic
For the whole state, I would put mine armor on,
Which I can scarcely bear.

CORIOLANUS.

What must I do?

MENENIUS.

Return to the tribunes.

CORIOLANUS.

Well,
What then? what then?

MENENIUS.

Repent what you have spoke.

CORIOLANUS.

For them? I cannot do it to the gods:
Must I then do't to them?

VOLUMNIA.

You are too absolute,
Though therein you can never be too noble
But when extremities speak.

I prithee now, my son,
Go to them with this bonnet in thy hand;
And thus far having stretch'd it (here be with them)
Thy knee bussing the stones, (for in such business
Action is eloquent, and the eyes of the ignorant
More learned than the ears,) waving thy head,
Which often thus correcting thy stout heart,
Now humble as the ripest mulberry,
That will not hold the handling: or say to them,
Thou art their soldier, and being bred in broils
Hast not the soft way which, thou dost confess,
Were fit for thee to use, as they to claim,
In asking their good loves: but thou wilt frame
Thyself, forsooth, hereafter theirs, so far
As thou hast power and person.

MENENIUS.

This but done,
Even as she speaks, why all their hearts were yours;
For they have pardons, being asked, as free
As words to little purpose.

VOLUMNIA.

Prithee, now,
Go and be rul'd: although I know thou hadst rather
Follow thine enemy in a fiery gulf
Than flatter him in a bower.

MENENIUS.

Only fair speech.

COMINIUS.

I think, 'twill serve, if he
Can thereto frame his spirit.

VOLUMNIA.

He must, and will:
Prithee, now, say you will, and go about it.

CORIOLANUS.

Must I go show them my unbarbed sconce? Must I
With my base tongue give to my noble heart
A lie, that it must bear? Well, I will do't:

Yet were there but this single plot to lose,
This mould of Marcius, they to dust should grind it,
And throw it against the wind. To the market-place!
You have put me now to such a part, which never
I shall discharge to the life.

VOLUMNIA.

I prithee, now, sweet son, as thou hast said
My praises made thee first a soldier, so
To have my praise for this, perform a part
Thou hast not done before.

CORIOLANUS.

Well, I must do't;
Away, my disposition, and possess me
Some harlot's spirit!

* * * * *

I will not do't:
Lest I surcease to honor mine own truth,
And by my body's action, teach my mind
A most inherent baseness.

VOLUMNIA.

At thy choice, then:
To beg of thee it is my more dishonor,
Than thou of them. Come all to ruin: let
Thy mother rather feel thy pride, than fear
Thy dangerous stoutness; for I mock at death
With as big heart as thou. Do as thou list—
Thy valiantness was mine, thou suck'dst it from me:
But owe thy pride myself.

CORIOLANUS.

Pray be content:
Mother, I am going to the market-place—
Chide me no more.

When the spirit of the mother and the son are brought into immediate collision, he yields before her: the warrior who stemmed alone the whole city of Corioli, who was ready to face " the steep Tarpeian death, or at wild horses' heels, —vagabond exile—flaying," rather than abate one jot of his proud will—shrinks at her rebuke. The haughty, fiery, overbearing temperament of Coriolanus, is drawn in such forcible and striking colors, that nothing can more impress us with the real grandeur and power of Volumnia's character, than his boundless submission to her will—his more than filial tenderness and respect.

> You gods! I prate,
> And the most noble mother of the world
> Leave unsaluted. Sink my knee i' the earth—
> Of thy deep duty more impression show
> Than that of common sons!

When his mother appears before him as a suppliant, he exclaims,

> My mother bows;
> As if Olympus to a molehill should
> In supplication nod.

Here the expression of reverence, and the magnificent image in which it is clothed, are equally characteristic both of the mother and the son.

Her aristocratic haughtiness is a strong trait in Volumnia's manner and character, and her supreme contempt for the plebeians, whether they are to be defied or cajoled, is very like what I have heard expressed by some high-born and high-bred women of our own day.

> I muse my mother
> Does not approve me further, who was wont
> To call them woollen vassals; things created
> To buy and sell with groats; to show bare heads
> In congregations; to yawn, be still, and wonder,
> When one but of my ordinance stood up
> To speak of peace or war.

And Volumnia reproaching the tribunes,

> 'Twas you incensed the rabble—

Cats, that can judge as fitly of his worth,
As I can of those mysteries which Heaven
Will not have earth to know.

There is all the Roman spirit in her exultation when the trumpets sound the return of Coriolanus.

Hark! the trumpets.
These are the ushers of Marcius: before him
He carries noise, and behind him he leaves tears.

And in her speech to the gentle Virgilia, who is weeping her husband's banishment—

Leave this faint puling! and lament as I do,
In anger—Juno-like!

But the triumph of Volumnia's character, the full display of all her grandeur of soul, her patriotism, her strong affections, and her sublime eloquence, are reserved for her last scene, in which she pleads for the safety of Rome, and wins from her angry son that peace which all the swords of Italy and her confederate arms could not have purchased. The strict and even literal adherance to the truth of history is an additional beauty.

Her famous speech, beginning "Should we be silent and not speak," is nearly word for word from Plutarch, with some additional graces of expression, and the charm of metre superadded. I shall give the last lines of this address, as illustrating that noble and irresistible eloquence which was the crowning ornament of the character. One exquisite touch of nature, which is distinguished by italics, was beyond the rhetorician and historian, and belongs only to the poet.

Speak to me, son;
Thou hast affected the fine strains of honor,
To imitate the graces of the gods;

To tear with thunder the wide cheeks o' the air,
And yet to charge thy sulphur with a bolt.
That should but rive an oak. Why dost not speak?
Think'st thou it honorable for a noble man
Still to remember wrongs? Daughter, speak you:
He cares not for your weeping. Speak thou, boy;
Perhaps thy childishness may move him more
Than can our reasons. There is no man in the world
More bound to his mother; yet here he lets me prate
Like one i' the stocks. Thou hast never in thy life
Show'd thy dear mother any courtesy:
When she, (poor hen!) fond of no second brood,
Has cluck'd thee to the wars, and safely home,
Laden with honor. Say my request 's unjust,
And spurn me back; but, if it be not so,
Thou art not honest, and the gods will plague thee
That thou restrain'st from me the duty which
To a mother's part belongs. He turns away—
Down, ladies: let us shame him with our knees.
To his surname Coriolanus 'longs more pride,
Than pity to our prayers; down, and end;
This is the last; so will we home to Rome,
And die among our neighbors. Nay, behold us:
This boy, that cannot tell what he would have,
But kneels, and holds up hands, for fellowship,
Does reason our petition with more strength
Than thou hast to deny 't.*

* The corresponding passage in the old English Plutarch runs thus;—"My son, why dost thou not answer me? Doest thou think it good altogether to give place unto thy choler and revenge, and thinkest thou it not honesty for thee to grant thy mother's request in so weighty a cause? Dost thou take it honorable for a nobleman to remember the wrongs and injuries done him, and dost not in like case think it an honest nobleman's part to be thankful for the goodness that parents do show to their children, acknowledging the duty and reverence they ought to bear unto them? No man living is more bound to show himself thankful in all parts and respects than thyself; who so universally showest all ingratitude. Moreover, my son' thou hast sorely taken of thy country, exacting grievous payments upon them in revenge of the injuries offered thee; besides thou hast

It is an instance of Shakspeare's fine judgment, that after this magnificent and touching piece of eloquence, which saved Rome, Volumnia should speak no more, for she could say nothing that would not deteriorate from the effect thus left on the imagination. She is at last dismissed from our admiring gaze amid the thunder of grateful exclamations.

> Behold our patroness,—the life of Rome.

CONSTANCE.

We have seen that in the mother of Coriolanus, the principal qualities are exceeding pride, self-will, strong maternal affection, great power of imagination, and energy of temper. Precisely the same qualities enter into the mind of Constance of Bretagne; but in her these qualities are so differently modified by circumstances and education, that not even in fancy do we think of instituting a comparison between the Gothic grandeur of Constance, and the more severe and classical dignity of the Roman matron.

The scenes and circumstances with which Shakspeare has surrounded Constance are strictly faithful to the old chronicles, and are as vividly as they are accurately represented. On the other hand, the hints on which the cha-

not hitherto showed thy poor mother any courtesy. And, therefore, it is not only honest, but due unto me, that without compulsion I should obtain my so just and reasonable request of thee. But since by reason I cannot persuade ye to it, to what purpose do I defer my last hope?" And with these words, herself, his wife, and children fell down upon their knees before him.

racter has been constructed are few and vague; but the portrait harmonizes so wonderfully with its historic background, and with all that later researches have discovered relative to the personal adventures of Constance, that I have not the slightest doubt of its individual truth. The result of a life of strange vicissitude; the picture of a tameless will, and high passions, for ever struggling in vain against a superior power;—and the real situation of women, in those chivalrous times, are placed before us in a few noble scenes. The manner in which Shakspeare has applied the scattered hints of history to the formation of the character, reminds us of that magician who collected the mangled limbs which had been dispersed up and down, reunited them into the human form, and reanimated them with the breathing and conscious spirit of life.

Constance of Bretagne was the only daughter and heiress of Conan IV. Duke of Bretagne; her mother was Margaret of Scotland, the eldest daughter of Malcolm IV.: but little mention is made of this princess in the old histories; but she appears to have inherited some portion of the talent and spirit of her father, and to have transmitted them to her daughter. The misfortunes of Constance may be said to have commenced before her birth, and took their rise in the misconduct of one of her female ancestors. Her great-grandmother Matilda, the wife of Conan III. was distinguished by her beauty and imperious temper, and not less by her gallantries. Her husband, not thinking proper to repudiate her during his lifetime, contented himself with disinheriting her son Hoel, whom he declared illegitimate; and bequeathed his dukedom to his daughter Bertha, and her husband Allan the Black, Earl of Richmond, who were proclaimed and acknowledged Duke and Duchess of Bretagne.

Prince Hoel, so far from acquiescing in his father's

will, immediately levied an army to maintain his rights, and a civil war ensued between the brother and sister, which lasted for twelve or fourteen years. Bertha, whose reputation was not much fairer than that of her mother Matilda, was succeeded by her son Conan IV.; he was young, and of a feeble vacillating temper, and after struggling for a few years against the increasing power of his uncle Hoel, and his own rebellious barons, he called in the aid of that politic and ambitious monarch Henry II. of England. This fatal step decided the fate of his crown and his posterity; from the moment the English set foot in Bretagne, that miserable country became a scene of horrors and crimes—oppression and perfidy on the one hand, unavailing struggles on the other. Ten years of civil discord ensued, during which the greatest part of Bretagne was desolated, and nearly a third of the population carried off by famine and pestilence. In the end, Conan was secured in the possession of his throne by the assistance of the English king, who, equally subtle and ambitious, contrived in the course of this warfare to strip Conan of most of his provinces by successive treaties; alienate the Breton nobles from their lawful sovereign, and at length render the duke himself the mere vassal of his power.

In the midst of these scenes of turbulence and bloodshed was Constance born, in the year 1164. The English king consummated his perfidious scheme of policy, by seizing on the person of the infant princess, before she was three years old, as a hostage for her father. Afterwards, by contracting her in marriage to his third son, Geoffrey Plantagenet, he insured, as he thought, the possession of the duchy of Bretagne to his own posterity.

From this time we hear no more of the weak, unhappy Conan, who, retiring from a fruitless contest, hid himself in some obscure retreat: even the date of his death is unknown. Meanwhile Henry openly claimed the duchy in behalf of his son Geoffrey and the Lady Constance; and their claims not being immediately acknowledged, he invaded Bretagne with a large army, laid waste the country, bribed or forced some of the barons into submission, murdered or imprisoned others; and, by the most treacherous and barbarous policy, contrived to keep possession of the country he had thus seized. However, in order to satisfy the Bretons, who were attached to the race of their ancient sovereigns, and to give some color to his usurpation, he caused Geoffrey and Constance to be solemnly crowned at Rennes, as Duke and Duchess of Bretagne. This was in the year 1169, when Constance was five, and Prince Geoffrey about eight years old. His father Henry continued to rule, or rather to ravage and oppress, the country in their name for about fourteen years, during which period we do not hear of Constance. She appears to have been kept in a species of constraint as a hostage rather than a sovereign; while her husband Geoffrey, as he grew up to manhood, was too much engaged in keeping the Bretons in order, and disputing his rights with his father, to think about the completion of his union with Constance, although his sole title to the dukedom was properly and legally in right of his wife. At length, in 1182, the nuptials were formally celebrated, Constance being then in her nineteenth year. At the same time, she was recognised as Duchess of Bretagne *de son chef*, (that is, in her own right,) by two acts of legislation, which are still preserved among the records of Bretagne, and bear her own seal and signature.

Those domestic feuds which embittered the whole life of Henry II., and at length broke his heart, are well known. Of all his sons, who were in continual rebellion against him, Geoffrey was the most undutiful, and the most formidable: he had all the pride of the Plantagenets,—all the warlike accomplishments of his two elder brothers, Henry and Richard; and was the only one who could compete with his father in talent, eloquence and dissimulation. No sooner was he the husband of Constance, and in possession of the throne of Bretagne, than he openly opposed his father; in other words, he maintained the honor and interests of his wife and her unhappy country against the cruelty and oppression of the English plunderers.* About three years after his marriage, he was invited to Paris for the purpose of concluding a league, offensive and defensive, with the French king; in this journey he was accompanied by the Duchess Constance, and they were received and entertained with royal magnificence. Geoffrey, who excelled in all chivalrous accomplishments, distinguished himself in the tournaments which were celebrated on the occasion; but unfortunately, after an encounter with a French knight, celebrated for his prowess, he was accidentally flung from his horse, and trampled to death in the lists before he could be extricated.

Constance, being now left a widow, returned to Bretagne, where her barons rallied round her, and acknowledged her as their sovereign. The Salique law did not prevail in Bretagne, and it appears that in those times the power of a female to possess and transmit the rights of sovereignty had been recognised in several instances; but Constance is the first woman who exercised those rights in her own person. She had one daughter, Elinor, born in the second year of her marriage, and a few months after her husband's death she gave birth to a son. The states of Bretagne were filled with exultation; they required that

* V. Daru. Histoire de Bretagne.

the infant prince should not bear the name of his father,—a name which Constance, in fond remembrance of her husband, would have bestowed on him—still less that of his grandfather Henry; but that of Arthur, the redoubted hero of their country, whose memory was worshipped by the populace. Though the Arthur of romantic and fairy legends,—the Arthur of the round table, had been dead for six centuries, they still looked for his second appearance among them, according to the prophecy of Merlin; and now with fond and short-sighted enthusiasm, fixed their hopes on the young Arthur as one destined to redeem the glory and independence of their oppressed and miserable country. But in the very midst of the rejoicings which succeeded the birth of the prince, his grandfather, Henry II., demanded to have the possession and guardianship of his person, and on the spirited refusal of Constance to yield her son into his power, he invaded Bretagne with a large army, plundering, burning, devastating the country as he advanced; he seized Rennes, the capital, and having by the basest treachery obtained possession of the persons, both of the young duchess aud her children, he married Constance forcibly to one of his own favorite adherents, Randal de Blondeville, Earl of Chester, and conferred on him the duchy of Bretagne, to be held as a fief of the English crown.

The Earl of Chester, though a brave knight, and one of the greatest barons of England, had no pretensions to so high an alliance, nor did he possess any qualities or personal accomplishments which might have reconciled Constance to him as a husband. He was a man of diminutive stature and mean appearance, but of haughty and ferocious manners, and unbounded ambition.* In a conference

* V. Sir Peter Leycester's Antiquities of Chester.

between this Earl of Chester and the Earl of Perche, in Lincoln cathedral, the latter taunted Randal with his insignificant person, and called him contemptuously, "*Dwarf.*" "Say'st thou so!" replied Randal; "I vow to God and our Lady, whose church this is, that ere long I will seem to thee high as that steeple!" He was as good as his word when, on ascending to the throne of Brittany, the Earl of Perche became his vassal.

We cannot know what measures were used to force this degradation on the reluctant and high-spirited Constance; it is only certain that she never considered her marriage in the light of a sacred obligation, and that she took the first opportunity of legally breaking from a chain which could scarcely be considered as legally binding. For about a year she was obliged to allow this detested husband the title of Duke of Bretagne, and he administered the government without the slightest reference to her will, even in form, till 1189, when Henry II. died, execrating himself and his undutiful children. Whatever great and good qualities this monarch may have possessed, his conduct in Bretagne was uniformly detestable. Even the unfilial behavior of his sons may be extenuated; for while he spent his life, and sacrificed his peace, and violated every principle of honor and humanity to compass their political aggrandizement, he was guilty of atrocious injustice towards them, and set them a bad example in his own person.

The tidings of Henry's death had no sooner reached Bretagne, than the barons of that country rose with one accord against his government, banished or massacred his officers; and, sanctioned by the Duchess Constance, drove Randal de Blondeville and his followers from Bretagne: he retired to his earldom of Chester, there to brood over his injuries, and meditate vengeance.

In the mean time, Richard I. ascended the English throne; soon afterwards he embarked on his celebrated expedition to the Holy Land, having previously declared Prince Arthur, the only son of Constance, heir to all his dominions.*

His absence and that of many of her own turbulent barons and encroaching neighbors, left to Constance and her harrassed dominions a short interval of profound peace. The historians of that period, occupied by the warlike exploits of the French and English kings in Palestine, made but little mention of the domestic events of Europe during their absence; but it is no slight encomium on the character of Constance, that Bretagne flourished under her government and began to recover from the effects of twenty years of desolating war. The seven years during which she ruled as an independent sovereign, were not marked by any events of importance; but in the year 1196 she caused her son Arthur, then nine years of age, to be acknowledged Duke of Bretagne by the States, and associated him with herself in all the acts of government.

There was more of maternal fondness than policy in this measure, and it cost her dear. Richard, that royal firebrand, had now returned to England: by the intrigues and representations of Earl Randal, his attention was turned to Bretagne. He expressed extreme indignation that Constance should have proclaimed her son Duke of Bretagne, and her partner in power, without his consent, he being the feudal lord and natural guardian of the young prince. After some excuses and representations on the part of Constance, he affected to be pacified, and a friendly interview was appointed at Pontorson, on the frontiers of Normandy.

* By the treaty of Messina, 1190.

We can hardly reconcile the cruel and perfidious scenes which follow with those romantic and chivalrous associations which illustrate the memory of Cœur-de-Lion—the friend of Blondel, and the antagonist of Saladin. Constance, perfectly unsuspicious of the meditated treason, accepted the invitation of her brother-in-law, and set out from Rennes with a small but magnificent retinue to join him at Pontorson. On the road, and within sight of the town, the Earl of Chester was posted with a troop of Richard's soldiery, and while the Duchess prepared to enter the gates, where she expected to be received with honor and welcome, he suddenly rushed from his ambuscade, fell upon her and her suite, put the latter to flight, and carried off Constance to the strong Castle of St. Jaques de Beavron, where he detained her a prisoner for eighteen months. The chronicle does not tell us how Randal treated his unfortunate wife during this long imprisonment; she was absolutely in his power, none of her own people were suffered to approach her, and whatever might have been his behavior towards her, one thing alone is certain, that so far from softening her feelings towards *him*, it seems to have added tenfold bitterness to her abhorence and her scorn.

The barons of Bretagne sent the Bishop of Rennes to complain of this violation of faith and justice, and to demand the restitution of the Duchess. Richard meanly evaded and temporized—he engaged to restore Constance to liberty on certain conditions, but this was merely to gain time. When the stipulated terms were complied with, and the hostages delivered, the Bretons sent a herald to the English king, to require him to fulfil his part of the treaty, and restore their beloved Constance. Richard replied with insolent defiance, refused to deliver up either the hostages or Constance, and marched his army into the heart of the country.

All that Bretagne had suffered previously was as nothing compared to this terrible invasion, and all that the humane and peaceful government of Constance had effected during seven years was at once annihilated. The English barons, and their savage and mercenary followers, spread themselves through the country, which they wasted with fire and sword. The castles of those who ventured to defend themselves were razed to the ground, the towns and villages plundered and burnt, and the wretched inhabitants fled to the caves and forests; but not even there could they find an asylum: by the orders and in the presence of Richard, the woods were set on fire, and hundreds either perished in the flames or were suffocated in the smoke.

Constance, meanwhile, could only weep in her captivity over the miseries of her country, and tremble with all a mother's fears for the safety of her son. She had placed Arthur under the care of William Desroches, the senechal of her palace, a man of mature age, of approved valor, and devotedly attached to her family. This faithful servant threw himself with his young charge, into the fortress of Brest, where he for some time defied the power of the English king.

But notwithstanding the brave resistance of the nobles and peolpe of Bretagne, they were obliged to submit to the conditions imposed by Richard. By a treaty concluded in 1198, of which the terms are not exactly known, Constance was delivered from her captivity, though not from her husband; but in the following year, when the death of Richard had restored her to some degree of independence, the first use she made of it was to *divorce herself* from Randal. She took this step with her usual precipitancy, not waiting for the sanction of the Pope, as was the custom in those days; and soon afterwards she gave her hand to Guy, Count de Thouars, a man of courage and integrity, who for some time maintained the cause of his wife and her son against the power of England. Arthur was now fourteen, and the legitimate heir of all the dominions of his uncle Richard. Constance placed him under the guardianship of the king of France, who knighted the young prince with his own hand, and solemnly swore to defend his rights against his usurping uncle John.

It is at this moment that the play of King John opens, and history is followed as closely as the dramatic form would allow, to the death of John. The real fate of poor Arthur, after he had been abandoned by the French, and had fallen into the hands of his uncle, is now ascertained; But according to the chronicle from which Shakspeare drew his materials, he was killed in attempting to escape from the castle of Falaise. Constance did not live to witness this consummation of her calamities; within a few months after Arthur was taken prisoner, in 1201, she died suddenly before she had attained her thirty-ninth year, but the cause of her death is not specified.

Her eldest daughter Elinor, the legitimate heiress of England, Normandy, and Bretagne, died in captivity, having been kept a prisoner in Bristol Castle from the age of fifteen. She was at that time so beautiful, that she was called proverbially, "La belle Bretonne," and by the English the "Fair Maid of Brittany." She, like her brother Arthur, was sacrificed to the ambition of her uncles. Of the two daughters of Constance by Guy de Thouars, the eldest, Alice, became the Duchess of Bretagne, and married the Count de Dreux, of the royal blood of France. The sovereignty of Bretagne was transmitted through her descendants in an uninterrupted line, till, by the marriage of the celebrated Anne de Bretagne with Charles VIII. of France, her dominions were for ever united with the French monarchy.

In considering the real history of Constance, three things must strike us as chiefly remarkable.

First, that she is not accused of any vice, or any act of injustice or violence; and this praise, though poor and negative, should have its due weight, considering the scanty records that remain of her troubled life, and the period at which she lived—a period in which crimes of the darkest dye were familiar occurrences. Her father, Conan, was considered as a gentle and amiable prince—"gentle even to feebleness;" yet we are told that on one occasion he acted over again the tragedy of Ugolino and Ruggiero, when he shut up the Count de Dol, with his two sons and his nephew, in a dungeon, and deliberately starved them to death: an event recorded without any particular comment by the old chroniclers of Bretagne. It also appears that during those intervals, when Constance administered the government of her states with some degree of independence, the country prospered under her sway, and that she possessed at all times the love of her people and the respect of her nobles.

Secondly, no imputation whatever has been cast on the honor of Constance, as a wife and as a woman. The old historians, who have treated in a very unceremonious style the levities of her great-grandmother Matilda, her grandmother Bertha, her godmother Constance, and her mother-in-law Elinor, treat the name and memory of *our* Lady Constance with uniform respect.

Her third marriage with Guy de Thouars, has been censured as impolitic, but has also been defended; it can hardly, considering her age, and the circumstances in which she was placed, be a just subject of reproach.

During her hated union with Randal de Blondeville, and the years past in a species of widowhood, she conducted herself with propriety,—at least I can find no reason to judge otherwise.

Lastly, we are struck by the fearless determined spirit, amounting at times to rashness, which Constance displayed on several occasions, when left to the free exercise of her own power and will; yet we see how frequently, with all this resolution and pride of temper, she became a mere instrument in the hands of others, and a victim to the superior craft or power of her enemies. The inference is unavoidable; there must have existed in the mind of Constance, with all her noble and amiable qualities, a deficiency somewhere,—a want of firmness, a want of judgment or wariness, and a total want of self-control.

* * * * *

In the play of King John, the three principal characters are the King, Falconbridge, and Lady Constance. The first is drawn forcibly and accurately from history; it reminds us of Titian's portrait of Cæsar Borgia, in which the hatefulness of the subject is redeemed by the masterly skill of the artist,—the truth, and power, and wonderful beauty of the execution. Falconbridge is the spirited creation of the poet.* Constance is certainly an historical personage; but the form which, when we meet it on the record of history, appears like a pale, indistinct shadow, half melted into its obscure back ground, starts before us into a strange relief and palpable breathing reality upon the page of Shakspeare.

* Malone says, that "in expanding the character of the bastard, Shakspeare seems to have proceeded on the following slight hint in an old play on the story of King John:

> Next them a bastard of the king's deceased—
> A hardy wild-head, rough and venturous."

It is easy to *say* this; yet who but Shakspeare could have expanded the last line into a Falconbridge?

Whenever we think of Constance, it is in her maternal character. All the interest which she excites in the drama turns upon her situation as the mother of Arthur. Every circumstance in which she is placed, every sentiment she utters, has a reference to him; and she is represented, through the whole of the scenes in which she is engaged, as alternately pleading for the rights, and trembling for the existence of her son.

The same may be said of the Merope. In the four tragedies of which her story forms the subject,* we see her but in one point of view, namely, as a mere impersonation of the maternal feeling. The poetry of the situation is every thing, the character nothing. Interesting as she is, take Merope out of the circumstances in which she is placed,—take away her son, for whom she trembles from the first scene to the last, and Merope in herself is nothing; she melts away into a name, to which we can affix no other characteristic by which to distinguish her. We recognize her no longer. Her position is that of an agonized mother; and we can no more fancy her under a different aspect, than we can imagine the statue of Niobe in a different attitude.

But while we contemplate the character of Constance, she assumes before us an individuality perfectly distinct from the circumstances around her. The action calls forth her maternal feelings, and places them in the most prominent point of view: but with Constance, as with a real human being, the maternal affections are a powerful instinct, modified by other faculties, sentiments, and im-

* The Greek Merope, which was esteemed one of the finest of the tragedies of Euripides, is unhappily lost; those of Maffei, Alfieri, and Voltaire, are well known. There is another Merope in Italian, which I have not seen—the English Merope is merely a bad translation from Voltaire.

pulses, making up the individual character. We think of her as a mother, because, as a mother distracted for the loss of her son, she is immediately presented before us, and calls forth our sympathy and our tears; but we infer the rest of her character from what we see, as certainly, and as completely as if we had known her whole course of life.

That which strikes us as the principal attribute of Constance is *power*—power of imagination, of will, of passion, of affection, of pride; the moral energy, that faculty which is principally exercised in self-control, and gives consistency to the rest, is deficient—or rather, to speak more correctly, the extraordinary development of sensibility and imagination, which lends to the character its rich poetical coloring, leaves the other qualities comparatively subordinate. Hence it is that the whole complexion of the character, notwithstanding its amazing grandeur, is so exquisitely feminine. The weakness of the woman, who by the very consciousness of that weakness is worked up to desperation and defiance, the fluctuations of temper and the bursts of sublime passion, the terrors, the impatience, and the tears, are all most true to feminine nature. The energy of Constance not being based upon strength of character, rises and falls with the tide of passion. Her haughty spirit swells against resistance, and is excited into frenzy by sorrow and disappointment; while neither from her towering pride, nor her strength of intellect, can she borrow patience to submit, or fortitude to endure. It is, therefore with perfect truth of nature that Constance is first introduced as pleading for peace.

> Stay for an answer to your embassy,
> Lest unadvised you stain your swords with blood;
> My Lord Chatillon may from England bring
> That right in peace, which here we urge in war,
> And then we shall repent each drop of blood,
> That hot, rash haste so indirectly shed.

And that the same woman, when all her passions are roused by the sense of injury, should afterwards exclaim,

War, war! No peace! peace is to me a war!

That she should be ambitious for her son, proud of his high birth and royal rights, and violent in defending them, is most natural; but I cannot agree with those who think that in the mind of Constance *ambition*—that is, the love or dominion for its own sake—is either a strong motive or a strong feeling; it could hardly be so where the natural impulses and the ideal power predominate in so high a degree. The vehemence with which she ass erts the just and legal rights of her son is that of a fond mother and a proud-spirited woman, stung with the sense of injury, and herself a reigning sovereign,—by birth and right, if not in fact; yet when bereaved of her son, grief not only "fills the room up of her absent child," but seems to absorb every other faculty and feeling—even pride and anger. It is true that she exults over him as one whom nature and fortune had destined to be *great*, but in her distraction for his loss, she thinks of him only as her "pretty Arthur."

O lord! my boy, my Arthur, my fair son!
My life, my joy, my food, my all the world!
My widow-comfort, and my sorrows' cure!

No other feeling can be traced through the whole of her frantic scene—it is grief only, a mother's heart-rending, soul-absorbing grief, and nothing else. Not even indignation, or the desire of revenge, interfere with its soleness and intensity. An ambitious woman would hardly have thus addressed the cold, wily Cardinal;

And, Father Cardinal, I have heard you say,
That we shall see and know our friends in heaven:
If that be true, I shall see my boy again;

For since the birth of Cain, the first male child,
To him that did but yesterday suspire,
There was not such a gracious creature born.
But now will canker sorrow eat my bud,
And chase the native beauty from his cheek,
And he will look as hollow as a ghost;
As dim and meagre as an ague's fit:
And so he'll die; and, rising so again,
When I shall meet him in the court of heaven
I shall not know him: therefore never, never
Must I behold my pretty Arthur more!

The bewildered pathos and poetry of this address could be natural in no woman, who did not unite, like Constance, the most passionate sensibility with the most vivid imagination.

It is true that Queen Elinor calls her on one occasion, "ambitious Constance," but the epithet is rather the natural expression of Elinor's own fear and hatred than really applicable. Elinor, in whom age had subdued all passions but ambition, dreaded the mother of Arthur as her rival in power, and for that reason only opposed the claims of the son.* But I conceive, that in a woman yet in the prime of life, and endued with the peculiar disposition of Constance, the mere love of power would be too much modified by fancy and feeling to be called a *passion*.

In fact, it is not pride, nor temper nor ambition, nor even maternal affection which in Constance gives the prevailing tone to the whole character—it is the predominance of the imagination. I do not mean in the conception of the dramatic portrait, but in the temperament of the woman herself. In the poetical, fanciful, excitable cast of her mind

* "Queen Elinor saw that if he were king, how his mother Constance would look to bear the most rule in the realm of England, till her son should come to a lawful age to govern of himself."—HOLINSHED.

—in the *excess* of the ideal power, tinging all her affections, exalting all her sentiments and thoughts, and animating the expression of both, Constance can only be compared to Juliet.

In the first place, it is through the power of imagination that when under the influence of excited temper, Constance is not a mere incensed woman; nor does she, in the style of Volumnia, "lament in anger Juno-like," but rather like a sybil in a fury. Her sarcasms come down like thunderbolts. In her famous address to Austria—

> O Lymoges! O Austria! thou dost shame
> That bloody spoil, thou slave! thou wretch! thou coward! &c.

it is as if she had concentrated the burning spirit of scorn, and dashed it in his face—every word seems to blister where it falls. In the scolding scene between her and Queen Elinor, the laconic insolence of the latter is completely overborne by the torrent of bitter contumely which bursts from the lips of Constance, clothed in the most energetic, and often in the most figurative expressions.

ELINOR.

Who's it that thou dost call usurper—France?

CONSTANCE.

Let me make answer—Thy usurping son.

ELINOR.

Out, insolent! thy bastard shall be king,
That thou may'st be a queen, and check the world!

CONSTANCE.

My bed was ever to thy son as true,
As thine was to thy husband; and this boy
Liker in feature to his father Geoffrey,
Than thou and John in manners: being as like
As rain to water, or devil to his dam.
My boy a bastard! by my soul, I think
His father never was so true begot;
It cannot be and if thou wert his mother.

ELINOR.

There's a good mother, boy that blots thy father.

CONSTANCE.

There's a good grandam, boy that would blot thee.

* * * * * *

ELINOR.

Come to thy grandam, child.

CONSTANCE.

Do, child,—go to its grandam, child;
Give grandam kingdom, and its grandam will
Give it a plum, a cherry, and a fig—
There's a good grandam.

ARTHUR.

Good, my mother, peace.
I would that I were low laid in my grave;
I am not worth this coil that's made for me.

ELINOR.

His mother shames him so, poor boy, he weeps.

CONSTANCE.

Now shame upon you, whe'r she does or no!
His grandam's wrongs, and not his mother's shame,
Draw those heaven-moving pearls from his poor eyes,
Which heaven shall take in nature of a fee—
Ay, with these chrystal beads heav'n shall be bribed
To do him justice, and revenge on you.

ELINOR.

Thou monstrous slanderer of heaven and earth.

CONSTANCE.

Thou monstrous injurer of heaven and earth,
Call me not slanderer; thou and thine usurp
The dominations, royalties and rights
Of this oppressed boy. This is thy eldest son's son
Unfortunate in nothing but in thee.

* * * * *

ELINOR.

Thou unadvised scold, I can produce
A will, that bars the title of thy son.

CONSTANCE.
Ay, who doubts that? A will—a wicked will—
A woman's will—a canker'd grandam's will;

KING PHILIP.
Peace, lady; pause, or be more moderate.

And in her very opposite mood, when struggling with the consciousness of her own helpless situation, the same susceptible and excitable fancy still predominates.

Thou shalt be punished for thus frighting me,
For I am sick, and capable of fears;
Oppressed with wrongs and therefore full of fears;
A widow, husbandless, subject to fears;
A woman, naturally born to fears;
And though thou now confess thou didst but just
With my vexed spirits I cannot take a truce,
But they will quake and tremble all this day.
What dost thou mean by shaking of thy head?
Why dost thou look so sadly on my son?
What means that hand upon that breast of thine?
Why holds thine eye that lamentable rheum,
Like a proud river peering o'er his bounds?
Be these sad signs confirmers of thy words?
* * * * * *
Fellow, begone; I cannot brook thy sight—
This news hath made thee a most ugly man!

It is the power of imagination which gives so peculiar a tinge to the maternal tenderness of Constance: she not only loves her son with the fond instinct of a mother's affection, but she loves him with her poetical imagination, exults in his beauty and his royal birth, hangs over him with idolatry, and sees his infant brow already encircled with the diadem. Her proud spirit, her ardent enthusiastic fancy, and her energetic self-will, all combine with her maternal love to give it that tone and character which belongs to her only; hence that most beautiful address to her son, which coming from the lips of Constance, is as full of nature and truth as of pathos and poetry, and which we could hardly sympathize with in any other.

ARTHUR.
I do beseech you, madam, be content.

CONSTANCE.
If thou, that bid'st me be content were grim,
Ugly, and slanderous to thy mother's womb,
Full of unpleasing blots and sightless stains;
Lame, foolish, crook'd, swart, prodigious,
Patched with foul moles and eye-offending marks,
I would not care—I then would be content;
For then I should not love thee; no, nor thou
Become thy great birth, nor deserve a crown.
But thou art fair; and at thy birth, dear boy!
Nature and fortune join'd to make thee great;
Of nature's gifts thon may'st with lillies boast,
And with the half-blown rose; but Fortune, O
She is corrupted, chang'd, and won from thee;
She adulterates hourly with thine uncle John;
And with her golden hand hath pluck'd on France
To tread down fair respect of sovereignty.

In this exceeding vivacity of imagination which in the end turns sorrow to frenzy, Constance is not only a bereaved and doating mother, but a generous woman, betrayed by her own rash confidence, in whose mind the sense of injury mingling with the sense of grief, and her impetuous temper conflicting with her pride, combine to overset her reason; yet she is not mad; and how admirably, how forcibly, she herself draws the distinction between the frantic violence of uncontrolled feeling and actual madness!

Thou art not holy to belie me so;
I am not mad; this hair I tear is mine;
My name is Constance; I was Geoffrey's wife;

Young Arthur is my son, and he is lost;
I am not mad; I would to heaven I were!
For then, 'tis like I should forget myself—
O, if I could, what grief should I forget.

Not only has Constance words at will, and fast as the passionate feelings rise in her mind they are poured forth with vivid, overpowering eloquence, but like Juliet she may be said to speak in pictures. For instance—

Why holds thine eye that lamentable rheum?
Like a proud river peering o'er its bounds.

And throughout the whole dialogue there is the same overflow of eloquence, the same splendor of diction, the same luxuriance of imagery; yet with an added grandeur, arising from habits of command, from the age, the rank, and the matronly character of Constance. Thus Juliet pours forth her love like a muse in a rapture: Constance raves in her sorrow like a Pythoness possessed with the spirit of pain. The love of Juliet is deep and infinite as the boundless sea; and the grief of Constance is so great, that nothing but the round world itself is able to sustain it.

I will instruct my sorrows to be proud;
For grief is proud and makes his owner stout.
To me, and to the state of my great grief,
Let kings assemble; for my grief's so great,
That no supporter but the huge firm earth
Can hold it up. Here I and Sorrow sit;
Here is my throne,—bid kings come bow to it!

An image more majestic, more wonderfully sublime was never presented to fancy; yet almost equal as a flight of poetry is her apostrophe to the heavens—

Arm, arm, ye heavens, against these perjured kings.
A widow calls!—be husband to me, heavens!

And again—

O that my tongue were in the thunder's mouth,
Then with a passion would I shake the world.

Not only do her thoughts start into images, but her feelings become persons; grief haunts her as a living presence:

Grief fills the room up of my absent child;
Lies in his bed, walks up and down with me;
Puts on his pretty looks, repeats his words,
Remembers me of all his gracious parts,
Stuffs out his vacant garments with his form;
Then have I reason to be fond of grief.

And death is welcomed as a bridegroom; she sees the visionary monster as Juliet *saw* "the bloody Tybalt festering in his shroud," and heaps one ghastly image upon another with all the wild luxuriance of a distempered fancy.

O amiable, lovely death!
Thou odoriferious stench! sound rottenness!
Arise forth from the couch of lasting night,
Thou hate and terror to prosperity,
And I will kiss thy detestable bones;
And put my eye-balls in thy vaulty brows;
And ring these fingers with thy household worms;
And stop this gap of breath with fulsome dust;
And be a carrion monster like thyself:
Come grin on me, and I will think thou smil'st,
And buss thee as thy wife! Misery's love,
O come to me!

Constance, who is a majestic being, is majestic in her very frenzy; majesty is also the characteristic of Hermione; but what a difference between *her* silent, lofty, uncomplaining despair, and the eloquent grief of Constance, whose wild lamentations, which come bursting forth clothed in the grandest, the most poetical imagery, not only melt, but absolutely electrify us.

On the whole, it may be said that pride and maternal affection form the basis of the character of Constance, as it is exhibited to us; but that these passions, in an equal degree common to many human beings, assume their peculiar and individual tinge from an extraordinary devlopment of intellect and fancy. It is the energy of passion which lends the character its concentrated power, as it is the prevalence of imagination throughout which dilates it into magnificence.

Some of the most splendid poetry to be met with in Shakspeare, may be found in the parts of Juliet and Constance—the most splendid, perhaps, excepting only the parts of Lear and Othello; and for the same reason,—that Lear and Othello as men, and Juliet and Constance as women, are distinguished by the predominance of the same faculties,—passion and imagination.

The sole deviation from history, which may be considered as essentially interfering with the truth of the situation, is the entire omission of the character of Guy de Thouars, so that Constance is incorrectly represented as in a state of widowhood, at a period when, in point of fact, she was married. It may be observed, that her marriage took place just at the period of the opening of the drama; that Guy de Thouars played no conspicuous part in the affairs of Bretagne till after the death of Constance, and that the mere presence of this personage, altogether superfluous in the action, would have completely destroyed the dramatic interest of the situation;—and what a situation! One more magnificent was never placed before the mind's eye than that of Constance, when, deserted and betrayed, she stands alone in her despair, amidst her false friends and her ruthless enemies!*—The image of the mother-eagle, wounded and bleeding to death, yet stretched over her

* King John, Act iii. Scene 1.

young in an attitude of defiance, while all the baser birds of prey are clamoring round her eirie, gives but a faint idea of the moral sublimity of this scene. Considered merely as a poetical or dramatic picture, the grouping is wonderfully fine: on one side, the vulture ambition of that mean-souled tyrant, John: on the other, the selfish, calculating policy of Philip; between them, balancing their passions in his hand, the cold, subtle, heartless Legate; the fiery, reckless Falconbridge; the princely Louis; the still unconquered spirit of that wrangling queen, old Elinor; the bridal loveliness and modesty of Blanche; the boyish grace and innocence of young Arthur; and Constance in the midst of them, in all the state of her great grief, a grand impersonation of pride and passion, helpless at once and desperate—form an assemblage of figures, each perfect in its kind, and, taken all together, not surpassed for the variety, force, and splendor of the dramatic and picturesque effect.

Elinor of Guienne, and Blanche of Castile, who form part of the group around Constance, are sketches merely, but they are strictly historical portraits and full of truth and spirit.

At the period when Shakspeare has brought these three women on the scene together, Elinor of Guinne, (the daughter of the last Duke of Guinne, and Aquitaine, and, like Constance, the heiress of a sovereign duchy,) was near the close of her long, various, and unquiet life—she was nearly seventy: and, as in early youth, her violent passions had overborne both principle and policy, so in her old age we see the same character, only modified by time: her strong intellect and love of power, unbridled by conscience or principle, surviving when other passions were extinguished, and rendered more dangerous by a degree of subtlety and self-command to which her youth had been a stranger. Her personal and avowed hatred for Constance, together with its motive, are mentioned by the old historians. Holinshed expressly says, that Queen Elinor was mightily set against her grandson Arthur, rather moved thereto by envy conceived against his mother than by any fault of the young prince, for that she knew and dreaded the high spirit of the Lady Constance.

Shakspeare has rendered this with equal spirit and fidelity.

QUEEN ELINOR.

What now, my son! have I not ever said,
How that ambitious Constance would not cease,
Till she had kindled France and all the world
Upon the right and party of her son?
This might have been prevented and made whole
With very easy arguments of love;
Which now the manage of two kingdoms must
With fearful bloody issue arbitrate.

KING JOHN.

Our strong possession and our right for us!

QUEEN ELINOR.

Your strong possession, much more than your right;
Or else it must go wrong with you and me.
So much my conscience whispers in your ear—
Which none but heaven, and you, and I, shall hear.

Queen Elinor preserved to the end of her life her influence over her children, and appears to have merited their respect. While intrusted with the government, during the absence of Richard I., she ruled with a steady hand, and made herself exceedingly popular; and as long as she lived to direct the councils of her son John, his affairs prospered. For that intemperate jealousy which converted her into a domestic firebrand, there was at least much cause, though little excuse. Elinor had hated and wronged the husband of her youth,* and she had afterwards to endure the negligence and innumerable infidelities of the husband whom she passionately loved:†—"and so the whirlygig of time brought in his revenges." Elinor died in 1203, a few months after Constance, and before the murder of Arthur—a crime which, had she lived, would probably never have been consummated; for the nature of Elinor, though violent, had no tincture of the baseness and cruelty of her son.

Blanche of Castile was the daughter of Alphonso IX. of Castile, and the grand-daughter of Elinor. At the time that she is introduced into the drama she was about fifteen, and her marriage with Louis VIII., then Dauphin, took place in the abrupt manner here represented; it is not often that political marriages have the same happy result. We are told by the historians of that time, that from the moment Louis and Blanche met, they were inspired by a mutual passion, and that during a union of more than twenty six years, they were never known to differ, nor ever spent more than a single day asunder.‡

In her exceeding beauty and blameless reputation; her love for her husband, and strong domestic affections; her pride of birth and rank; her feminine gentleness of deportment; her firmness of temper; her religious bigotry; her love of absolute power and her upright and conscientious administration of it,—Blanche greatly resembled Maria

* Louis VII. of France, whom she was accustomed to call, in contempt, *the monk*. Elinor's adventures in Syria, whither she accompanied Louis on the second Crusade, would form a romance.

† Henry II., of England. It is scarcely necessary to observe that the story of Fair Rosamand as far as Elinor is concerned, is a mere invention of some ballad maker of later times.

‡ V. Mezerai.

Theresa of Austria. She was, however, of a more cold and calculating nature; and in proportion as she was less amiable as a woman, did she rule more happily for herself and others. There cannot be a greater contrast than between the acute understanding, the steady temper, and the cool intriguing policy of Blanche, by which she succeeded in disuniting and defeating the powers arrayed against her and her infant son, and the rash confiding temper and susceptible imagination of Constance, which rendered herself and her son easy victims to the fraud or ambition of others. Blanche, during forty years, held in her hand the destinies of the greater part of Europe, and is one of the most celebrated names recorded in history—but in what does she survive to us except in a name? Nor history, nor fame, though "trumpet tongued," could do for *her* what Shakspeare and poetry have done for Constance. The earthly reign of Blanche is over, her sceptre broken, and her power departed. When will the reign of Constance cease? when will *her* power depart? Not while this world is a world, and there exist in it human souls to kindle at the touch of genius, and human hearts to throb with human sympathies!

* * * *

There is no female character of any interest in the play of Richard II. The queen (Isabelle of France) enacts the same passive part in the drama that she does in history.

The same remark applies to Henry IV. In this admirable play there is no female character of any importance; but Lady Percy, the wife of Hotspur, is a very lively and beautiful sketch: she is sprightly, feminine, and fond, but without any thing energetic or profound, in mind or feeling. Her gaiety and spirit in the first scenes, are the result of youth and happiness, and nothing can be more natural that the utter dejection and brokenness of heart which follow her husband's death: she is no heroine for war or tragedy; she has no thought of revenging her loss, and even her grief has something soft and quiet in its pathos. Her speech to her father-in-law, Northumberland, in which she entreats him "not to go to the wars," and at the same time pronounces the most beautiful eulogium on her heroic husband, is a perfect piece of feminine eloquence, both in the feeling and in the expression.

Almost every one knows by heart Lady Percy's celebrated address to her husband, beginning,

O, my good lord, why are you thus alone?

And that of Portia to Brutus, in Julius Cæsar,

* * * * You've ungently, Brutus,
Stol'n from my bed.

The situation is exactly similar, the topics of remonstrance are nearly the same: the sentiments and the style as opposite as are the characters of the two women. Lady Percy is evidently accustomed to win more from her fiery lord by caresses than by reason: he loves her in his rough way "as Harry Percy's wife" but she has no real influence over him—he has no confidence in her.

LADY PERCY.

* * * * In faith,
I'll know your business, Harry, that I will;
I fear my brother Mortimer doth stir
About this title, and hath sent for you
To line his enterprise, but if you go—

HOTSPUR.

So far afoot, I shall be weary, love!

The whole scene is admirable, but unnecessary here, be-because it illustrates no point of character in her. Lady

Percy has no *character*, properly so called; whereas, that of Portia is very distinctly and faithfully drawn from the outline furnished by Plutarch. Lady Percy's fond upbraidings, and her half playful, half pouting entreaties, scarcely gain her husband's attention. Portia, with true matronly dignity and tenderness, pleads her right to share her husband's thoughts, and proves it too.

> I grant I am a woman, but withal,
> A woman that Lord Brutus took to wife—
> I grant I am a woman, but withal,
> A woman well reputed—Cato's daughter.
> Think you, I am no stronger than my sex,
> Being so father'd and so husbanded?
>
> * * * *
>
> BRUTUS.
>
> You are my true and honorable wife—
> As dear to me, as are the ruddy drops
> That visit my sad heart!

Portia, as Shakspeare has truly felt and represented the character, is but a softened reflection of that of her husband Brutus: in him we see an excess of natural sensibility, an almost womanish tenderness of heart, repressed by the tenets of his austere philosophy: a stoic by profession, and in reality the reverse—acting deeds against his nature by the strong force of principle and will. In Portia there is the same profound and passionate feeling, and all her sex's softness and timidity, held in check by that self-discipline, that stately dignity, which she thought became a woman "so fathered and so husbanded." The fact of her inflicting on herself a voluntary wound to try her own fortitude, is perhaps the strongest proof of this disposition. Plutarch relates, that on the day on which Cæsar was assassinated, Portia appeared overcome with terror, and even swooned away, but did not in her emotion utter a word which could affect the conspirators. Shakspeare has rendered this circumstance literally.

PORTIA.
I prithee, boy, run to the senate-house,
Stay not to answer me, but get thee gone.
Why dost thou stay?

LUCIUS.
To know my errand, madam.

PORTIA.
I would have had thee there and here again,
Ere I can tell thee what thou should'st do there.
O constancy! be strong upon my side!
Set a huge mountain 'tween my heart and tongue!
I have a man's mind, but a woman's might.
*   *   *   Ah me! how weak a thing
The heart of woman is!—O, I grow faint, &c.

There is another beautiful incident related by Plutarch, which could not well be dramatized. When Brutus and Portia parted for the last time in the island of Nisida, she restrained all expression of grief that she might not shake *his* fortitude: but afterwards, in passing through a chamber in which there hung a picture of Hector and Andromache, she stopped, gazed upon it for a time with a settled sorrow, and at length burst into a passion of tears.*

If Portia had been a Christian, and lived in later times, she might have been another Lady Russell; but she made a poor stoic. No factitious or external control was sufficient to restrain such an exuberance of sensibility and fancy: and those who praise the *Philosophy* of Portia, and

* When at Naples, I have often stood upon the rock, at the extreme point of Posilippo, and looked down upon the little island of Nisida, and thought of this scene till I forgot the Lazeretto which now deforms it;—deforms it, however, to the fancy only, for the building itself, as it rises from amid the vines, the cypresses, and fig-trees which embosom it, looks beautiful at a distance.

the *heroism* of her death, certainly mistook the character altogether. It is evident, from the manner of her death, that it was not deliberate self-destruction, "after the high Roman fashion," but took place in a paroxysm of madness, caused by over-wrought and suppressed feeling, grief, terror, and suspense. Shakspeare has thus represented it;—

BRUTUS.

O, Cassius! I am sick of many griefs!

CASSIUS.

Of your philosophy you make no use,
If you give place to accidental evils.

BRUTUS.

No man bears sorrow better—Portia's dead.

CASSIUS.

Ha!—Portia?

BRUTUS.

She is dead.

CASSIUS.

How 'scap'd I killing when I crossed you so?
O insupportable and touching loss—
Upon what sickness?

BRUTUS.

Impatient of my absence,
And grief that young Octavius with Mark Antony
Had made themselves so strong—(for with her death
These tidings came)—*with this she fell distract*,
And, her attendants absent, swallowed fire.

So much for woman's philosophy!

MARGARET OF ANJOU.

MALONE has written an essay, to prove from external and internal evidence, that the three parts of King Henry VI., were not originally written by Shakspeare, but altered by him from two old plays,* with considerable improvements and additions of his own. Burke, Porson, Dr. Warbourton, and Dr. Farmer, pronounced this piece of criticism, convincing and unanswerable; but Dr. Johnson and Stevens would not be convinced, and moreover, have contrived, to answer the *unanswerable.* "Who shall decide when doctors disagree?" The only arbiter in such a case is one's own individual taste and judgment. To me it appears that the three parts of Henry VI. have less of poetry and passion, and more of unnecessary verbosity and inflated language, than the rest of Shakspeare's works; that the continual exhibition of treachery, bloodshed, and violence, is revolting, and the want of unity of action, and of a pervading interest, oppressive and fatiguing; but also that there are splendid passages in the Second and Third Parts, such as Shakspeare alone could have written; —and this is not denied by the most sceptical.†

* "The Contention of the two houses of York and Lancaster," in two parts, supposed by Malone to have been written about 1590.

† I abstain from making any remarks on the character of Joan of Arc, as delineated in the First Part of Henry VI.; first, because I do not in my conscience attribute it to Shakspeare; and secondly, because in representing her according to the vulgar English traditions, as half sorceress, half enthusiast, and in the end, corrupted by pleasure and ambition, the truth of history, and the truth of nature, justice, and common sense, are equally violated. Schiller has treated the character nobly; but in making Joan the slave of passion, and the victim of love, instead of the victim of patriotism, has com-

Among the arguments against the authenticity of these plays, the character of Margaret of Anjou has not been adduced, and yet to those who have studied Shakspeare in his own spirit, it will appear the most conclusive of all. When we compare her with his other female characters, we are struck at once by the want of family likeness; Shakspeare was not always equal, but he had not two *manners*, as they say of painters. I discern his hand in particular parts, but I cannot recognise his spirit in the conception of the whole: he may have laid on some of the colors, but the original design has a certain hardness and heaviness, very unlike his usual style. Magaret of Anjou, as exhibited in these tragedies, is a dramatic portrait of considerable truth, and vigor, and consistency—but she is not one of Shakspeare's women. He who knew so well in what true greatness of spirit consisted—who could excite our respect and sympathy, even for a Lady Macbeth, would never have given us a heroine without a touch of heroism: he would not have portrayed a high-hearted woman, struggling unsubdued against the strangest vicissitudes of fortune, meeting reverses and disasters, such as would have broken the most masculine spirit, with unsha-

mitted, I think, a serious error in judgment and feeling; and I cannot sympathize with Madame de Stael's defence of him on this particular point. There was no occasion for this deviation from the truth of things, and from the dignity and spotless purity of the character. This young enthusiast with her religious reveries, her simplicity, and heroism, her melancholy, her sensibility, her fortitude, her perfectly feminine bearing in all her exploits, (for though she so often led the van of battle unshrinking, while death was all round she never struck a blow, nor stained her consecrated sword with blood,—another point in which Schiller has wronged her,)—this heroine and martyr, over whose last moments we shed burning tears of pity and indignation, remains yet to be treated as a dramatic character, and I know but one person capable of doing this.

ken constancy, yet left her without a single personal quality which would excite our interest in her bravely endured misfortunes ;—and this too in the very face of history. He would not have given us, in lieu of the magnanimous queen, the subtle and accomplished French woman, a mere "Amazonian trull," with every coarser feature of depravity and ferocity ; he would have redeemed her from unmingled detestation ; he would have breathed into her some of his own sweet spirit—he would have given the woman a soul.

The old chronicler Hall informs us, that Queen Margaret "excelled all others as well in beauty and favor, as wit and policy, and was in stomach and courage more like to a man than to a woman." He adds, that after the espousals of Henry and Margaret, "the King's friends fell from him, the lords of the realm fell in division among themselves ; the Commons rebelled against their natural prince ; fields were foughten ; many thousands slain ; and, finally, the king was deposed, and his son slain ; and his queen sent home again with as much misery and sorrow as she was received with pomp and triumph."

This passage seems to have furnished the ground-work of the character as it is developed in these plays with no great depth or skill. Margaret is portrayed with all the exterior graces of her sex ; as bold and artful, with spirit to dare, resolution to act, and fortitude to endure ; but treacherous, haughty, dissembling, vindictive, and fierce. The bloody struggle for power in which she was engaged, and the companionship of the ruthless iron men around her, seem to have left her nothing of womanhood but the heart of a mother—that last stronghold of our feminine nature ! So far the character is consistently drawn : it has something of the power, but none of the flowing ease of Shakspeare's manner. There are fine materials not well applied; there is poetry in some of the scenes and speeches; the situations are often exceedingly poetical; but in the character of Margaret herself, there is not an atom of poetry. In her artificial dignity, her plausible wit, and her endless volubility, she would remind us of some the most admired heroines of French Tragedy, but for that unlucky box on the ear which she gives the Duchess of Gloster,—a violation of tragic decorum, which of course destroys all parallel.

Having said thus much, I shall point out some of the finest and most characteristic scenes in which Margaret appears. The speech in which she expresses her scorn of her meek husband, and her impatience of the power exercised by those fierce overbearing barons, York, Salisbury, Warwick, Buckingham, is very fine, and conveys as faithful an idea of those feudal times as of the woman who speaks. The burst of female spite with which she concludes, is admirable—

> Not all these lords do vex me half so much
> As that proud dame, the lord Protector's wife.
> She sweeps it through the court with troops of ladies,
> More like an empress than Duke Humphrey's wife.
> Strangers in court do take her for the queen:
> She bears a duke's revenues on her back,
> And in her heart she scorns our poverty.
> Shall I not live to be avenged on her?
> Contemptuous base-born callet as she is!
> She vaunted 'mongst her minions 'tother day,
> The very train of her worst wearing gown
> Was better worth than all my father's lands,
> Till Suffolk gave two dukedoms for his daughter.

Her intriguing spirit, the facility with which she enters into the murderous confederacy against the good Duke Humphrey, the artful plausibility with which she endeavors to turn suspicion from herself—confounding her gentle consort by mere dint of words—are exceedingly characteristic, but not the less revolting.

Her criminal love for Suffolk, (which is a dramatic incident, not an historic fact,) gives rise to the beautiful parting scene in the third act; a scene which it is impossible to read without a thrill of emotion, hurried away by that power and pathos which forces us to sympathize with the eloquence of grief, yet excites not a momentary interest either for Margaret or her lover. The ungoverned fury of Margaret in the first instance, the manner in which she calls on Suffolk to curse his enemies, and then shrinks back overcome by the violence of the spirit she had herself evoked, and terrified by the vehemence of his imprecations; — the transition of her mind, from the extremity of rage to tears and melting fondness, have been pronounced and justly, to be in Shakspeare's own manner.

> Go, speak not to me—even now begone.
> O go not yet! Even thus two friends condemn'd
> Embrace, and kiss, and take ten thousand leaves,
> Loather a hundred times to part than die.
> Yet now farewell; and farewell life with thee!

which is followed by that beautiful and intense burst of passion from Suffolk —

> 'Tis not the land I care for, wert thou hence;
> A wilderness is populous enough,
> So Suffolk had thy heavenly company:
> For where thou art, there is the world itself,
> With every several pleasure in the world;
> And where thou art not, desolation!

In the third part of Henry the Sixth, Margaret, engaged in the terrible struggle for her husband's throne, appears to rather more advantage. The indignation against Henry, who had pitifully yielded his son's birthright for the privilege of reigning unmolested during his own life, is worthy of her, and gives rise to a beautiful speech. We are here inclined to sympathize with her: but soon after follows the murder of the Duke of York; and the base revengeful spirit and atrocious cruelty with which she insults over him, unarmed and a prisoner,—the bitterness of her mockery, and the unwomanly malignity with which she presents him with the napkin stained with the blood of his youngest son, and "bids the father wipe his eyes withal," turn all our sympathy into aversion and horror. York replies in the celebrated speech, beginning—

> She-wolf of France, and worse than wolves of France,
> Whose tongue more poisons than the adder's tooth—

and taunts her with the poverty of her father, the most irritating topic he could have chosen.

> Hath that poor monarch taught thee to insult?
> It needs not, nor it boots thee not, proud queen,
> Unless the adage must be verified,
> That beggars, mounted, ride their horse to death.
> 'Tis beauty, that doth oft make women proud,
> But, God he knows, thy share thereof is small.
> 'Tis virtue that doth make them most admired;
> The contrary doth make thee wondered at.
> 'Tis government that makes them seem divine,
> The want thereof makes thee abominable.
> * * * * *
> O tiger's heart, wrapped in a woman's hide!
> How couldst thou drain the life-blood of the child
> To bid the father wipe his eyes withal,
> And yet be seen to bear a woman's face?
> Women are soft, mild, pitiful, and flexible.
> Thou stern, obdurate, flinty, rough, remorseless!

By such a woman as Margaret is here depicted, such a

speech could be answered only in one way—with her dagger's point—and thus she answers it.

It is some comfort to reflect that this trait of ferocity is not historical: the body of the Duke of York was found, after the battle, among the heaps of slain, and his head struck off; but even this was not done by the command of Margaret.

In another passage the truth and consistency of the character of Margaret are sacrificed to the march of the dramatic action, with a very ill effect. When her fortunes were at the very lowest ebb, and she had sought refuge in the court of the French king, Warwick, her most formidable enemy, upon some disgust he had taken against Edward the Fourth, offered to espouse her cause, and proposed a match between the prince her son, and his daughter Anne of Warwick—the "gentle Lady Anne," who figures in Richard the Third. In the play, Margaret embraces the offer without a moment's hesitation:* we are disgusted by her versatile policy, and a meanness of spirit in no way allied to the magnanimous forgiveness of her terrible adversary. The Margaret of history sternly resisted this degrading expedient. She could not, she said, pardon from her heart the man who had been the primary cause of all her misfortunes. She mistrusted Warwick, despised him for the motives of his revolt from Edward, and considered that to match her son into the family of her enemy from mere policy, was a species of degradation. It took Louis the Eleventh, with all his art and eloquence, fifteen days to wring a reluctant consent, accompanied with tears, from this high-hearted woman.

* See Henry VI. Part III. Act iii. Scene 3—

QUEEN MARGARET.

Warwick, those words have turned my hate to love—
And I forgive and quite forget old faults,
And joy, that thou becom'st King Henry's friend.

The speech of Margaret to her council of generals before the battle of Tewkesbury, (Act v. Scene v.) is as remarkable a specimen of false rhetoric, as her address to the soldiers on the eve of the fight, is of true and passionate eloquence.

She witnesses the final defeat of her arm y, the massacre of her adherents, and the murder of her son ; and though the savage Richard would willingly have put an end to her misery, and exclaims very pertinently—

> Why should she live to fill the world with words?

she is dragged forth unharmed, a woful spectacle of extremest wretchedness, to which death would have been an undeserved relief. If we compare the clamorous and loud exclaims of Margaret after the slaughter of her son, to the ravings of Constance, we shall perceive where Shakspeare's genius did *not* preside, and where it *did*. Margaret, in bold defiance of history, but with fine dramatic effect, is introduced again in the gorgeous and polluted court of Edward the Fourth. There she stalks around the seat of her former greatness, like a terrible phantom of departed majesty, uncrowned, unsceptered, desolate, powerless—or like a vampire thirsting for blood—or like a grim prophetess of evil, implicating that ruin on the head of her enemies, which she lived to see realized. The scene following the murder of the princes in the tower, in which Queen Elizabeth and the Duchess of York sit down on the ground bewailing their desolation, and Margaret suddenly appears from behind them, like the very personification of woe, and seats herself beside them, revelling in their despair, is, in the general conception and effect, grand and appalling.

THE DUCHESS.

> O, Harry's wife, triumph not in my woes ;
> God witness with me, I have wept for thine!

QUEEN MARGARET.

Bear with me, I am hungry for revenge,
And now I cloy me with beholding it.
Thy Edward he is dead, that killed my Edward:
Thy other Edward dead, to quit my Edward—
Young York he is but boot, because both they
Match not the high perfection of my loss.
Thy Clarence he is dead that stabbed my Edward;
And the beholders of this tragic play,
The adulterate Hastings, Rivers, Vaughan, Grey,
Untimely smothered in their dusky graves.
Richard yet lives, hell's black intelligencer,
Only reserved their factor, to buy souls
And send them thither. But at hand, at hand,
Ensues his piteous, and unpitied end—
Earth gapes, hell burns, fiends roar for him; saints pray
To have him suddenly conveyed from hence.
Cancel his bond of life, dear God, I pray,
That I may live to say, the dog is dead!*

She should have stopped here; but the effect thus powerfully excited is marred and weakened by so much superfluous rhetoric, that we are tempted to exclaim with the old Duchess of York—

Why should calamity be full of words?

* Horace Walpole observes, that it is evident from the conduct of Shakspeare, that the house of Tudor retained all their Lancastrian prejudices even in the reign of Queen Elizabeth. In his play of Richard the Third, he seems to deduce the woes of the house of York from the curses which Queen Margaret had vented against them; and he could not give that weight to her curses, without supposing a right in her to utter them.

QUEEN KATHARINE OF ARRAGON.

To have a just idea of the accuracy and beauty of this historical portrait, we ought to bring immediately before us those circumstances of Katharine's life and times, and those parts of her character, which belong to a period previous to the opening of the play. We shall then be better able to appreciate the skill with which Shakspeare has applied the materials before him.

Katharine of Arragon, the fourth and youngest daughter of Ferdinand, King of Arragon, and Isabella of Castile, was born at Alcala, whither her mother had retired to winter after one of the most terrible campaigns of the Moorish war—that of 1485.

Katharine had derived from nature no dazzling qualities of mind, and no striking advantages of person. She inherited a tincture of Queen Isabella's haughtiness and obstinacy of temper, but neither her beauty nor her splendid talents. Her education, under the direction of that extraordinary mother, had implanted in her mind the most austere principles of virtue, the highest ideas of female docorum, the most narrow and bigoted attachment to the forms of religion, and that excessive pride of birth and rank, which distinguished so particularly her family and her nation. In other respects, her understanding was strong, and her judgment clear. The natural turn of her mind was simple, serious, and domestic, and all the impulses of her heart kindly and benevolent. Such was Katharine; such, at least, she appears, on a reference to the chronicles of her times, and particularly from her own letters, and the papers written or dictated by herself which relate to her divorce, all of which are distinguished by the same artless simplicity of style, the same quiet good sense, the same resolute, yet gentle spirit, and fervent piety.

When five years old, Katharine was solemnly affianced to Arthur, Prince of Wales, the eldest son of Henry VII.; and in the year 1501, she landed in England, after narrowly escaping shipwreck on the southern coast, from which every adverse wind conspired to drive her. She was received in London with great honor, and immediately on her arrival united to the young prince. He was then fifteen, and Katharine in her seventeenth year.

Arthur, as it is well known, survived his marriage only five months; and the reluctance of Henry VII. to refund the splendid dowry of the infanta, and forego the advantages of an alliance with the most powerful prince of Europe, suggested the idea of uniting Catharine to his second son Henry; after some hesitation, a dispensation was procured from the pope, and she was betrothed to Henry in her eighteenth year. The prince, who was then only twelve years old, resisted as far as he was able to do so, and appears to have really felt a degree of horror at the idea of marrying his brother's widow. Nor was the mind of King Henry at rest; as his health declined, his conscience reproached him with the equivocal nature of the union into which he had forced his son; and the vile motives of avarice and expediency which had governed him on the occasion. A short time previous to his death, he dissolved the engagement, and even caused Henry to sign a paper in which he solemnly renounced all idea of a future union with the infanta. It is observable that Henry signed this paper with reluctance, and that Katharine, instead of being sent back to her own country, still remained in England.

It appears that Henry, who was now about seventeen,

had become interested for Katharine, who was gentle and amiable. The difference of years was rather a circumstance in her favor; for Henry was just at that age, when a youth is most likely to be captivated by a woman older than himself; and no sooner was he required to renounce her, than the interest she had gradually gained in his affections, became, by opposition, a strong passion. Immediately after his father's death, he declared his resolution to take for his wife the lady Katharine of Spain, and none other; and when the matter was discussed in council, it was urged that, besides the many advantages of the match in a political point of view, she had given "so much proof of virtue and sweetness of condition, as they knew not where to parallel her." About six weeks after his accession, June 3, 1509, the marriage was celebrated with truly royal splendor, Henry being then eighteen, and Katharine in her twenty-fourth year.

It has been said with truth, that if Henry had died while Katharine was yet his wife and Wolsey was minister, he would have left behind him the character of a magnificent, popular, and accomplished prince, instead of that of the most hateful ruffian and tyrant who ever swayed these realms. Notwithstanding his occasional infidelities, and his impatience at her midnight vigils, her long prayers, and her religious austerities, Catharine and Henry lived in harmony together. He was fond of openly displaying his respect and love for her, and she exercised a strong and salutary influence over his turbulent and despotic spirit. When Henry set out on his expedition to France, in 1513, he left Katharine regent of the kingdom during his absence, with full powers to carry on the war against the Scots, and the Earl of Surry at the head of the army, as her lieutenant-general. It is curious to find Katharine—the pacific, and unpretending Katharine—describing herself as having "her heart set to war," and "horrible busy" with making "standards, banners, badges, scarfs, and the like."* Nor was this mere silken preparation—mere dalliance with the pomp and circumstance of war; for within a few weeks afterwards, her general defeated the Scots in the famous battle of Flodden-field, where James IV. and most of his nobility were slain.†

Katharine's letter to Henry, announcing this event, so strikingly displays the piety and tenderness, the quiet simplicity, and real magnanimity of her character, that there cannot be more apt and beautiful illustration of the exquisite truth and keeping of Shakspeare's portrait.

SIR,

My Lord Howard hath sent me a letter, open to your grace, within one of mine, by the which ye shall see at length the great victory that our Lord hath sent your subjects in your absence: and for this cause, it is no need herein to trouble your grace with long writing; but to my thinking, this battle hath been to your grace, and all your realm, the greatest honor that could be, and more than ye should win all the crown of France, thanked be God for it! And I am sure your grace forgetteth not to do this, which shall be cause to send you many more such great victories as I trust he shall do. My husband, for haste, with Rouge-cross, I could not send your grace the piece of the king of Scots' coat, which John Glyn now bringeth. In this your grace shall see how I can keep my promise, sending you for your banners a king's coat. I thought to send himself unto you, but our Englishmen's hearts would not suffer it. It should have been better for him to have been in

* See her letters in Ellis's Collection.

† Under similar circumstances, one of Katharine's predecessors, Philippa of Hainault, had gained in her husband's absence the battle of Neville Cross, in which David Bruce was taken prisoner.

peace than have this reward, but all that God sendeth is for the best. My Lord of Surry, my Henry, would fain know your pleasure in the burying of the king of Scots' body, for he hath written to me so. With the next messenger your grace's pleasure may be herein known. And with this I make an end, praying God to send you home shortly: for without this, no joy here can be accomplished—and for the same I pray. And now go to our Lady at Walsyngham, that I promised so long ago to see.

At Wolburn, the 16th day of September, (1513.)

I send your grace herein a bill, found in a Scottishman's purse, of such things as the French king sent to the said King of Scots, to make war against you, beseeching you to send Mathew hither as soon as the messenger cometh with tidings of your grace.

Your humble wife and true servant,

KATHARINE.*

The legality of the King's marriage with Katharine remained undisputed till 1527. In the course of that year, Anna Bullen first appeared at court, and was appointed maïd of honor to the queen; and then, and not till then, did Henry's union with his brother's wife "creep too near his conscience." In the following year, he sent special messengers to Rome, with secret instructions; they were required to discover (among other "hard questions") whether if the queen entered a religious life, the king might have the Pope's dispensation to marry again; and whether, if the king (for the better inducing the queen thereto) would enter himself into a religious life, the Pope would dispense with the king's vow, and leave her there?

* Ellis's Collection. We must keep in mind that Katharine was a foreigner, and till after she was seventeen, never spoke or wrote a word of English.

Poor Katharine! we are not surprised to read that when she understood what was intended against her "she labored with all those passions which jealousy of the king's affection, sense of honor, and the legitimation of her daughter, could produce, laying in conclusion the whole fault on the Cardinal." It is elsewhere said, that Wolsey bore the queen ill-will, in consequence of her reflecting with some severity on his haughty temper and very unclerical life.

The proceedings were pending for nearly six years, and one of the causes of this long delay, in spite of Henry's impatient and despotic character, is worth noting. The old chronicle tells us, that though the men generally, and more particularly the priests and the nobles, sided with Henry in this matter; yet all the ladies of England were against it. They justly felt that the honor and welfare of no woman was secure, if after twenty years of union, she might be thus deprived of all her rights as a wife; the clamor became so loud and general, that the king was obliged to yield to it for a time, to stop the proceedings, and to banish Anna Bullen from the court.

Cardinal Campeggio, called by Shakspeare, Campeius, arrived in England in October, 1528. He at first endeavored to persuade Katharine to avoid the disgrace and danger of contesting her marriage by entering a religious house; but she rejected his advice with strong expressions of disdain. "I am," said she. "the king's true wife, and to him married; and if all doctors were dead, or law or learning far out of men's minds at the time of our marriage, yet I cannot think that the court of Rome, and the whole church of England, would have consented to a thing unlawful and detestable as you call it.—Still I say I am his wife, and for him will I pray."

About two years afterwards, Wolsey died, (in November,

1530,)—the king and queen met for the last time, on the 14th of July, 1531. Until that period, some outward show of respect and kindness had been maintained between them; but the king then ordered her to repair to a private residence, and no longer to consider herself as his lawful wife. "To which the virtuous and mourning queen replied no more than this, that to whatever place she removed, nothing could remove her from being the king's wife. And so they bid each other farewell; and from this time the king never saw her more."* He married Anna Bullen in 1532, while the decision relative to his former marriage was still pending. The sentence of divorce, to which Katharine never would submit was finally pronounced by Cranmer in 1533, and the unhappy queen, whose health had been gradually declining through these troubles of heart, died January 29, 1536, in the fiftieth year of her age.

Thus the action of the play of Henry VIII. includes events which occurred from the impeachment of the Duke of Buckingham in 1521, to the death of Katharine in 1536. In making the death of Katharine precede the birth of Queen Elizabeth, Shakspeare has committed an anachronism, not only pardonable but necessary. We must remember that the construction of the play required a happy termination, and that the birth of Elizabeth, before or after the death of Katharine, involved the question of her legitimacy. By this slight deviation from the real course of events, Shakspeare has not perverted historic facts, but merely sacrificed them to a higher principle, and in doing so has not only preserved dramatic propriety, and heightened the poetical interest, but has given a strong proof of his delicacy and his judgment.

* Hall's Chronicle.

If we also call to mind that in this play Katharine is properly the heroine, and exhibited from first to last as the very "queen of earthly queens;" that the whole interest is thrown round her and Wolsey—the one the injured rival, the other the enemy of Anna Bullen—and that it was written in the reign and for the court of Elizabeth, we shall yet further appreciate the moral greatness of the poet's mind, which disdained to sacrifice justice and the truth of nature to any time-serving expediency.

Schlegel observes somewhere, that in the literal accuracy and apparent artlessness with which Shakspeare has adapted some of the events and characters of history to his dramatic purposes, he has shown equally his genius and his wisdom. This, like most of Schlegel's remarks, is profound and true; and in this respect Katharine of Arragon may rank as the triumph of Shakspeare's genius and his wisdom. There is nothing in the whole range of poetical fiction in any respect resembling or approaching her; there is nothing comparable, I suppose, but Katharine's own portrait by Holbein, which, equally true to the life, is yet as far inferior as Katharine's person was inferior to her mind. Not only has Shakspeare given us here a delineation as faithful as it is beautiful, of a peculiar modification of character; but he has bequeathed us a precious moral lesson, in this proof that virtue alone,—(by which I mean here the union of truth or conscience with benevolent affection—the one the highest law, the other the purest impulse of the soul,)—that such virtue is a sufficient source of the deepest pathos and power without any mixture of foreign or external ornament; for who but Shakspeare would have brought before us a queen and a heroine of tragedy, stripped her of all pomp of place and circumstance, dispensed with all the usual sources of poetical interest, as youth, beauty, grace, fancy, commanding intellect; and without any appeal to our imagination, without violation of historical truth, or any sacrifices of the other dramatic personages, for the sake of effect, could depend on the moral principle alone, to touch the very springs of feeling in our bosoms, and melt and elevate our hearts through the purest and holiest impulses of our nature!

The character when analyzed, is, in the first place, distinguished by *truth*. I do not only mean its truth to nature, or its relative truth arising from its historic fidelity and dramatic consistency, but *truth* as a quality of the soul: this is the basis of the character. We often hear it remarked that those who are themselves perfectly true and artless, are in this world the more easily and frequently deceived—a common-place fallacy; for we shall ever find that truth is as undeceived as it is undeceiving, and that those who are true to themselves and others may now and then be mistaken, or in particular instances duped by the intervention of some other affection or quality of the mind; but they are generally free from illusion, and they are seldom imposed upon in the long run by the shows of things and superfices of characters. It is by this integrity of heart and clearness of understanding, this light of truth within her own soul, and not through any acuteness of intellect, that Katharine detects and exposes the real character of Wolsey, though unable either to unravel his designs, or to defeat them.

> * * * My lord, my lord,
> I am a simple woman, much too weak
> T' oppose your cunning.

She rather intuitively feels than knows his duplicity, and in the dignity of her simplicity she towers above his arrogance as much as she scorns his crooked policy. With this essential truth are combined many other qualities, natural or acquired, all made out by the same uncompromising breath of execution and fidelity of pencil, united with the utmost delicacy of feeling. For instance, the apparent contradiction arising from the contrast between Katharine's natural disposition and the situation in which she is placed ; her lofty Castilian pride and her extreme simplicity of language and deportment; the inflexible resolution with which she asserts her right, and her soft resignation to unkindness and wrong; her warmth of temper breaking through the meekness of a spirit subdued by a deep sense of religion ; and a degree of austerity tinging her real benevolence ;—all these qualities, opposed yet harmonizing, has Shakspeare placed before us in a few admirable scenes.

Katharine is at first introduced as pleading before the king in behalf of the commonalty, who had been driven by the extortions of Wolsey into some illegal excesses. In this scene, which is true to history, we have her upright reasoning mind, her steadiness of purpose, her piety and benevolence, placed in a strong light. The unshrinking dignity with which she opposes without descending to brave the Cardinal, the stern rebuke addressed to the Duke of Buckingham's surveyor, are finely characteristic ; and by thus exhibiting Katharine as invested with all her conjugal rights and influence, and royal state, the subsequent situations are rendered more impressive. She is placed in the first instance on such a height in our esteem and reverence, that in the midst of her abandonment and degradation, and the profound pity she afterwards inspires, the first effect remains unimpaired, and she never falls beneath it.

In the beginning of the second act, we are prepared for the proceedings of the divorce, and our respect for Katharine heightened by the general sympathy for " the good queen," as she is expressively entitled, and by the following beautiful eulogium on her character uttered by the Duke of Norfolk:

> He (Wolsey) counsels a divorce—the loss of her
> That like a jewel, hath hung twenty years
> About his neck, yet never lost her lustre.
> Of her that loves him with that excellence
> That angels love good men with. Even of her,
> That when the greatest stroke of fortune falls,
> Will bless the king!

The scene in which Anna Bullen is introduced as expressing her grief and sympathy for her royal mistress, is exquisitely graceful.

> Here's the pang that pinches:
> His highness having lived so long with her, and she
> So good a lady, that no tongue could ever
> Pronounce dishonor of her—by my life
> She never knew harm doing. O now, after
> So many courses of the sun enthron'd,
> Still growing in a majesty and pomp— the which
> To leave is a thousand-fold more bitter, than
> 'Tis sweet at first to acquire. After this process,
> To give her the avaunt! it is a pity
> Would move a monster.
>
> OLD LADY.
>
> Hearts of the most hard temper
> Melt and lament for her.
>
> ANNE.
>
> O, God's will! much better
> She ne'er had known pomp; though it be temporal
> Yet if that quarrel, fortune, do divorce
> It from the bearer, 'tis a sufferance, panging
> As soul and body's severing.
>
> OLD LADY.
>
> Alas, poor lady!
> She's a stranger now again.

ANNE.

So much the more
Must pity drop upon her. Verily,
I swear, 'tis better to be lowly born,
And range with humble livers in content,
Than to be perk'd up in a glistering grief,
And wear a golden sorrow.

How completely, in the few passages appropriated to Anna Bullen, is her character portrayed! with what a delicate and yet luxuriant grace is she sketched off, with her gaiety and her beauty, her levity, her extreme nobility, her sweetness of disposition, her tenderness of heart, and, in short, all her *femalities!* How nobly has Shakspeare done justice to the two women, and heightened our interest in both, by placing the praises of Katharine in the mouth of Anna Bullen! and how characteristic of the latter, that she should first express unbounded pity for her mistress, insisting chiefly on her fall from her regal state and wordly pomp, thus betraying her own disposition—

For she that had all the fair parts of woman,
Had, too, a woman's heart, which ever yet
Affected eminence, wealth, and sovereignty.

That she should call the loss of temporal pomp, once enjoyed, "a sufferance equal to soul and body's severing;" that she should immediately protest that she would not herself be a queen—" No, good troth! not for all the riches under heaven!"—and not long afterwards ascend without reluctance that throne and bed from which her royal mistress had been so cruelly divorced!—how natural!—The portrait is not less true and masterly than that of Katharine; but the character is overborne by the superior moral firmness and intrinsic excellence of the latter. That we may be more fully sensible of this contrast, the beautiful scene just alluded to immediately precedes Katharine's trial at Blackfriars, and the description of Anna Bullen's triumphant beauty at her coronation, is placed immediately before the dying scene of Katharine; yet with equal good taste and good feeling, Shakspeare has constantly avoided all personal collision between the two characters; nor does Anna Bullen ever appear as queen except in the pageant of the procession, which in reading the play is scarcely noticed.

To return to Katharine. The whole of the trial scene is given nearly verbatim from the old chronicles and records, but the dryness and harshness of the law proceedings is tempered at once, and elevated by the genius and the wisdom of the poet. It appears, on referring to the historical authorities, that when the affair was first agitated in council, Katharine replied to the long expositions and theological sophistries of her opponents with resolute simplicity and composure:—"I am a woman, and lack wit and learning to answer these opinions; but I am sure that neither the king's father nor my father would have condescended to our marriage, if it had been judged unlawful. As to your saying that I should put the case to eight persons of this realm for quietness of the king's conscience, I pray Heaven to send his grace a quiet conscience: and this shall be your answer, that I say I am his lawful wife, and to him lawfully married, though not worthy of it; and in this point I will abide till the court of Rome, which was privy to the beginning, have made a final ending of it."*

Katharine's appearance in the court at Blackfriars, attended by a noble troop of ladies and prelates of her counsel, and her refusal to answer the citation, are historical.† Her speech to the king—

* Hall's Chronicle, p. 781.

† The court at Blackfriars sat on the 28th of May, 1529. "The queen being called, accompanied by the four bishops and others of

Sir, I beseech you to do me right and justice,
And to bestow your pity on me, &c. &c.

is taken word for word, (as nearly as the change from prose to blank verse would allow,) from the old record in Hall. It would have been easy for Shakspeare to have exalted his own skill, by throwing a coloring of poetry and eloquence into this speech, without altering the sense or sentiment; but by adhering to the calm argumentative simplicity of manner and diction natural to the woman, he has preserved the truth of character without lessening the pathos of the situation. Her challenging Wolsey, as "a foe to truth," and her very expression, "I utterly refuse —yea, from my soul *abhor* you for my judge," are taken from fact. The sudden burst of indignant passion towards the close of this scene,

In one who ever yet
Had stood to charity, and displayed the effects
Of disposition gentle, and of wisdom
O'ertopping woman's power;

is taken from nature, though it occurred on a different occasion.*

Lastly, the circumstances of her being called back after she had appealed from the court, and angrily refusing to return, is from the life. Master Griffith, on whose arm

her counsel, and a great company of ladies and gentlewomen following her; and after her obeisance, sadly and with great gravity, she appealed from them to the court of Rome."—*See Hall and Cavendish's Life of Wolsey.*

The account which Hume gives of this scene is very elegant; but after the affecting *naivete* of the old chroniclers, it is very cold and unsatisfactory.

* "The Queen answered the Duke of Suffolk very highly and obstinately, with many high words; and suddenly, in a fury, she departed from him into her privy chamber."—*Vide Hall's Chronicle.*

she leaned, observed that she was called; "On, on," quoth she, "it maketh no matter, for it is no indifferent court for me, therefore I will not tarry. Go on your ways."*

King Henry's own assertion, "I dare to say, my lords, that for her womanhood, wisdom, nobility, and gentleness, never prince had such another wife; and therefore if I would willingly change her, I were not wise,"—is thus beautifully paraphrased by Shakspeare:

> That man i' the world who shall report he has
> A better wife, let him in nought be trusted,
> For speaking false in that! Thou art alone,
> If thy rare qualities, sweet gentleness,
> Thy meekness, saint-like;—wife-like government,
> Obeying in commanding; and thy parts,
> Sovereign and pious else, could speak thee out
> The queen of earthly queens. She's nobly born,
> And like her true nobility she has
> Carried herself towards me.

The annotators on Shakspeare have all observed the close resemblanco between this fine passage—

> Sir,
> I am about to weep, but thinking that
> We are a queen, or long have dreamed so, certain
> The daughter of a king—my drops of tears
> I'll turn to sparks of fire;

and the speech of Hermione—

> I am not prone to weeping as our sex
> Commonly are, the want of which vain dew
> Perchance shall dry your pities; but I have
> That honorable grief lodged here, which burns
> Worse than tears drown.

* Vide Cavendish's Life of Wolsey.

But these verbal gentlemen do not seem to have felt that the resemblance is merely on the surface, and that the two passages could not possibly change places, without a manifest violation of the truth of character. In Hermione it is pride of sex merely: In Katharine it is pride of place and pride of birth. Hermione, though so superbly majestic, is perfectly independent of her regal state: Katharine, though so meekly pious, will neither forget hers, nor allow it to be forgotten by others for a moment. Hermione, when deprived of that "crown and comfort of her life," her husband's love, regards all things else with despair and indifference, except her feminine honor; Katharine, divorced and abandoned, still with true Spanish pride stands upon respect, and will not bate one atom of her accustomed state.

> Though unqueened, yet like a queen,
> And daughter to a king, inter me!

The passage—

> A fellow of the royal bed, that owns
> A moiety of the throne—a great king's daughter,
> Here standing
> To prate and talk for life and honor 'fore
> Who please to come to hear,*

Would apply nearly to both queens, yet a single sentiment nay, a single sentence, could not possibly be transferred from one character to the other. The magnanimity, the noble simplicity, the purity of heart, the resignation in each—how perfectly equal in degree! how diametrically opposite in kind!†

* Winter's Tale, Act ii. Scene 1.

† I have constantly abstained from considering any of these characters with a reference to the theatre, yet I cannot help remarking

Once more to return to Katharine.

We are told by Cavendish, that when Wolsey and Campeggio visited the queen by the king's order, she was found at work among her women, and came forth to meet the cardinals with a skein of white thread hanging about her neck; that when Wolsey addressed her in Latin, she interrupted him, saying, "Nay, good my lord, speak to me in English, I beseech you; although I understand Latin." "Forsooth then," quoth my lord, "madam, if it please your grace, we come both to know your mind, how ye be disposed to do in this matter between the king and you, and also to declare secretly our opinions and our counsel unto you, which we have intended of very zeal and obedience that we bear to your grace." "My lords, I thank you then," quoth she, "of your good wills; but to make answer to your requests I cannot so suddenly, for I was set among my maidens at work, thinking full little of any such matter, wherein there needeth a longer deliberation, and a better head than mine, to make answer to so noble wise men as ye be. I had need of good counsel in this case, which toucheth me so near; and for any counsel or friendship that I can find in England, they are nothing to my purpose or profit. Think you, I pray you, my lords, will any Englishman counsel, or be friendly unto me, against the king's pleasure, they being his subjects? Nay, forsooth, my lords! and for my counsel, in whom I do

that if Mrs. Siddons, who excelled equally in Hermione and Katharine, and threw such majesty of demeanor, such power, such picturesque effect, into both, could likewise feel and convey the infinite contrast between the ideal grace, the classical repose and imaginative charm thrown around Hermione, and the matter of fact, artless, prosaic nature of Katharine; between the poetical grandeur of the former, and the moral dignity of the latter,—then she certainly exceeded all that I could have imagined possible, even to her wonderful powers.

intend to put my trust, they be not here; they be in Spain, in my native country.* Alas! my lords! I am a poor woman, lacking both wit and understanding sufficiently to answer such approved wise men as ye be both, in so weighty a matter. I pray you to extend your good and indifferent minds in your authority unto me, for I am a simple woman, destitute and barren of friendship and counsel, here in a foreign region; and as for your counsel, I will not refuse, but be glad to hear."

It appears, also, that when the Archbishop of York and Bishop Tunstall waited on her at her house near Huntingdon, with the sentence of the divorce, signed by Henry, and confirmed by act of parliament, she refused to admit its validity, she being Henry's wife, and not his subject. The bishop describes her conduct in his letter: "She being therewith in great choler and agony, and always interrupting our words, declared that she would never leave the name of queen, but would persist in accounting herself the king's wife till death." When the official letter, containing minutes of their conference, was shown to her, she seized a pen, and dashed it angrily across every sentence in which she was styled *Princess-dowager*.

If now we turn to that inimitable scene between Katharine and the two cardinals, (act III. scene I.) we shall observe how finely Shakspeare has condensed these incidents, and unfolded to us all the workings of Katharine's proud yet feminine nature. She is discovered at work with

* This affecting passage is thus rendered by Shakspeare.

Nay, forsooth, my friends,
They that must weigh out my afflictions—
They that my trust must grow to, live not here—
They are, as all my other comforts, far hence,
In mine own country, lords.

Henry. VIII. *Act.* 3. *Sc.* 1.

some of her women—she calls for music "to soothe her soul, grown sad with troubles"—then follows the little song, of which the sentiment is so well adapted to the occasion, while its quaint yet classic elegance, breathes the very spirit of those times, when Surry loved and sung.

SONG.

Orpheus with his lute made trees,
And the mountain-tops, that freeze,
  Bow themselves when he did sing:
To his music, plants and flowers
Ever sprung, as sun and showers
  There had made a lasting spring.

Every thing that heard him play,
Even the billows of the sea,
  Hung their heads and then lay by.
In sweet music is such art,
Killing care, and grief of heart,
  Fall asleep, on hearing, die.

They are interrupted by the arrival of the two cardinals. Katharine's perception of their subtlety—her suspicion of their purpose—her sense of her own weakness and inability to contend with them, and her mild subdued dignity, are beautifully represented, as also the guarded self-command with which she eludes giving a definitive answer; but when they counsel her to that which she, who knows Henry, feels must end in her ruin, then the native temper is roused at once, to use Tunstall's expression, "the choler and the agony" burst forth in words.

Is this your Christian counsel? Out upon ye:
Heaven is above all yet; there sits a Judge
That no king can corrupt.

WOLSEY.

Your rage mistakes us.

QUEEN KATHARINE.

The more shame for ye! Holy men I thought ye,

29

Upon my soul, two reverend cardinal virtues;
But cardinal sins, and hollow hearts I fear ye:
Mend them, for shame, my lords; is this your comfort,
The cordial that ye bring a wretched lady!

With the same force of language, and impetuous yet dignified feeling, she asserts her own conjugal truth and merit, and insists upon her rights.

Have I lived thus long (let me speak myself,
Since virtue finds no friends) a wife, a true one,
A woman, (I dare say, without vain glory,)
Never yet branded with suspicion?
Have I with all my full affections
Still met the king—loved him next heaven, obeyed him?
Been out of fondness superstitious to him—
Almost forgot my prayers to content him,
And am I thus rewarded? 'tis not well, lords, &c.

My lord, I dare not make myself so guilty,
To give up willingly that noble title
Your master wed me to; nothing but death
Shall e'er divorce my dignities.

And this burst of unwonted passion is immediately followed by the natural reaction; it subsides into tears, dejection, and a mournful self-compassion.

Would I had never trod this English ground,
Or felt the flatteries that grow upon it.
What will become of me now, wretched lady?
I am the most unhappy woman living.
Alas! poor wenches! where are now your fortunes?
[*To her women.*
Shiwrecked upon a kingdom, where no pity,
No friends, no house, no kindred weep for me!
Almost no grave allowed me! Like the lily that once
Was mistress of the field and flourished,
I'll hang my head and perish.

Dr. Johnson observes on this scene, that all Katharine's distresses could not save her from a quibble on the word *cardinal.*

Holy men I thought ye,
Upon my soul, two reverend cardinal virtues,
But cardinal sins, and hollow hearts, I fear ye!

When we read this passage in connexion with the situation and sentiment, the scornful play upon the words is not only appropriate and natural, it seems inevitable. Katharine, assuredly, is neither an imaginative nor a witty personage, but we all acknowledge the truism, that anger inspires wit, and wherever there is passion there is poetry. In the instance just alluded to, the sarcasm springs naturally out from the bitter indignation of the moment. In her grand rebuke of Wolsey, in the trial scene, how just and beautiful is the gradual elevation of her language, till it rises into that magnificent image!

You have by fortune and his highness' favors,
Gone slightly o'er low steps, and now are mounted,
Where powers are your retainers, &c.

In the depth of her affliction, the pathos as naturally clothes itself in poetry.

Like the lily
That once was mistress of the field, and flourish'd,
I'll hang my head and perish.

But these, I believe, are the only instances of imagery throughout; for in general, her language is plain and energetic. It has the strength and simplicity of her character, with very little metaphor and less wit.

In approaching the last scene of Katharine's life, I feel as if about to tread within a sanctuary, where nothing befits us but silence and tears; veneration so strives with compassion, tenderness with awe.*

* Dr. Johnson is of opinion, that this scene "is above any other part of Shakspeare's tragedies, and perhaps above any scene of any other poet, tender and pathetic; without gods, or furies, or poisons, or precipices; without the help of romantic circumstances, without improbable sallies of poetical lamentation, and without any throes of tumultuous misery."

I have already observed, that in judging of Shakspeare's characters

We must suppose a long interval to have elapsed since Katharine's interview with the two cardinals. Wolsey was disgraced and poor Anna Bullen at the height of her short-lived prosperity. It was Wolsey's fate to be detested by both queens. In the pursuance of his own selfish and ambitious designs, he had treated both with perfidy; and one was the remote, the other the immediate, cause of his ruin.*

The ruffian king, of whom one hates to think, was bent on forcing Katharine to concede her rights, and illegitimize her daughter in favor of the offspring of Anna Bullen; she steadily refused, was declared contumacious, and the sentence of divorce pronounced in 1533. Such of her attendants as persisted in paying her the honors due to a queen were driven from her household, those who consented to serve her as princess dowager, she refused to admit into her presence, so that she remained unattended, except by a few women, and her gentleman usher, Griffith. During the last eighteen months of her life she resided at Kimbolton. Her nephew, Charles V., had offered her an asylum and princely treatment; but Katharine, broken in

as of persons we meet in real life, we are swayed unconsciously by our own habits and feelings, and our preference governed more or less by our individual prejudices or sympathies. Thus, Dr. Johnson, who has not a word to bestow on Imogen, and who has treated poor Juliet as if he had been in truth "the very beadle to an amorous sigh," does full justice to the character of Katharine, because the logical turn of his mind, his vigorous intellect, and his austere integrity, enabled him to appreciate its peculiar beauties; and, accordingly, we find that he gives it, not only unqualified, but almost exclusive admiration; he goes so far as to assert, that in this play the genius of Shakspeare comes in and goes out with Katharine.

* It will be remembered that in early youth Anna Bullen was betrothed to Lord Henry Percy, who was passionately in love with her. Wolsey, to serve the king's purposes, broke of this match, and forced Percy into an unwilling marriage with Lady Mary Talbot. "The stout Earl of Northumberland," who arrested Wolsey at York, was this very Percy; he was chosen for this mission by the interference of Anna Bullen:—a piece of vengeance truly feminine in its mixture of sentiment and spitefulness, and every way characteristic of the individual woman.

heart and declining in health, was unwilling to drag the spectacle of her misery and degradation into a strange country; she pined in her loneliness, deprived of her daughter, receiving no consolation from the pope, and no redress from the emperor. Wounded pride, wronged affection, and a cankering jealousy of the woman preferred to her, (which, though it never broke out into unseemly words, is enumerated as one of the causes of her death,) at length wore out a feeble frame. "Thus," says the chronicle, "Queen Katharine fell into her last sickness, and though the king sent to comfort her through Chapuys, the emperor's ambassador, she grew worse and worse, and finding death now coming, she caused a maid attending on her to write to the king to this effect:—

My most dear Lord, King, and Husband.

The hour of my death now approaching, I cannot choose but, out of the love I bear you, advise you of your soul's health, which you ought to prefer before all considerations of the world or flesh whatsoever, for which yet you have cast me into many calamities, and yourself into many troubles; but I forgive you all, and pray God to do so likewise; for the rest I commend unto you Mary our daughter, beseeching you to be a good father to her as I have heretofore desired. I must entreat you also to respect my maids, and give them in marriage, which is not much, they being but three, and all my other servants, a year's pay besides their due, lest otherwise they be unprovided for: lastly, I make this vow, that mine eyes desire you above all things.—Farewell!*

* The king is said to have wept on reading this letter, and her body being interred at Peterbro', in the monastery, for honor of her memory it was preserved at the dissolution, and erected into a bishop's see. *Herbert's Life of Henry VIII.*

She also wrote another letter to the ambassador, desiring that he would remind the king of her dying request and urge him to do her this last right.

What the historian relates, Shakspeare realizes. On the wonderful beauty of Katharine's closing scene we need not dwell, for that requires no illustration. In transferring the sentiments of her letter to her lips, Shakspeare has given them added grace, and pathos, and tenderness, without injuring their truth and simplicity; the feelings, and almost the manner of expression, are Katharine's own. The severe justice with which she draws the character of Wolsey, is extremely characteristic; the benign candor with which she listens to the praise of him "whom living she most hated," is not less so. How beautiful her religious enthusiasm!—the slumber which visits her pillow, as she listens to that sad music she called her knell! her awakening from the vision of celestial joy to find herself still on earth—

> Spirits of peace! where are ye? are ye gone,
> And leave me here in wretchedness behind ye?

how unspeakably beautiful! And to consummate all in one final touch of truth and nature, we see that consciousness of her own worth and integrity which had sustained her through all her trials of heart, and that pride of station for which she had contended through long years,—which had become more dear by opposition, and by the perseverance with which she had asserted it,—remaining the last strong feeling upon her mind, to the very last hour of existence,

> When I am dead, good wench,
> Let me be used with honor;—strew me over
> With maiden flowers, that all the world may know
> I was a chaste wife to my grave: enbalm me,
> Then lay me forth—although unqueen'd, yet like
> A queen, and daughter to a king, inter me—
> I can no more—

In the epilogue to this play,* it is recommended—

——To the merciful construction of good women,
For *such a one* we show'd them—

alluding to the character of Queen Katharine. Shakspeare has, in fact, placed before us a queen and a heroine, who in the first place, and above all, is a good woman; and I repeat, that in doing so, and in trusting for all his effect to truth and virtue, he has given a sublime proof of his genius and his wisdom,—for which, among many other obligations, we women remain his debtors.

* Written (as the commentators suppose,) not by Shakspeare, but by Ben Johnson.

LADY MACBETH.

I doubt whether the epithet *historical* can properly apply to the character of Lady Macbeth; for though the subject of the play be taken from history, we never think of her with any reference to historical associations, as we do with regard to Constance, Volumnia, Katharine of Arragon, and others. I remember reading some critique, in which Lady Macbeth was styled the "*Scottish queen*," and methought the title, as applied to *her*, sounded like a vulgarism. It appears that the real wife of Macbeth—she, who lives only in the obscure record of an obscure age, bore the very unmusical appellation of Graoch, and was instigated to the murder of Duncan, not only by ambition, but by motives of vengeance. She was the granddaughter of Kenith the Fourth, killed in 1003, fighting against Malcolm the Second, the father of Duncan. Macbeth reigned over Scotland from the year 1039 to 1056: —but what is all this to the purpose? The sternly magnificent creation of the poet stands before us independent of all these aids of fancy—she is Lady Macbeth; as such she lives, she reigns, and is immortal in the world to imagination. What earthly title could add to her grandeur? what human record or attestation strengthen our impression of her reality?

Characters in history move before us like a procession of figures in *basso relievo:* we see one side only, that which the artist chose to exhibit to us; the rest is sunk in the block: the same characters in Shakspeare are like the statues *cut out* of the block, fashioned, finished, tangible in every part: we may consider them under every aspect, we may examine them on every side. As the classical times, when the garb did not make the man, were peculiarly favorable to the development and delineation of the human form, and have handed down to us the purest models of strength and grace—so the times in which Shakspeare lived, were favorable to the vigorous delineation of natural character. Society was not then one vast conventional masquerade of manners. In his revelations, the accidental circumstances are to the individual character, what the drapery of the antique statue is to the statue itself; it is evident, that, though adapted to each other, and studied relatively, they were also studied separately. We trace through the folds the fine and true proportions of the figure beneath; they seem and are independent of each other to the practised eye, though carved together from the same enduring substance; at once perfectly distinct and eternally inseparable. In history we can but study character in relation to events, to situation and circumstances, which disguise and encumber it: we are left to imagine, to infer, what certain people must have been, from the manner in which they have acted or suffered. Shakspeare and nature bring us back to the true order of things; and showing us what the human being *is*, enable us to judge of the possible as well as the positive result in acting and suffering. Here, instead of judging the individual by his actions, we are enabled to judge of action by a reference to the individual. When we can carry this power into the experience of real life, we shall perhaps be more just to one another, and not consider ourselves aggrieved, because we cannot gather figs from thistles and grapes from thorns.

In the play or poem of Macbeth, the interest of the story is so engrossing, the events so rapid and so appalling, the accessories so sublimely conceived and so skilfully combined, that it is difficult to detach Lady Macbeth from the dramatic situation, or consider her apart from the terrible associations of our first and earliest impression. As the vulgar idea of a Juliet—that all beautiful and heaven gifted child of the south—is merely a love-sick girl in white satin, so the common-place idea of Lady Macbeth, though endowed with the rarest powers, the loftiest energies, and the profoundest affections, is nothing but a fierce, cruel woman, brandishing a couple of daggers, and exciting her husband to butcher a poor old king.

Even those who reflect more deeply are apt to consider rather the mode in which a certain character is manifested, than the combination of abstract qualities making up that individual human being; so what should be last, is first; effects are mistaken for causes, qualities are confounded with their results, and the perversion of what is essentially good, with the operation of positive evil. Hence it is, that those who can feel and estimate the magnificent conception and poetical development of the character, have overlooked the grand moral lesson it conveys; they forget that the crime of Lady Macbeth terrifies us in proportion as we sympathise with her; and that this sympathy is in proportion to the degree of pride, passion, and intellect we may ourselves possess. It is good to behold and to tremble at the possible result of the noblest faculties uncontrolled or perverted. True it is, that the ambitious women of these civilized times do not murder sleeping kings: but are there therefore no Lady Macbeths in the world? no woman, who, under the influence of a diseased or excited appetite for power or distinction, would sacrifice the happiness of a daughter, the fortunes of a husband; the principles of a son and peril their own souls?

The character of Macbeth is considered as one of the most complex in the whole range of Shakspeare's dramatic creations. He is represented in the course of the action under such a variety of aspects; the good and evil qualities of his mind are so poised and blended, and instead of being gradually and successively developed, evolve themselves so like shifting lights and shadows playing over the "unstable waters," that his character has afforded a continual and interesting subject of analysis and contemplation. None of Shakspeare's personages have been treated of more at large; none have been more minutely criticised and profoundly examined. A single feature in his character—the question, for instance, as to whether his courage be personal and constitutional, or excited by mere desperation—has been canvassed, asserted, and refuted, in two masterly essays.

On the other hand, the character of Lady Macbeth resolves itself into few and simple elements. The grand features of her character are so distinctly and prominently marked, that though acknowledged to be one of the poet's most sublime creations, she has been passed over with comparatively few words: generally speaking, the commentators seem to have considered Lady Macbeth rather with reference to her husband, and as influencing the action of the drama, than as an individual conception of amazing power, poetry, and beauty: or if they do individualize her, it is ever with those associations of scenic representation which Mrs. Siddons has identified with the character, Those who have been accustomed to see it arrayed in the form and lineaments of that magnificent woman, and developed with her wonder-working powers, seem satisfied to leave it there, as if nothing more could be said or added.*

* Mrs. Siddons left among her papers in analysis of the character of Lady Macbeth, which I have never seen; but I have heard her say, that after playing the part for thirty years, she never read it

But the generation which beheld Mrs. Siddons in her glory is passing away, and we are again left to our own unassisted feelings, or to all the satisfaction to be derived from the sagacity of critics, and the reflections of commentators. Let us turn to them for a moment.

Dr. Johnson, who seems to have regarded her as nothing better than a kind of ogress, tells us in so many words that "Lady Macbeth is merely detested." Schlegel dismisses her in haste, as a species of female fury. In the two essays on Macbeth already mentioned, she is passed over with one or two slight allusions. The only justice that has yet been done to her is by Hazlitt in the "Characters of Shakspeare's Plays." Nothing can be finer than his remarks as far as they go, but his plan did not allow him sufficient space to work out his own conception of the character, with the minuteness it requires. All that he says is just in sentiment, and most eloquent in the expression: but in leaving some of the finest points altogether untouched, he has also left us in doubt whether he even felt or perceived them; and this masterly criticism stops short of the *whole* truth—it is a little superficial, and a little too harsh.

In the mind of Lady Macbeth, ambition is represented as the ruling motive, an intense overmastering passion, which is gratified at the expense of every just and generous principle, and every feminine feeling. In the pursuit of her object, she is cruel, treacherous and daring. She is

over without discovering in it something new, she had an idea that Lady Macbeth must from her celtic origin have been a small, fair, blue-eyed woman. Bonduca, Tredegonde, Brunchault, and other Amazons of the gothic ages were of this complexion; yet I cannot help fancying Lady Macbeth dark, like Black Agnes of Douglas—a sort of Lady Macbeth in her way.

doubly, trebly dyed in guilt and blood, for the murder she instigates is rendered more frightful by disloyalty and ingratitude, and by the violation of all the most sacred claims of kindred and hospitality. When her husband's more kindly nature shrinks from the perpetration of the deed of horror, she, like an evil genius, whispers him on to his damnation. The full measure of her wickedness is never disguised, the magnitude and atrocity of her crime is never extenuated, forgotten, or forgiven, in the whole course of the play. Our judgment is not bewildered, nor our moral feeling insulted, by the sentimental jumble of great crimes, and dazzling virtues, after the fashion of the German school, and of some admirable writers of our own time. Lady Macbeth's amazing power of intellect, her inexorable determination of purpose, her superhuman strength of nerve, render her as fearful in herself as her deeds are hateful; yet she is not a mere monster of depravity, with whom we have nothing in common—nor a meteor, whose destroying path we watch in ignorant affright and amaze. She is a terrible impersonation of evil passions and mighty powers, never so far removed from our own nature, as to be cast beyond the pale of our sympathies; for the woman herself remains a woman to the last,—still linked with her sex and with humanity.

This impression is produced partly by the essential truth in the conception of the character, and partly by the manner in which it is evolved; by a combination of minute and delicate touches, in some instances by speech, in others by silence; at one time by what is revealed, at another by what we are left to infer. As in real life, we perceive distinctions in character we cannot always explain, and receive impressions for which we cannot always account, without going back to the beginning of an acquaintance, and recalling many and trifling circumstances—looks, and tones, and words ;—thus to explain that hold which Lady Macbeth, in the midst of all her atrocities, still keeps upon our feelings, it is necessary to trace minutely the action of the play, as far as she is concerned in it, from its very commencement to its close.

We must then bear in mind, that the first idea of murdering Duncan is not suggested by Lady Macbeth to her husband ; it springs within *his* mind, and is revealed to us, before his first interview with his wife,—before she is introduced or even alluded to.

MACBETH.

This supernatural soliciting
Cannot be ill ; cannot be good. If ill,
Why hath it given me earnest of success,
Commencing in a truth ? I am thane of Cawdor—
If good, why do I yield to that suggestion,
Whose horrid image doth unfix my hair,
And make my seated heart knock at my ribs,
Against the use of nature ?

It will be said, that the same " horrid suggestion" presents itself spontaneously to her, on the reception of his letter ; or rather that the letter itself acts upon her mind, as the prophecy of the Wierd sisters on the mind of her husband, kindling the latent passion for empire into a quenchless flame. We are prepared to see the train of evil, first lighted by hellish agency, extend itself to *her* through the medium of her husband ; but we are spared the more revolting idea that it originated with her. The guilt is thus more equally divided than we should suppose, when we hear people pitying " the noble nature of Macbeth," bewildered and goaded on to crime, solely or chiefly by the instigation of his wife.

It is true that she afterwards appears the more active agent of the two ; but it is less through her pre-eminence in wickedness, than through her superiority of intellect. The eloquence—the fierce fervid eloquence with which she bears down the relenting and reluctant spirit of her husband, the dexterous sophistry with which she wards off his objections, her artful and affected doubts of his courage,—the sarcastic manner in which she lets fall the word coward—a word which no man can endure from another, still less from a woman, and least of all from a woman he loves—and the bold address with which she removes all obstacles, silences all arguments, overpowers all scruples, and marshals the way before him, absolutely make us shrink before the commanding intellect of the woman, with a terror in which interest and admiration are strangely mingled.

LADY MACBETH.

He has almost supp'd: why have you left the chamber?

MACBETH.

Hath he asked for me?

LADY MACBETH.

Know you not he has?

MACBETH.

We will proceed no further in this business:
He hath honored me of late, and I have bought
Golden opinions from all sorts of people,
Which would be worn now in their newest gloss,
Not cast aside so soon.

LADY MACBETH.

Was the hope drunk,
Wherein you dressed yourself? hath it slept since,
And wakes it now to look so green and pale
At what it did so freely? From this time
Such I account thy love. Art thou afeard
To be the same in thine own act and valour,
As thou art in desire? Wouldst thou have that

Which thou esteem'st the ornament of life,
And live a coward in thine own esteem;
Letting I dare not wait upon I would,
Like the poor cat in the adage?

MACBETH.

Prythee, peace:
I dare do all that may become a man:
Who dares do more is none.

LADY MACBETH.

What beast was it then,
That made you break this enterprize to me?
Where you durst do it, there you were a man;
And to be more than what you were, you would
Be so much more the man. Nor time, nor place
Did then adhere, and yet you would make both;
They have made themselves, and that their fitness now
Does unmake you. I have given suck, and know
How tender 'tis to love the babe that milks me:
I would, while it were smiling in my face,
Have plucked my nipple from his boneless gums,
And dashed the brains out, had I so sworn, as you
Have done to this.

MACBETH.

If we should fail,—

LADY MACBETH.

We fail.*
But screw your courage to the sticking-place,
And we'll not fail.

*In her impersonation of the part of Lady Macbeth, Mrs. Siddons adopted successively three different intonations in giving the words *we fail.* At first a quick contemptuous interrogation—"We fail?" Afterwards with the note of admiration—*We fail!* and an accent of indignant astonishment, laying the principal emphasis on the word *we*, *we* fail! Lastly she fixed on what I am convinced is the true reading—we fail. With the simple period, modulating her voice to a deep, low resolute tone, which settled the issue at once—as though she had said, "if we fail, why then we fail, and all is over." This is consistent with the dark fatalism of the character and the sense of the line following, and the effect was sublime, almost awful.

Again, in the murdering scene, the obdurate inflexibility of purpose with which she drives on Macbeth to the execution of their project, and her masculine indifference to blood and death, would inspire unmitigated disgust and horror, but for the involuntary consciousness that it is produced rather by the exertion of a strong power over herself, than by absolute depravity of disposition and ferocity of temper. This impression of her character is brought home at once to our very hearts with the most profound knowledge of the springs of nature within us, the most subtle mastery over their various operations, and a feeling of dramatic effect not less wonderful. The very passages in which Lady Macbeth displays the most savage and relentless determination, are so worded as to fill the mind with the idea of sex, and place the *woman* before us in all her dearest attributes, at once softening and refining the horror, and rendering it more intense. Thus when she reproaches her husband for his weakness—

From this time,
Such I account thy love!

Again—

Come to my woman's breast,
And take my milk for gall, ye murdering ministers,
That no compunctious visitings of nature
Shake my fell purpose, &c.

I have given suck, and know how tender 'tis
To love the babe that milks me, &c.

And lastly, in the moment of extremest horror comes that unexpected touch of feeling, so startling, yet so wonderfully true to nature—

Had he not resembled my father as he slept,
I had done it!

Thus, in one of Weber's or Beethoven's grand symphonies, some unexpected—soft minor chord or passage will steal on the ear, heard amid the magnificent crash of harmony, making the blood pause, and filling the eye with unbidden tears.

It is particularly observable, that in Lady Macbeth's concentrated, strong nerved ambition, the ruling passion of her mind, there is yet a touch of womanhood; she is ambitious less for herself than for her husband. It is fair to think this, because we have no reason to draw any other inference either from her words or actions. In her famous soliloquy, after reading her husband's letter, she does not once refer to herself. It is of him she thinks: she wishes to see her husband on the throne, and to place the sceptre within *his* grasp. The strength of her affections adds strength to ambition. Although in the old story of Boethius we are told that the wife of Macbeth "burned with unquenchable desire to bear the name of queen," yet in the aspect under which Shakspeare has represented the character to us, the selfish part of this ambition is kept out of sight. We must remark also, that in Lady Macbeth's reflections on her husband's character, and on that milkiness of nature, which she fears "may impede him from the golden round," there is no indication of female scorn: there is exceeding pride, but no egotism in the sentiment or the expression; no want of wifely and womanly respect and love for *him*, but, on the contrary, a sort of unconsciousness of her own mental superiority, which she betrays rather than asserts as interesting in itself as it is most admirably conceived and delineated.

Glamis thou art, and Cawdor, and shalt be
What thou art promised:—yet do I fear thy nature;
It is too full o' the milk of human kindness,
To catch the nearest way, thou wouldst be great;

Art not without ambition; but without
The illness should attend it. What thou wouldst highly,
That wouldst thou holily; wouldst not play false,
And yet wouldst wrongly win: thou'dst have great Glamis,
That which cries, *This thou must do, if thou have it;*
And that which rather thou dost fear to do
Than wishest should be undone. Hie thee hither,
That I may pour my spirits in thine ear,
And chastise with the valour of my tongue
All that impedes thee from the golden round;
Which fate and metaphysical* aid doth seem
To have thee crowned withal.

Nor is there any thing vulgar in her ambition: as the strength of her affections lends to it something profound and concentrated, so her splendid imagination invests the object of her desire with its own radiance. We cannot trace in her grand and capacious mind that it is the mere baubles and trappings of royalty which dazzle and allure her: hers is the sin of the "star-bright apostate," and she plunges with her husband into the abyss of guilt, to procure for "all their days and nights, sole sovereign sway and masterdom." She revels, she luxuriates in her dream of power. She reaches at the golden diadem, which is to sear her brain; she perils life and soul for its attainment with enthusiam as perfect, a faith as settled, as that of the martyr, who sees at the stake heaven and its crowns of glory opening upon him.

Great Glamis! worthy Cawdor!
Greater than both, by the all-hail *hereafter!*
Thy letters have transported me beyond
This ignorant present, and I feel now
The future in the instant!

* *Metaphysical* is here use in the sense of spiritual or preternatural.

This is certainly the very rapture of ambition! and those who have heard Mrs. Siddons pronounce the word *hereafter*, cannot forget the look, the tone; which seemed to give her auditors a glimpse of that awful *future*, which she, in her prophetic fury, beholds upon the instant.

But to return to the text before us; Lady Macbeth having proposed the object to herself, and arrayed it with an ideal glory, fixes her eye steadily upon it, soars far above all womanish feelings and scruples to attain it, and stoops upon her victim with the strength and velocity of a vulture; but having committed unflinchingly the crime necessary for the attainment of her purpose, she stops there. After the murder of Duncan, we see Lady Macbeth, during the rest of the play, occupied in supporting the nervous weakness, and sustaining the fortitude of her husband; for instance, Macbeth is at one time on the verge of frenzy, between fear and horror, and it is clear that if she loses her self-command, both must perish—

MACBETH.

One cried, God help us! and Amen! the other,
As they had seen me with these hangmans' hands
Listening their fear, I could not say *Amen!*
When they did cry *God bless us!*

LADY MACBETH.

Consider it not so deeply

MACBETH.

But wherefore could not I pronounce amen?
I had most need of blessing, and amen
Stuck in my throat.

LADY MACBETH.

These deeds must not be thought on
After these ways: so, it will make us mad.

MACBETH.

Methought I heard a voice cry,
"Sleep no more." &c. &c.

LADY MACBETH.
What do you mean? who was it that thus cried?
Why, worthy Thane,
You do unbend your noble strength to think,
So brainsickly of things.—Go, get some water, &c. &c.

Afterwards in Act 3d, she is represented as muttering to herself,

Nought's had, all's spent
When our desire is got without content.

Yet immediately addresses her moody and conscience-stricken husband—

How now, my lord? why do you keep alone,
Of sorriest fancies your companions making,
Using those thoughts, which should indeed have died
With them they think on? Things without remedy
Should be without regard: what's done, is done.

But she is no where represented as urging him on to new crimes; so far from it, that when Macbeth darkly hints his purposed assassination of Banquo, and she inquires his meaning, he replies,

Be innocent of the knowledge, dearest chuck,
Till thou approve the deed.

The same may be said of the destruction of Macduff's family. Every one must perceive how our detestation of the woman had been increased, if she had been placed before us as suggesting and abetting those additional cruelties into which Macbeth is hurried by his mental cowardice.

If my feeling of Lady Macbeth's character be just to the conception of the poet, then she is one who could steel herself to the commission of a crime from necessity and expediency, and be daringly wicked for a great end, but not likely to perpetrate gratuitous murders from any vague or selfish fears. I do not mean to say that the perfect confidence existing between herself and Macbeth could possibly leave her in ignorance of his actions or designs: that heart-broken and shuddering allusion to the murder of Lady Macduff (in the sleeping scene) proves the contrary:

> The thane of Fife had a wife; where is she now?

But she is no where brought before us in immediate connexion with these horrors, and we are spared any flagrant proof of her participation in them. This may not strike us at first, but most undoubtedly has an effect on the general bearing of the character, considered as a whole.

Another more obvious and pervading source of interest arises from that bond of entire affection and confidence which, through the whole of this dreadful tissue of crime and its consequences, unites Macbeth and his wife; claiming from us an involuntary respect and sympathy, and shedding a softening influence over the whole tragedy. Macbeth leans upon her strength, trusts in her fidelity, and throws himself on her tenderness.

> O full of scorpions is my mind, dear wife!

She sustains him, calms him, soothes him—

> Come on,
> Gentle my lord, sleek o'er your rugged looks;
> Be bright and jovial 'mong your guests to night.

The endearing epithets, the terms of fondness in which he addresses her, and the tone of respect she invariably maintains towards him, even when most exasperated by his vacillation of mind and his brain-sick terrors, have, by the very force of contrast, a powerful effect on the fancy.

By these tender redeeming touches we are impressed with a feeling that Lady Macbeth's influence over the affections of her husband, as a wife and a woman, is at least equal to her power over him as a superior mind. Another thing has always struck me. During the supper scene in which Macbeth is haunted by the spectre of the murdered Banquo, and his reason appears unsettled by the extremity of his horror and dismay, her indignant rebuke, her low whispered remonstrance, the sarcastic emphasis with which she combats his sick fancies, and endeavors to recall him to himself, have an intenseness, a severity, a bitterness, which makes the blood creep.

LADY MACBETH.

Are you a man?

MACBETH.

Ay, and a bold one, that dare look on that
Which might appal the devil.

LADY MACBETH.

O proper stuff!
This is the very painting of your fear—
This is the air-drawn dagger, which you said
Led you to Duncan. O, these flaws and starts
(Impostors to true fear) would well become
A woman's story at a winter's fire,
Authorized by her grandam. Shame itself!
Why do you make such faces? When all's done
You look but on a stool.
What! quite unmann'd in folly?

Yet when the guests are dismissed, and they are left alone, she says no more, and not a syllable of reproach or scorn escapes her; a few words in submissive reply to his questions, and an entreaty to seek repose, are all she permits herself to utter. There is a touch of pathos and of tenderness in this silence which has always affected me beyond expression; it is one of the most masterly and most beautiful traits of charactor in the whole play.

Lastly, it is clear that in a mind constituted like that of Lady Macbeth, and not utterly depraved and hardened by the habit of crime, conscience must wake some time or other, and bring with it remorse closed by despair, and despair by death. This great moral retribution was to be displayed to us—but how? Lady Macbeth is not a woman to start at shadows; she mocks at air drawn daggers; she sees no imagined spectres rise from the tomb to appal or accuse her.* The towering bravery of *her* mind disdains the visionary terrors which haunt her weaker husband. We know, or rather we feel, that she who could give a voice to the most direful intent, and call on the spirits that wait on mortal thoughts to "unsex her," and stop up all access and passage of remorse"—to that remorse would have given no tongue nor sound; and that rather than have uttered a complaint, she would have held her breath and died. To have given her a confidant, though in the partner of her guilt, would have been a degrading resource, and have disappointed and enfeebled all our previous impressions of her character; yet justice is to be done, and we are to be made acquainted with that which the woman herself would have suffered a thousand deaths of torture rather than have betrayed. In the sleeping scene we have a glimpse into the depths of that inward hell; the seared brain and broken heart are laid bare before us in the helplessness of slumber. By a judgment the most sublime ever imagined, yet the most unforced, natural, and

* Mrs. Siddons, I believe had an idea that Lady Macbeth beheld the Spectre of Banquo in the supper scene, and that her self control and presence of mind enabled her to surmount her consciousness of the ghastly presence. This would be superhuman, and I do not see that either the character or the text bear out this supposition.

inevitable, the sleep of her who murdered sleep is no longer repose, but a condensation of resistless horrors, which the prostrate intellect and the powerless will can neither bafle nor repel. We shudder and are satisfied; yet our human sympathies are again touched: we rather sigh over the ruin than exult in it; and after watching her through this wonderful scene with a sort of fascination, we dismiss the unconscious, helpless, despair-stricken murderess, with a feeling which Lady Macbeth, in her waking strength, with all her awe-commanding powers about her could never have excited.

It is here especially we perceive that sweetness of nature which in Shakspeare went hand in hand with his astonishing powers. He never confounds that line of demarcation which eternally separates good from evil, yet he never places evil before us without exciting in some way a consciousness of the opposite good which shall balance and relieve it.

I do deny that he has represented in Lady Macbeth, a woman "*naturally cruel*,"* "*invariably savage*,"† or endued with "*pure demoniac firmness*,"‡—if ever there could have existed a woman to whom such phrases could apply—a woman without touch of modesty, pity, or fear, —Shakspeare knew that a thing so monstrous was unfit for all the purposes of poetry. If Lady Macbeth had been *naturally* cruel, she needed not so solemnly to have abjured all pity, and called on the spirits that wait on mortal thoughts to *unsex* her; nor would she have been loved to excess by a man of Macbeth's character; for it is the sense of intellectual energy and strength of will, overpowering her feminine nature, which draws from him that burst of intense admiration—

* Cumberland. † Professor Richardson. ‡ Forster's Essays.

Bring forth men-children only!
For thy undaunted metal should compose
Nothing but males.

If she had been *invariably* savage, her love would not have comforted and sustained her husband in his despair, nor would her uplifted dagger have been arrested by a dear and venerable image rising between her soul and its fell purpose. If endued with *pure demoniac firmness*, her woman's nature would not, by the reaction, have been so horribly avenged,—she would not have died of remorse and despair.

We cannot but observe that through the whole of the dialogue appropriated to Lady Macbeth, there is something very peculiar and characteristic in the turn of expression; her compliments, when she is playing the hostess or the queen, are elaborately elegant and verbose; but, when in earnest, she speaks in short energetic sentences—sometimes abrupt, but always full of meaning; her thoughts are rapid and clear, her expressions forcible, and the imagery like sudden flashes of lightning: all the foregoing extracts exhibit this, but I will venture one more, as an immediate illustration.

MACBETH.

My dearest love,
Duncan comes here to-night.

LADY MACBETH.

And when goes hence?

MACBETH.

To-morrow as he purposes.

LADY MACBETH.

O never
Shall sun that morrow see!
Thy face, my Thane, is as a book, where men
May read strange matters. To beguile the time:
Look like the time, bear welcome in your eye,

Your tongue, your hand; look like the innocent flower
But be the serpent under it.

What would not the firmness, the self-command, the enthusiasm, the intellect, the ardent affections of this woman have performed, if properly directed? But the object being unworthy of the effort, the end is disappointment, despair, and death.

The power of religion could alone have controlled such a mind; but it is the misery of a very proud, strong, and gifted spirit, wtthout sense of religion, that instead of looking upward to find a superior, it looks round and sees all things as subject to itself. Lady Macbeth is placed in a dark, ignorant, iron age; her powerful intellect is slightly tinged with its credulity and superstition; but she has no religious feeling to restrain the force of will. She is a stern fatalist in principle and action; "what is done, is done," and would be done over again under the same circumstances; her remorse is without repentance, or any reference to an offended Deity; it arises from the pang of a wounded conscience, the recoil of the violated feelings of nature; it is the horror of the past, not the terror of the future; the torture of self condemnation, not the fear of judgment; it is strong as her soul, deep as her guilt, fatal as her resolve, and terrible as her crime.

If it should be objected to this view of Lady Macbeth's character, that it engages our sympathies in behalf of a perverted being, and that to leave her so strong a power upon our feelings in the midst of such supreme wickedness, involves a moral wrong, I can only reply in the words of Dr. Channing, that "in this, and the like case, our interest fastens on what is *not* evil in the character—that there is something ennobling in the consciousness, however awakened, of the energy which resides in the mind; and many a virtuous man has borrowed new strength from the force, constancy, and dauntless courage of evil agents."* This is true; and might he not have added that many a powerful and gifted spirit has learnt humility and self-government, from beholding how far the energy which resides in mind may be degraded and perverted?

In general, when a woman is introduced into a tragedy to be the presiding genius of evil in herself, or the cause of evil to others, she is either too feebly or too darkly portrayed; either crime is heaped on crime, and horror on horror, till our sympathy is lost in incredulity, or the stimulus is sought in unnatural or impossible situations, or in situations that ought to be impossible, (as in the Myrrha or the Cenci,) or the character is enfeebled by a mixture of degrading propensities and sexual weakness, as in Vittoria Corombona. But Lady Macbeth, though so supremely wicked, and so consistently feminine, is still kept aloof from all base alloy. When Shakspeare created a female character purely detestable, he made her an accessary, never a principal. Thus Regan and Goneril are two powerful sketches of selfishness, cruelty, and ingratitude; we abhor them whenever we see or think of them, but we think very little about them, except as necessary to the action of the drama. They are to cause the madness of Lear, and to call forth the filial devotion of Cordelia, and their depravity is forgotten in its effects. A comparison has been made between Lady Macbeth and the Greek Clytemnestra (in the Agamemnon of Æschylus.) The Clytemnestra of Sophocles is something more in Shakspeare's spirit, for she is something less impudently atrocious; but, considered as a woman, and an individual,

* See Dr. Channing's remarks on Satan, in his essay "On the Character and writings of Milton."

would any one compare this shameless adulteress, cruel murderess, and unnatural mother, with Lady Macbeth? Lady Macbeth herself would certainly shrink from the approximation.*

The Electra of Sophocles comes nearer to Lady Macbeth as a poetical conception, with this strong distinction, that she commands more respect and esteem, and less sympathy. The murder in which she participates is ordained by the oracle—is an act of justice, and therefore less a murder than a sacrifice. Electra is drawn with magnificent simplicity, and intensity of feeling and purpose, but there is a want of light and shade, and relief. Thus the scene in which Orestes stabs his mother within her chamber, and she is heard pleading for mercy, while Electra stands forward, listening exultingly to her mother's cries, and urging her brother to strike again, "another blow! another!" &c., is terribly fine, but the horror is too shocking, too *physical*—if I may use such an expression; it will not surely bear a comparison with the murdering scene in Macbeth, where the exhibition of various passions—the irresolution of Macbeth, the bold determination of his wife, the deep suspense, the rage of the elements

* The vision of Clytemnestra the night before she is murdered, in which she dreams that she has given birth to a dragon, and that in laying it to her bosom, it draws blood instead of milk, has been greatly admired; but I suppose that those who most admire it would not place it in comparison with Lady Macbeth's sleeping scene. Lucy Ashton, in the bride of Lammermoor, is a domestic Lady Macbeth; but the development being in the narrative, not the dramatic form, it follows hence that we have a masterly portrait, not a complete individual; and the relief of poetry and sympathy being wanting, the detestation she inspires is so unmixed as to be almost intolerable: consequently, the character, considered in relation to the other personages of the story is perfect; but abstractedly it is imperfect; a basso relievo—not a *statue*.

without, the horrid stillness within, and the secret feeling of that infernal agency, which is ever present to the fancy, even when not visible on the scene—throw a rich coloring of poetry over the whole, which does not take from "the present horror of the time," and yet relieves it. Shakspeare's blackest shadows are like those of Rembrandt; so intense, that the gloom which brooded over Egypt in her day of wrath was pale in comparison,—yet so transparent that we seem to see the light of heaven through their depth.

In the whole compass of dramatic poetry there is but one female character which can be placed near that of Lady Macbeth;—the MEDEA. Not the vulgar voluble fury of the Latin tragedy, nor the Medea in a hoop petticoat of Corneille, but the genuine Greek Medea—the Medea of Euripides.*

There is something in the *Medea* which seizes irresistibly on the imagination. Her passionate devotion to Jason, for whom she had left her parents and country—to whom she had given all,

> And would have drawn the spirit from her breast
> Had he but asked it, sighing forth her soul
> Into his bosom,—†

the wrongs and insults which drive her to desperation—the horrid refinement of cruelty with which she plans and executes her revenge upon her faithless husband—the gush of fondness with which she weeps over her children, whom

* A comparison has already been made in an article in the "Reflector." It will be seen on a reference to that very masterly Essay, that I differ from the author in his conception of Lady Macbeth's character.

† Appolonius of Rhodeas.—Vide Elton's specimens of the Classics.

in the next moment she devotes to destruction in a paroxysm of insane fury, carry the terror and pathos of tragic situation to their extreme height. But if we may be allowed to judge through the medium of a translation, there is a certain hardness in the manner of treating the character which in some degree defeats the effect. Media talks too much: her human feelings and superhuman power are not sufficiently blended. Taking into consideration the different impulses which actuate Medea and Lady Macbeth, as love, jealousy, and revenge on the one side, and ambition on the other; we expect to find more of female nature in the first than in the last; and yet the contrary is the fact: at least, my own impression, as far as a woman may judge of a woman, is, that although the passions of Medea are more feminine, the character is less so; we seem to require more feeling in her fierceness, more passion in her frenzy; something less of poetical abstraction,—less art, fewer words; her delirious vengeance we might forgive, but her calmness and subtlety are rather revolting.

These two admirable characters, placed in contrast to each other, afford a fine illustration of Schlegel's distinction between the ancient or Greek drama, which he compares to Sculpture, and the modern or romantic drama, which he compares to painting. The gothic grandeur, the rich chiar'oscuro, and deep toned colors of Lady Macbeth, stand thus opposed to the classical elegance and mythological splendor, the delicate yet inflexible outline of the Medea. If I might be permitted to carry this illustration still further, I would add, that there exists the same distinction between the lady Macbeth and the Medea, as between the Medusa of Leonardo da Vinci and the Medusa of the Greek gems and bas reliefs. In the painting the horror of the subject is at once exalted and softened by the most vivid coloring, and the most magical contrast of light and shade. We gaze—until from the murky depths of the back ground the serpent hair seems to stir and glitter as if instinct with life, and the head itself, in all its ghastliness, and brightness, appears to rise from the canvas with the glare of reality. In the Medusa of sculpture how different is the effect on the imagiuation! We have here the snakes convolving round the winged and graceful head: the brows contracted with horror and pain: but every feature is chiselled into the most regular and faultless perfection; and amid the gorgon terrors, there rests a marbly, fixed supernatural grace, which without reminding us for a moment of common life or nature, stands before us a presence, a power, and an enchantment!